Child Abuse Compensa

CHILD ABUSE COMPENSATION CLAIMS

A practitioner's guide

Elizabeth-Anne Gumbel QC
Malcolm Johnson
Richard Scorer

The Law Society

ISBN 1–85328–717 2

Published in 2002 by the Law Society
113 Chancery Lane, London WC2A 1PL

Typeset by Columns Design Ltd, Reading
Printed by Antony Rowe Ltd, Chippenham, Wilts

Contents

CONTENTS

About the authors

Elizabeth-Anne Gumbel QC is a personal injury lawyer at 199 Strand Chambers, she has a particular interest in child abuse compensation claims and is instructed in a number of group actions arising out of abuse of children in local authority care or in institutions; she has acted for both claimants and defendants. Reported cases in which she has appeared include: *X (Minors)* v. *Bedfordshire CC* [1995] 2 AC 633; *Barrett* v. *London Borough of Enfield* [1999] 3 WLR 79; *W* v. *Essex CC* [1995] Fam 90; *S* v. *Gloucestershire CC* [2001] Fam 313; *T* v. *Surrey CC* [1994] 4 All ER 577; *Z and Others* v. *UK* [2001] 2 FLR 612.

Malcolm Johnson is a solicitor at Steel & Shamash, where he specialises in personal injury. He is Secretary of the Association of Child Abuse Lawyers (ACAL). He handles a variety of cases involving child abuse. He has written articles on the subject of child abuse in the legal press and has also developed and presented training programmes for lawyers.

Richard Scorer is a solicitor and partner at Pannone & Partners where he specialises in personal injury. He is an executive officer of the Association of Child Abuse Lawyers (ACAL). He has written articles on the subject of child abuse compensation claims and has represented claimants in the North Wales litigation as well as bringing claims against the Catholic Church and other childcare institutions.

Foreword

It is a sad reflection on the nature of our society that this book is needed at all. The abuse of children, on the scale revealed by law reports and public enquiries reports over the last twenty years, is both perplexing and disturbing. Lawyers can only pick up the pieces, punish the offenders, identify those who enabled the abuse to happen and compensate the victims.

This book provides a valuable, indeed invaluable, aid to lawyers performing that task. The book is a work of scholarship. It is also a practical guide of great utility to any solicitor or barrister, who is instructed in a civil claim concerning child abuse.

The book is written by practitioners with direct practical experience of the field. It is fortified by thorough analysis of the case law and the statutory framework. It contains much useful information, which is not readily accessible to lawyers.

I have read the manuscript with growing interest and admiration. The qualities that impress are clarity, comprehensiveness and reliability.

The authors have created a sensible structure (which is not easy when addressing a diffuse area of law) and they have stuck to it faithfully. This structure will stand the authors in good stead, when they come to write further editions.

I have no hesitation in commending this book to the legal profession.

Mr Justice Rupert Jackson
Royal Courts of Justice
15 October 2001

Preface and acknowledgements

Child abuse compensation claims are a new and developing area of the law. This is the first book that deals specifically with these types of claims. This book is intended to give both detailed analysis of the relevant areas of the law and practical guidance in dealing with child abuse compensation claims. It is written for both claimant and defendant lawyers.

It is assumed that the reader will be a personal injury lawyer and therefore the book does not intend to cover the basic principles of personal injury litigation. It aims to give specific guidance in what is fast becoming a new specialism.

The book states the law as at 31 July 2001. The authors will be publishing updates at six-monthly intervals (see Updates, p. 253 for details). However, the reader is advised to monitor developments in this constantly changing area of the law.

We are grateful to Henry Witcomb of 199 Strand Chambers for drafting the statements of case for the claimant and defendant and to Patrick Sadd of 199 Strand Chambers for his advice on the Schedule of Loss and Case Management Directions.

We are also grateful to the following for their comments and help with the text:

Dr Audrey Oppenheim, Consultant Psychiatrist,
Alder Hey Children's Hospital

Deirdre Healy, Pannone & Partners

Suzanne Heald, Pannone & Partners

Susan Snow, Steel & Shamash

Jeremy Rosenblatt, 4 Paper Buildings

Responsibility for the final text is, however, ours alone.

Table of cases

Table of statutes

Table of statutory instruments and European legislation

EUROPEAN LEGISLATION

Table of reports and inquiries

CHAPTER 1

The background and history of child abuse claims

1.1 THE BACKGROUND TO CIVIL CLAIMS

1.1.1 The investigation of child abuse has permeated the work of family courts and criminal courts for decades. Until the 1990s such investigation principally focused on the activities of the individual abuser, usually a person living within the child's home or community. The sexual and physical abuse of children by those specifically employed to care for them professionally such as teachers, social workers and care workers was rarely investigated. Such investigation as did occur was directed at the activities of the individual abuser, it was not directed towards the school, care home or local authority employer who had responsibility for protecting the child. Civil claims alleging that a public authority or institution was responsible for exposing a child to the activities of the abuser are an area of litigation which can properly be identified as having its origins in the 1990s. Before that, the only means of obtaining compensation was through the criminal injuries compensation schemes. The first scheme for compensating victims of crimes of violence was introduced in 1964. The original scheme was introduced on 1 August 1964 but no claim could be made where the victim and the abuser were living together as members of the same family until the scheme was altered on 1 October 1979. The Criminal Injury Compensation schemes are discussed in detail in Chapter 6.

1.1.2 Sexual and physical abuse of children by those in positions of trust with children has of course been perpetrated for many decades. Abusers and their employers have denied both the fact and the extent of the abuse. This has led to the present situation where abuse is being investigated by the police and by means of civil litigation many years after the events. An article in *The Independent*, 8 January 2001 identified 98 police investigations in 34 police forces in England, Wales and Northern Ireland into historic child abuse. Paedophiles operating as far back as the 1950s are now being convicted of serious sexual offences and sentenced to long terms of imprisonment. The complainants, some now in their fifties, are having to relate the events of their childhood to police and in criminal courts. In the course of this process complainants have come to recognise that not only their abusers but also the public authorities and institutions employing the abusers should be held accountable for the damage done.

1.2   THE INQUIRIES

1.2.1   An important factor which has led to greater understanding of child abuse has been the extensive investigation carried out by a series of public and independent inquiries. High-profile inquiries have brought to public attention the accounts of abuse in private institutions, schools, approved schools and local authority children's homes (see Chapter 2 paras. 2.2.17 to 2.2.22). These inquiries began, as noted, as far back as the 1950s with the investigation of physical abuse. Only more recently has sexual abuse been thoroughly investigated. The following inquiries are examples of those that have played a role in identifying the nature and extent of child abuse over the last 50 years.

Disturbances at the Carlton Approved School

1.2.2   This Inquiry, *Disturbances at the Carlton Approved School on 29 and 30 August 1959* (Report of Inquiry by Mr Victor Durand QC, January 1960, Cmnd. 937) was set up to investigate the state of discipline at Carlton Approved School in the aftermath of a series of incidents. The scope of the investigation included the relations between the staff and pupils and any other matters that might explain the disturbances. In investigating the reasons for protests by boys in this approved school the Inquiry found that there were incidents of inappropriate use of physical punishment. In the course of the Inquiry 33 boys made allegations of ill-treatment and the Inquiry made findings that a number of staff were on occasion too quick to resort to slapping boys and that they had handled boys unnecessarily aggressively. The report of the Inquiry gives a helpful general summary of the working of the approved school system at the time (*Disturbances at the Carlton Approved School*, paras. 7–41).

Administration of punishment at Court Lees Approved School

1.2.3   This Inquiry, *Administration of Punishment at Court Lees Approved School* (Report of Inquiry by Brian Gibbens QC, August 1967, Cmnd. 3367) investigated the alleged excessive use of corporal punishment in an approved school. The Inquiry was set up following reports in the press and the receipt by the Home Office of photographs showing the injuries suffered by boys being caned at the school. The photographs were found to have been taken by a teacher at the school. After initial investigation the Home Office set up an independent inquiry. The Inquiry made limited findings in respect of the use of excessive corporal punishment and breaches of the Approved School Rules 1933 and 1949 (Rules made pursuant to para. 1(1) of the Fourth Schedule to the Children and Young Persons Act 1933). Rule 34 of the Approved School Rules 1933 lists the punishments that may be administered including corporal punishment. Rule 34(iv) provides that every effort shall be made to enforce discipline without resort to corporal punishment; Rule 35 lays down the specific requirements for the use of corporal punishment including type of cane. The approach of the Inquiry was 'not to accept the evidence of any boy, if it contradicted a member of staff, unless it was particularly convincing or was corroborated by other evidence' (*Administration of Punishment at Court Lees Approved School*, para. 28).

1.2.4   A number of inquiries followed in the 1970s and 1980s into individual cases of child abuse. Well-known examples are:

- Jasmine Beckford, London Borough of Brent and Brent Health Authority, published December 1985;
- Kimberley Carlile, London Borough of Greenwich and Greenwich Health Authority, published December 1987;
- Tyra Henry, London Borough of Lambeth, published 1987.

1.2.5   Through the period of these inquiries sexual abuse emerged as a shocking and widespread problem. The difficult issues involved in detecting and dealing with suspicion of sexual abuse were addressed by the *Cleveland Report*.

Report of the Inquiry into Child Abuse in Cleveland 1987

1.2.6   This Inquiry, *Report into Child Abuse in Cleveland 1987* (Cm 412, London, HMSO, 1988) was conducted by Lady Justice Butler-Sloss (now the President of the Family Division). The terms of reference of the Inquiry were:

To examine the arrangements for dealing with suspected cases of child abuse in Cleveland since 1 January 1987, including in particular cases of child sexual abuse, and to make recommendations.

1.2.7 After an Inquiry lasting 74 days, the *Cleveland Report* made a number of specific recommendations to social workers, doctors and the police as to how child abuse inquiries could be managed better. This Inquiry brought to the public attention the particular difficulties in dealing with allegations involving child sexual abuse.

1.2.8 The report and recommendations emphasised the need to listen carefully to what the child is saying and to treat the child 'as a person and not an object of concern' (Ibid., p. 245). Chapter 12 of the Report 'Listening to the child' set out the need to take seriously the child's account and to exercise particular care in the way that children are interviewed. The report's first recommendation asserted the need:

    a. To recognise and describe the extent and the problem of child sexual abuse;

    b. To receive more accurate data of the abuse which is identified.

(Ibid.)

1.2.9 Other recommendations emphasised the need for inter-agency co-operation and the danger of placing too great a reliance on the paediatric evidence alone. Detailed recommendations are made as to how professionals should treat children and parents in the course of child abuse investigations. Further specific recommendations are directed at social services, the police, the medical profession and the area review committees (Ibid., pp. 246–8).

1.2.10 Following the Cleveland Inquiry, further independent inquiries investigated child abuse in different areas. Lord Clyde's report of *The Inquiry into the Removal of Children from Orkney in February 1991* (London, HMSO, 1992) investigated removal of children from homes in Orkney following allegation of abuse in their homes. Allan Levy QC and Barbara Kahan conducted an inquiry into abuse in children's homes in Staffordshire. *The Pindown Experience and the Protection of Children: The Report of The Staffordshire Child Care Inquiry* (Staffordshire County Council, 1991). A. Kirkwood QC (now Mr Justice Kirkwood) conducted an inquiry into the activities of Frank Beck in a Leicestershire children's home (*The Leicestershire Inquiry 1992*, Leicestershire Social Services, 1993). The Pindown Inquiry and the Beck Inquiry were particularly potent examples of the potential for abuse of children within institutions by those entrusted with their care. The timing of these Inquiries coincided with the introduction and implementation of the Children Act 1989 (see para. 1.3).

Report of the Tribunal of Inquiry into the Abuse of Children in Care in the Former County Council Areas of Gwynedd and Clwyd since 1974

1.2.11   In February 2000 the report of Sir Ronald Waterhouse *Report of the Tribunal of Inquiry into the Abuse of Children in Care in the Former County Council Areas of Gwynedd and Clwyd since 1974* (February 2000, HC 201) was published. This investigated the abuse of children in care in North Wales. The report, *Lost in Care*, investigated abuse in 20 residential establishments and seven foster homes in Clwyd together with nine residential establishments and eight foster homes in Gwynedd. The Inquiry covered the period from 1974 to 1990. The report provides an extensive and helpful history of the local authority regimes in place and the problems that arose within the care system after the reorganisation of local government and the implementation of the Local Authority Social Services Act 1970. The Inquiry concluded that there was widespread sexual and physical abuse in local authority community homes, private residential establishments, residential schools, homes run by communities and in foster homes. The Inquiry found that the quality of care provided in all the institutions it examined was below an acceptable standard. Further, there was found to be misuse of secure accommodation and inadequate provision of education. Many other criticisms were made of the systems adopted for looking after children removed from home into care.

In respect of secure accommodation, s.24(2) Children and Young Persons Act 1969 gave power to a local authority to restrict a child's liberty subject to regulations made by the Secretary of State under s.43(2)(c) of the 1969 Act. Pursuant to these powers, regulations 11 to 14 of the Community Homes Regulations 1972 were implemented and provided for strict time limits on the use of secure accommodation.

A new scheme was implemented from January 1984 in s.21A Child Care Act 1980 and secure accommodation is now subject to the provisions of s.25 Children Act 1989.

1.3   THE CHILDREN ACT 1989

1.3.1   The Act received the Royal Assent on 16 November 1989; all but a small number of provisions did not come into force until October 1991. The Act was designed to achieve a complete overhaul of the legislation relating to children and to simplify the extraordinarily piecemeal and complex position that existed previously (see Chapter 2). The Act is described in the title as:

5

> An Act to reform the law relating to children; to provide for local authority services for children in need and others, to amend the law with respect to children's homes, voluntary homes and voluntary organisations; to make provision with respect to fostering, child minding and day care for young children and adoption; and for connected purposes.

1.3.2 The Children Act 1989 begins with what is effectively the 'overriding objectives' (cf. Part 1 Civil Procedure Rules 1998). Section 1 provides that:

- when a court determines any question in respect of a child's upbringing or child's property then 'the child's welfare shall be the paramount consideration';
- in general, any delay in determining any question relating to a child's upbringing is likely to prejudice the child's welfare;
- the court shall not make any orders unless to do so would be better for the child than making no order.

1.3.3 An Introduction to the Children Act 1989 described how:

> The law about caring for, bringing up and protecting children was inconsistent and fragmented across the face of the statute book. The Children Act brings about radical changes and improvements in the law and provides a single and consistent statement of it. (*An Introduction to the Children Act 1989*, London, HMSO, 1989, DoH, p. 1).

And:

> The Act rests on the belief that children are best looked after within the family with both parents playing a full part and without resort to legal proceedings. That belief is reflected in:
>
> - the new concept of parental responsibility;
> - the ability of unmarried fathers to share that responsibility by agreement with the mother;
> - the local authorities' duty to give support for children and their families;
> - the local authorities' duty to return a child looked after by them to the family unless this is against the child's interests;
> - the local authorities' duty to ensure contact with the child's parents whenever possible for a child looked after by them away from home.

1.3.4 This policy was in sharp contrast to the position under earlier legislation (see Chapter 2) where children were removed from their parents into care through a number of routes including the Juvenile Court. Children placed in approved schools frequently had little or no contact with their parents and cancellation of such home leave as they were entitled to was routinely implemented as a form of punishment. The plight of such children in the years between the reorganisation of children's departments into social services departments in the 1970s and the implementation of the Children Act 1989 was examined in the North Wales Inquiry described in paragraph 1.2.11.

1.4 THE EVOLUTION OF CIVIL PROCEEDINGS

1.4.1 Civil claims for compensation arising out of child abuse only became significant in the 1990s, although the cases summarised in para. 1.5 do include some isolated earlier claims. The Inquiries referred to in para. 1.2 highlighted the fact that children are at risk of physical, sexual and emotional abuse not only in their homes and communities but also within the care system. Police inquiries arising out of the activities of Frank Beck in Leicestershire and his conviction in 1991 brought further attention to the problems that children in care might be exposed to (see para. 1.5.29)

1.4.2 The cases summarised in para. 1.5 demonstrate the way the civil courts have in a short space of time grappled with the public policy issues involved in setting parameters for claims in this developing area.

1.4.3 Some of the earliest reported civil claims for compensation arising out of child abuse were claims brought by victims of abuse against their abusers. The best-known example is the case of *Stubbings* v. *Webb* [1993] AC 498. In that case the claimant was born in 1957 and, at the age of 2, was placed by a local authority in the care of foster parents who later adopted her. In 1987 the claimant brought proceedings against her adoptive father and stepbrother claiming damages arising out of the sexual abuse she suffered as a foster child and then as an adopted child. The House of Lords held that claims were properly categorised as trespass claims and not as negligence claims and should have a limitation period of six years. This period is fixed and not susceptible to any discretionary extension. The claimant was not entitled to rely on any argument that she only had the requisite knowledge to bring proceedings after she had seen a psychiatrist in 1984 pursuant to ss.11 and 14 Limitation Act 1980. Further, she could not rely on s.33 Limitation Act 1980. These sections were held only to apply to cases of negligence, nuisance or breach of duty.

1.4.4 In considering the case of *Stubbings and others* v. *the United Kingdom* [1997] 1 FLR 105, the European Court did not follow the Commission who found violations of Article 14 (discrimination) in conjunction with Article 6 (lack of access to court). The European Court found that the restriction imposed by the Limitation Act 1980 was within the margin of appreciation allowed to the United Kingdom in circumscribing access to court. In the course of its judgment, however, the Court stated:

7

> There has been a developing awareness in recent years of the range of problems caused by child abuse and its psychological effects on victims, and it is possible that the rules on limitation of actions applying in Member States of the Council of Europe may have to be amended to make special provision for this group of claimants in the near future.
>
> *Stubbings and others* v. *the United Kingdom* (para. 56 at 119G)

1.4.5 The case of *Stubbings* v. *Webb* gave rise to the anomalous position in the case of *S* v. *W and another (Child abuse: Damages)* [1995] 1 FLR 862. In *S* v. *W* a claim was brought by a claimant against her father. The father had been convicted of five counts of incest involving the claimant and had been sentenced to four years' imprisonment. The claimant also brought proceedings against her mother who had known of the abuse and failed to protect her from it. The Court of Appeal confirmed that the claim against the father was statute barred following *Stubbings* v. *Webb*. However, the Court of Appeal accepted that the claim could proceed against the mother, who was alleged to have negligently failed to prevent the father abusing the claimant. In respect of the mother, the claimant could rely on ss.11, 14 and 33 Limitation Act 1980. The Court of Appeal described how:

> It was a claim against the mother for an entirely independent tort involving acts of omission by her, such as constituted on her part a breach of her common law duty to take care of her child and not to expose that child to the unnecessary risk of injury or further injury.
>
> *S* v. *W* (Russell LJ at 866)

And:

> As has been pointed out, the result of the judge's ruling was, as he rightly said, illogical and surprising. That fact, is a good reason for inviting the attention of the Law Commission to the interrelation of these provisions and to the absence of any longstop limitation period of this and any other parts of the Act, for example section 28 of the Act which deals with persons under a disability.
>
> *S* v. *W* (Sir Ralph Gibson at 867)

1.4.6 By 1995 the position had been reached whereby claims arising out of the abuse of children could be brought against the abuser for assault and trespass provided they were brought within six years of the claimant reaching majority (or while the claimant was a patient) – see Chapter 5. In practical terms such claims would only provide compensation for victims of abuse if the abuser had the means to satisfy a judgment. However, if a person could be identified who had failed to protect the child from abuse, then potentially a claim could be brought outside the primary limitation period, provided the claimant could show a later date of knowledge or persuade the court to exercise its discretion to allow the action to proceed.

1.5   SUMMARY OF CLAIMS AGAINST PUBLIC AUTHORITIES

S v. *Walsall Borough Council and others* [1985] 1 WLR 1150

1.5.1   The claimant was born in 1972 and taken into care in 1974, she was placed by the defendant local authority with foster parents (the second and third defendants). While living with the foster parents, the claimant sustained severe third-degree burns to the soles of her feet. In 1976 the claimant issued proceedings in negligence against the foster parents and local authority. The County Court judge was unable to determine how the claimant's injuries had been sustained as the foster parents were unable to explain them. He found they had not been caused through any deliberate mistreatment but must have been caused negligently. The judge further found that the local authority was not vicariously liable for the foster parents' negligence.

1.5.2   The Court of Appeal upheld the decision. In the Court of Appeal the claim was not put on the basis that the local authority was negligent in its choice of foster parents or in its supervision of them. Rather, it was alleged that it was vicariously liable for the acts of the foster parents who were its servants or agents. The Court of Appeal investigated the relationship between the local authority and the foster parents. Oliver LJ (as he then was) having examined the Children Act 1948 and the Boarding-Out of Children Regulations 1955 stated:

> It seems to me, the statute and the regulations show quite clearly that this is a statutory scheme and that the relationship between the child and the local authority, and indeed between the child and foster parents, is one which is regulated, in my judgment simply and solely by the provisions of the statutory scheme. It seems to me that this is entirely inconsistent with the notion that the foster parents are in any way the agents of the local authority in carrying out their duties. It is the duty of the local authority to provide accommodation for the child, and the duty is satisfied by the provision of the accommodation by boarding out, and I do not think that the foster parents are in any way fulfilling the local authority's duty to provide accommodation. *They are the means by which the local authority carries out its own duty.* It certainly does not seem to me consistent with the statutory scheme that they should be treated as agents of the local authority.
>
> *S* v. *Walsall BC* (at 1155 E–H)

1.5.3   The nature of the relationship between the local authority and its foster parents is an issue which runs through many of the cases in different ways. Subsequent cases consider:

- the duties of the local authority towards its own foster parents, *W* v. *Essex County Council* [1998] 3 WLR 534;

- the need for local authorities to select foster parents carefully (*Surtees v. Kingston-Upon-Thames Borough Council* [1991] 2 FLR 559; *H* v. *Norfolk County Council* [1997] 1 FLR 384 and *S* v. *Gloucestershire County Council* [2000] 3 All ER 346);

- the extent to which a local authority is required to supervise the activities of foster parents so that children in their care remain safe (*Surtees v. Kingston-Upon-Thames Borough Council* [1991] 2 FLR 559, *H* v. *Norfolk County Council* [1997] 1 FLR 384 and *S* v. *Gloucestershire County Council* [2000] 3 All ER 346).

Surtees v. *Kingston-Upon-Thames Borough Council* [1991] 2 FLR 559

1.5.4   This case like *S.* v. *Walsall BC* also concerned a child who suffered scalded feet while in foster care. The claimant was born on 8 April 1964 and placed with foster parents by the local authority when she was 2 years old. On 9 August 1966 the claimant suffered very serious third-degree burns to her feet involving virtually complete destruction of the skin and tissues of the soles of her left foot. The claimant issued proceedings against the local authority in 1985. The statement of claim dated 13 May 1985 alleged negligence and breach of statutory duty against the local authority on the basis that the authority was vicariously liable for the acts of the foster parents. Thereafter the claimant commenced a separate action against the foster parents themselves for negligently or deliberately causing injury to the claimant. The trial judge, Leggatt J. (as he then was) found the injuries were not caused deliberately and there was no appeal against that finding. The judge further found that the injury was caused by the claimant climbing into the washbasin and accidentally knocking the hot-water tap so as to pour hot water on herself. The claimant unsuccessfully appealed against this finding and unsuccessfully argued that the foster parent was negligent even on her own account of events.

1.5.5   Stocker LJ described how:

> the duty imposed on [the foster mother] was to take such care as, in all the circumstances, was reasonable to ensure that the [claimant] was not exposed to unnecessary risk of injury, the standard of care being that of a careful parent in the prevailing circumstances.
> *Surtees* v. *Kingston-Upon-Thames Borough Council* (at 570)

1.5.6   In respect of the claim against the local authority, it was argued on behalf of the claimant that the local authority was negligent in that it:

> (a)   boarded [the claimant] out with the [foster parents] without proper investigation;

10

(b) allowed the [foster parents] to foster [the claimant] without proper preparation;

(c) failed to heed what were referred to as 'the warning signs'; and

(d) failed to visit [the claimant] and the [foster parents] during July 1966.

Surtees v. *Kingston Upon Thames Borough Council* (at 571)

Stocker LJ found that:

the claim against the local authority was bound to fail unless the injuries were deliberately inflicted.

He pointed out that the training and supervision of foster parents would not have prevented accidents by negligence. Sir Browne-Wilkinson VC (as he then was) agreed with the judgment of Stocker LJ and stated that:

we should be slow to characterise as negligent the care which ordinary loving and careful mothers are able to give to individual children, given the rough-and-tumble of home life.

Surtees v. *Kingston-Upon-Thames Borough Council* (at 583–4)

1.5.7 The claim against the foster parents therefore failed (by a majority) in the Court of Appeal as the claimant was unable to establish negligence on the part of the foster parents. The claim against the local authority failed as the claimant could not establish any responsibility on the part of the local authority for the acts of foster parent in the absence of deliberate harm to the child.

1.5.8 In a dissenting judgment Beldam LJ was critical of the local authority and pointed out that:

This department had assumed parental responsibility for the appellant. I am confident that no caring parent would have accepted as satisfactory the conflicting and perfunctory accounts recorded without interviewing and taking a full statement from Mrs H and any other witnesses. Unhappily, the appellant had no-one else to look after her rights, and if she had a right to compensation for this serious disablement, it depended on a very much more thorough investigation than was carried out.

Surtees v. *Kingston-Upon-Thames Borough Council* (at 572)

1.5.9 Further, Beldam LJ concluded that in the circumstances of this case he would have found the foster parents liable for the injury as they had not discharged the burden placed on them of showing how the accident could have occurred without negligence.

1.5.10 The case was decided on its own facts but is of interest as it includes a further analysis of the relationship between a local authority and its foster parents. Stocker LJ in the *obiter* passage set out above at para. 1.5.5

suggests that there could be liability on the part of a local authority for deliberate acts of foster parents in circumstances where the local authority was negligent in the choice of foster parents or its supervision of the placement. This case was relied upon by the claimant in the case of *H* v. *Norfolk CC* [1997] 1 FLR 384 at 390, but note that the Court of Appeal stated 'all *dicta* in [the Surtees] case now necessarily fall to be re-examined in the light of Lord Browne-Wilkinson's speech in the *Bedfordshire* case'. The *H* v. *Norfolk* case has now itself been overruled by *S* v. *Gloucestershire* CC [2000] 3 All ER 346.

P and others v. *Harrow London Borough Council* [1993] 1 FLR 723

1.5.11 The claimants lived in the area administered by Harrow local education authority but were not in the care of the local authority. While attending an independent boarding school approved by the Secretary of State for Education as suitable for children with emotional and behavioural difficulties the claimants suffered sexual abuse from the headmaster. The headmaster was subsequently convicted of offences of buggery and sexual assault and sentenced to 12 years' imprisonment. The claims brought against Harrow London Borough Council for breach of statutory duty and negligence were struck out by Mr Justice Potter (as he then was). He found no duty of care was owed by the local authority given it had not had the day-to-day control of the school, did not employ the staff there and had no rights of inspection. The local authority was entitled to rely on the right to approval given for the school by the Secretary of State. Applying the test in *Caparo Industries plc* v. *Dickman* [1990] 2 AC 605, the judge found assaults of the type complained of were not foreseeable, there was no relationship of proximity between the education authority and children at an independent school in respect of the physical safety of those children and it was not just fair and reasonable to impose a duty of care.

T (A minor) v. *Surrey County Council and others* [1994] 4 All ER 577

1.5.12 This was a claim brought by a child against a local authority, a childminder and the childminder's husband. The claimant alleged he had suffered brain damage while in the care of the childminder who was registered by the local authority. Scott Baker J. found that the childminder had inflicted non-accidental injury on the child by shaking. Another child (S) placed with the same childminder had earlier suffered brain damage while in her care. Local authority investigation at the time S sustained injury had concluded that the damage to S resulted from a congenital disposition of S to injury. When the claimant's mother had made inquiries of the local authority about the childminder, an employee of the local authority had told the mother there was no reason why her child could not be placed with the childminder. The employee had not told the mother of the earlier incident of brain damage occurring to a child in the childminder's care.

1.5.13 Scott Baker J. found that the local authority did not owe a common law duty of care to a child placed with a registered childminder. However, on the facts of this case the local authority were liable for negligent misstatement. The employee of the local authority had effectively reassured the mother about the childminder and this constituted a negligent misstatement. On the basis of *Hedley Byrne & Co Ltd* v. *Heller & Partners Ltd* [1964] AC 465, there had been an assumption of responsibility by the local authority and reliance by the mother.

X (Minors) v. *Bedfordshire County Council* [1995] 2 AC 633

1.5.14 This House of Lords' decision is critical to an understanding of how child abuse claims against public authorities and others have come to be formulated. The House of Lords heard five linked appeals: two involved child abuse claims against local authorities; three involved claims against education authorities. In each case the public authority had applied to strike out the claim for failure to show a cause of action (pursuant to Rules of the Supreme Court Order 18 rule 19, then in force). The House of Lords' decision defined the state of the law in respect of public authority liability as it was in 1995. Against the background of this analysis, subsequent decisions of the House of Lords and the Court of Appeal have identified areas of responsibility in respect of child abuse.

1.5.15 In *X (Minors)* v. *Bedfordshire County Council,* Lord Browne-Wilkinson gave the leading speech and began by classifying private law claims into four categories:

    (a)   actions for breach of statutory duty *simpliciter* (breach of a statutory requirement irrespective of carelessness);

    (b)   actions based solely on the careless performance of a statutory duty in the absence of any other common law right of action;

    (c)   actions based on a common law duty of care arising out of the imposition of a statutory duty or from the performance of it;

    (d)   misfeasance in public office.

(at 720H)

Misfeasance in public office was not discussed in detail in *X (Minors)* v. *Bedfordshire County Council*, but has since been considered by the House of Lords in *Three Rivers District Council* v. *Bank of England (No. 3)* [2000] 2 WLR 15.

1.5.16 Lord Browne-Wilkinson described how in respect of (a), breach of statutory duty *simpliciter*, a private law right of action would only arise in very limited and specific cases. It did not cover a scheme of social welfare which was passed not just for the benefit of individuals but for the benefit of society as a whole, *X (Minors)* v. *Bedfordshire County Council* (at 732B). In respect of (b) Lord Browne-Wilkinson stated that in order to found a cause of action based on careless performance of a statutory power or duty it was necessary to show that a duty of care arose at common law. The statutory duty therefore was only relevant to the backdrop. The statute might explain why the public authority was carrying out an act at all. The existence of the statutory duty did not in itself create a duty of care, *X (Minors)* v. *Bedfordshire County Council* (at 735A). Effectively, to succeed in a claim for compensation against a local authority in the area of child welfare it was necessary to establish a common law duty of care (category (c)). In order to show such a duty existed it was necessary to satisfy the criteria for the three-stage test in *Caparo Industries plc* v. *Dickman*.

1.5.17 Lord Browne-Wilkinson summarised the position as follows:

> If the [claimant's] complaint alleges carelessness not in the taking of a discretionary decision to do some act, but in the practical manner in which that act has been performed (e.g. the running of a school) the question whether or not there is a common law duty of care falls to be decided by applying the usual principles ie those laid down in *Caparo Industries plc* v. *Dickman* [1990] 2 AC 605, 617–18 . Was the damage to the [claimant] reasonably foreseeable? Was the relationship between the [claimant] and the Defendant sufficiently proximate? Is it just and reasonable to impose a duty of care? However, the question whether there is a common law duty and if so its ambit, must be profoundly influenced by the statutory framework within which the acts complained of were done.
>
> *X (Minors)* v. *Bedfordshire County Council* (at 739A–C)

1.5.18 Following this analysis by Lord Browne-Wilkinson, claims against a local authority for breach of statutory duty (as opposed to breach of common law duty) in the area of child care are unlikely to succeed. However, it will nearly always be relevant to examine the statutory framework against which a local authority is alleged to have a common law duty of care in respect of a child. Prior to the Children Act 1989 (see para. 1.3) the statutory framework for the exercise of local authority functions in respect of children was extremely complex. The relevant statutory framework is analysed in Chapter 2.

1.5.19 The first child abuse case in the *X (Minors)* v. *Bedfordshire County Council* litigation was the case of X. This was a claim brought on behalf of five children in the same family. The Official Solicitor acted as the children's litigation friend. The children had been born between October 1982 and May 1990. In October 1992 the local authority took steps to seek care orders in respect of all five children and final orders were made in April 1993. When received into care, the children were found to be severely damaged by the neglect and abuse they had suffered at home. The family had been known to social services since 1987 and it was alleged that the local authority should have acted more quickly and effectively to protect them from the neglect and abuse they suffered at home. The alleged facts in *X (Minors)* v. *Bedfordshire County Council* are set out in detail in the dissenting judgment of Sir Thomas Bingham MR (as he then was) in the Court of Appeal (at 653H–655E). This summary was adopted by Lord Browne-Wilkinson in the House of Lords (at 741–2).

1.5.20 The second child abuse case in the same litigation before the House of Lords was *M (A minor)* v. *Newham London Borough Council*. This was a claim brought by a child and her mother against a local authority, a health authority and a psychiatrist. The claimants alleged that the child had been removed from her home into local authority care because of the negligence of the three defendants in believing the child was at risk of sexual abuse if she remained in her home. The claimants alleged that the social worker and the psychiatrist had failed to investigate the facts with proper care and thoroughness. Had they done so they would have correctly identified the alleged abuser (who did not live in the home) and they would not have removed the child from home. The mother and child alleged they suffered psychiatric damage as a result of the enforced separation. *X (Minors)* v. *Bedfordshire County Council* (at 742G/H–744C).

1.5.21 In analysing the legal principles applicable to the facts in the cases of *X (Minors)* v. *Bedfordshire County Council* and *M (A minor)* v. *Newham London Borough Council*, Lord Browne-Wilkinson first considered the possible direct liability of the public authorities (as distinct to the possible vicarious liability). In respect of direct liability, *X (Minors)* v. *Bedfordshire County Council* (at 749D/F/G), he stated that:

- some of the allegations were justiciable and would not require the court to consider policy matters; the claim should not be struck out as non-justiciable;
- some of the decisions of the local authority might be shown to be so unreasonable as to be outside the ambit of the local authority's discretion and the claim should not be struck out on this basis;

- the local authority accepted that there was a relationship of proximity between it and the claimant children;

- the local authority accepted that it was foreseeable that the claimant children would suffer injury if the local authority carried out its statutory duties negligently;

- the issue was whether it was just fair and reasonable to superimpose a common law duty of care on the local authority in relation to the performance of its statutory duties to protect children

1.5.22 Lord Browne-Wilkinson agreed with the view of Sir Thomas Bingham MR set out in his dissenting judgment in the Court of Appeal that:

> The public policy consideration which has the first claim on the loyalty of the law is that wrongs should be remedied and that very potent counter considerations are required to override that policy.
>
> *X (Minors)* v. *Bedfordshire County Council* (at 749G and 663C–D)

1.5.23 Having stressed this test, Sir Thomas Bingham MR found there were no such overriding counter-considerations. The House of Lords disagreed with that view. Lord Browne-Wilkinson (with whom the other members of the Committee agreed) found there were such potent counter-considerations. Lord Browne-Wilkinson described these counter-considerations as follows:

- A common law duty of care would cut across the whole statutory system set up for protection of children at risk, the system is interdisciplinary involving the participation of the police, educational bodies, doctors and others. It would be unfair to make one body alone responsible and too difficult to disentangle liability between the participating bodies.

- The task of the local authority and its servants in dealing with children at risk is extraordinarily delicate.

- If liability were imposed local authorities might adopt a more defensive approach to their duties.

- The relationship between the social worker and the child's parents is frequently one of conflict. The risk of costly and vexatious litigation is a very high one which cannot be ignored.

- The statutory complaints procedure and the ombudsman provide an alternative route to air grievances (although not to recover compensation).

- There were no analogous existing categories of negligence from which to make an incremental extension.

> *X (Minors)* v. *Bedfordshire County Council* (at 749F/G–751G)

1.5.24 Lord Browne-Wilkinson then considered the possible vicarious liability of the public authorities for the acts of their employees in dealing with the claimants. However, he found there could be no such liability as:

> The social workers and the psychiatrists were retained by the local authority to advise the local authority not the [claimants].
> *X (Minors)* v. *Bedfordshire County Council* (at 752G)

The position was said to be analogous to an insurance doctor who owes duties to the insurance company who employs him but not to the insured whom he examines (other than a duty not to directly injure the insured). Lord Nolan gave a dissenting speech on this discrete point, *X (Minors)* v. *Bedfordshire County Council* (at 771H–772B).

1.5.25 Neither of the cases in respect of social services functions before the House of Lords in the *X (Minors)* v. *Bedfordshire County Council* litigation involved a claim by a child suffering ill-treatment or abuse while in the care of the local authority or other institution. In *X* v. *Bedfordshire* the claimants were five children who suffered abuse at home and alleged they should have been removed from home to avoid such abuse; in *M* v. *Newham* a child who alleged she was safe at home and removed into care unnecessarily alleged she suffered injury from being separated from her mother. Although the child in *M (A minor)* v. *Newham London Borough Council* was taken into care, the damage alleged was the separation of the family not the standard of treatment the child received in care.

1.5.26 In dealing with the education cases in the *X (Minors)* v. *Bedfordshire County Council* litigation, Lord Browne-Wilkinson hinted that the situation could be different where a child was placed in an institution run by a local authority. In analysing the position of a school (whether run by a public authority or a private institution), Lord Browne-Wilkinson pointed out that such an institution would owe a duty to the child to keep him safe.

> The question therefore is whether the headmaster of any school whether private or public, or a teaching adviser in under a duty to his pupils to exercise skill and care in advising on their educational needs? *It is accepted that a school and the teachers at the school are under a duty to safeguard the physical well-being of the pupil: Van Oppen* v. *Clerk to the Bedford Charity Trustees* [1990] 1 WLR 235 but there is no case where a school or teacher has been held liable for negligent advice relating to the educational needs of a pupil. The defendant authority maintains that there is no duty of care in relation to such advice. In my judgment a school which accepts a pupil assumes responsibility not only for his physical well-being but also for his educational needs. The education of the pupil is the very purpose for which the child goes to the school. The head teacher, being responsible for the school, himself comes under a duty of care to exercise the reasonable skills of a headmaster in relation to such educational needs. If it comes to the attention of the headmaster that a pupil is under-performing he does owe a

duty to take such steps as a reasonable teacher would consider appropriate to try to deal with such under-performance. To hold that in such circumstances, the head teacher could properly ignore the matter and make no attempt to deal with it would fly in the face not only of society's expectations of what a school will provide but also of the fine traditions of the teaching profession itself.

X (Minors) v. *Bedfordshire County Council* (at 765H–766C)

1.5.27 In relation to a school, Lord Browne-Wilkinson therefore set out the duties of the authority and its employees, including teachers, both to keep the pupils safe from personal injury and to provide them with a reasonable level of education.

1.5.28 The analysis in *X (Minors)* v. *Bedfordshire County Council* was the beginning of the detailed investigation of the principles applicable to public authorities in respect of children at risk of abuse by others. The decision now has to be read in the light of the subsequent decisions of the House of Lords and of the European Court as discussed in the following paragraphs.

Various claimants v. *Leicestershire County Council* (Potts J. 2 April 1996, unreported)

1.5.29 These claims were brought by a group of claimants who suffered abuse at children's homes in Leicestershire in which Frank Beck was employed. Frank Beck was found guilty on 17 counts involving sexual and physical assault of those in his charge. The offences for which he was convicted included four counts of buggery and one of rape. Frank Beck was sentenced to life imprisonment on these counts and to a total of 24 years' imprisonment on other counts. By the date of the civil trial, Frank Beck had died in prison.

1.5.30 In the course of the hearing before Mr Justice Potts, Leicestershire County Council accepted liability on the following basis:

1. There was a duty at common law to take reasonable care to avoid or prevent a [claimant] suffering personal injury while in the Defendants' care.

2. The Defendants were in breach of that duty in each case.

3. For the avoidance of doubt the breach of duty was in the failure of the Defendants, through their managers, to:

    (i) inspect and monitor The Poplars, Radcliffe Road and the Beeches.

4. It is accepted that where a [claimant] establishes that he/she was:

    (i) subjected to regression;

    (ii) provoked into a temper tantrum;

18

(iii) subjected to a physical assault;

(iv) subjected to a sexual assault,

whether under the guise of therapy or not, such [claimant] is entitled to damages for such injury as he/she may prove arose as a result.

5. For the avoidance of doubt the nature and extent of the abuse alleged is not admitted, nor is the alleged causation of the symptoms.

6. In the cases of H, B, I, I and L limitation is in issue.

Various claimants v. *Leicestershire County Council*
(transcript p. 4)

1.5.31 Limitation was later conceded and damages were assessed by Potts J. The highest award was that in the case of L who spent three years at Ratcliffe Children's home where she was abused by Frank Beck, *Various claimants* v. *Leicestershire County Council* (transcript p. 32). She was raped, buggered, physically assaulted and was subjected to forced regression. This claimant was awarded:

- £80,000 for pain, suffering and loss of amenity;
- £40,000 for lost earning capacity;
- £25,000 for cost of therapy.

The awards in this case were later used to assist Scott Baker J. in assessing damages in the North Wales Cases, *Various Claimants* v. *Flintshire County Council* (Scott Baker J. 26 July 2000)

H v. *Norfolk County Council* [1997] 1 FLR 384 (CA 10 May 1996)

1.5.32 In this case Mr Justice Harrison struck out a claim brought by a claimant against a local authority. The claimant was taken into care at the age of 4; he alleged he had suffered physical and sexual abuse by foster parents while he was placed with them between the ages of 5 and 14. The Court of Appeal refused the claimant permission to appeal against the striking-out of the claim. The Court of Appeal agreed with Harrison J., that the policy considerations were indistinguishable from those in *X (Minors)* v. *Bedfordshire County Council* as set out in para. 1.5.23 in respect of child abuse claims.

1.5.33 The House of Lords in *Barrett* v. *Enfield London Borough Council* [1999] 3 WLR 79 did not find it necessary to decide whether the decision in *H* v. *Norfolk County Council* was correct. Subsequently, the Court of Appeal in *S* v. *Gloucestershire County Council* [2000] 3 All ER 346 found that the decision in *H* v. *Norfolk* did not survive the reasoning in *Barrett* v. *Enfield London Borough Council* and should no longer be considered correct.

W v. *Essex County Council* [1999] Fam 90, [1998] 3 WLR 534

1.5.34 A claim was brought by foster parents and their own children against the local authority. A foster child (G) was placed in the claimants' household by the local authority after the parents had been told no child with a history of sexual abuse would be placed with them. The claimants alleged G had sexually abused the children in the foster family causing physical and psychiatric injury to the children and psychiatric damage to the parents. It was alleged that the local authority was aware before placing G in the family that he had received a caution in respect of an incident of sexual assault. Mr Justice Hooper refused to strike out the children's claims in negligence. He struck out the parents' claims in negligence and all the claims for breach of contract and misfeasance in public office.

1.5.35 The Court of Appeal (by a majority, Stuart-Smith LJ dissenting) upheld the decision of Hooper J. not to strike out the claims by the children. The Court of Appeal further upheld the decision of Hooper J., that the claim by the parents for psychiatric damage should be struck out.

1.5.36 The Court of Appeal gave the local authority leave to petition the House of Lords in respect of the children's claims in negligence. The Court of Appeal refused the parents leave to petition. Subsequently, the House of Lords granted the parents leave to petition. After the decision in *Barrett* v. *Enfield London Borough Council*, the local authority abandoned its appeal to the House of Lords. The parents appeal to the House of Lords was heard in January 2000 and the appeal against strike-out allowed, *W* v. *Essex County Council* [2000] 2 WLR 601.

C v. *Devon County Council* (CA, 29 June 1998, unreported)

1.5.37 The claimant claimed damages against the local authority in respect of alleged sexual abuse by a care worker. He claimed the abuse began while he was resident at an approved school and continued after he left the school. The alleged abuser was later convicted of sexual offences in respect of other children. The local authority applied to strike out the claim on the basis it disclosed no cause of action. HH Judge Wigmore refused to strike out the claim in negligence and the Court of Appeal refused the defendant leave to appeal against the decision not to strike out the claim. The case was said by the Court of Appeal to turn on its own facts and to be distinguishable from the decision in *H* v. *Norfolk County Council*.

T v. *North Yorkshire County Council* [1999] IRLR 98 (CA 9 July 1998)

1.5.38   The claimant was a pupil at a special school. He was sexually assaulted by the deputy headmaster of the school, an employee of the local authority. The assault took place on a school trip to Spain. A claim was brought against the local authority alleging vicarious liability for the assault by the deputy headmaster. No claim was brought in negligence. The Court of Appeal ruled the local authority could not be liable for sexual assaults as such assaults were necessarily outside the scope of the employee's duties. The Court of Appeal noted that that there was no allegation pleaded that the local authority owed any direct duty to the claimant to ensure that he was safe on the trip to Spain or that the local authority was itself negligent. This case has now been overruled by the House of Lords in the case of *Lister and others* v. *Hesley Hall Ltd* [2001] 2 WLR 1311 (see paragraph 1.5.52 below).

Barrett v. *London Borough of Enfield* [1999] 3 WLR 79

1.5.39   The claimant in this case had been in care from the age of 10 months until 18 years. It was alleged there had been no proper planning of his case after receipt into care, that he had never been found a satisfactory placement and that as a result of the mismanagement of his welfare by the local authority he had suffered psychiatric damage. HH Judge Brandt (reversing the district judge) struck out the claim and the Court of Appeal confirmed the decision. The House of Lords allowed the claimant's appeal against the striking out of the claim and held that it was arguable that a duty of care was owed by a local authority to a child in care. Lord Slynn described how:

> In summary the *Bedfordshire* case establishes that decisions by local authorities whether or not to take a child into care with all the difficult aspects that involves and all the disruption which may come about are not ones which the courts will review by way of a claim for damages in negligence . . . The question in the present case is different since the child was taken into care; it is therefore necessary to consider whether any acts or omissions and if so what kinds of acts or omissions can ground a claim in negligence. The fact that no completely analogous claim has been accepted by the courts previously points to the need for caution and the need to proceed 'incrementally' and 'by analogy with decided cases'.
>
> *Barrett* v. *London Borough of Enfield* (at 94D)

Lord Slynn concluded:

> In the present case the allegations which I have summarised are largely directed to the way in which the powers of the local authority were exercised. It is arguable (and that is all we are concerned with in this case at this stage) that if some of the allegations are made out, a duty of care was owed and was broken. Others involve the exercise of a discretion which the court may consider to be non justiciable – e.g. whether it was right to arrange adoption at all, though the question of whether adoption was ever considered and if not, why not, may be a matter for investigation in a claim in negligence. I do not think it right to go through each allegation in detail to assess the chances of it being justiciable. The claim is of an on-going failure of duty and must be seen as a whole. I do not think it is the right approach to look only at each detailed allegation and to ask whether that in itself could have caused the injury.
>
> *Barrett* v. *London Borough of Enfield* (at 98F)

1.5.40 In this case the House of Lords considered the proper standard by which to test the potential liability of a public authority for negligence. The House of Lords concluded that social workers and other staff were entitled to rely on the principle in *Bolam* v. *Friern Hospital Management Committee* [1957] 1 WLR 582. Lord Hutton stated:

> I consider where a [claimant] claims damages for personal injuries which he alleges have been caused by decisions negligently taken in the exercise of a statutory discretion, and provided that the decisions do not involve issues of policy which the courts are ill-equipped to adjudicate upon it is preferable for the courts to decide the validity of the [claimant's] claim by applying directly the common law concept of negligence than by applying as a preliminary test the public law concept of *Wednesbury* unreasonableness (see *Associated Provincial Picture Houses Ltd* v. *Wednesbury Corporation* [1948] 1 KB 223).
>
> *Barrett* v. *London Borough of Enfield* (at 111)

1.5.41 The case of *Barrett* v. *London Borough of Enfield* provided a further review of the public policy considerations in the area of social welfare responsibility. For a detailed analysis of the impact of this decision see: Craig, P. and Fairgrieve, D. '*Barrett*, negligence and discretionary powers', [1999] PL, winter 1999: 626. The case also provided an opportunity for the House of Lords to consider the European Court's decision in the case of *Osman* v. *UK* [1999] 1 FLR 193 in the period between the passing of the Human Rights Act 1998 and its implementation in October 2000.

Palmer v. *Tees Health Authority* [2000] PIQR P1

1.5.42 The claimant's daughter, aged 4, was abducted and sexually assaulted and murdered by a man named Armstrong who was a psychiatric patient. The claimant sued the health authority for damages for bereavement and for her own psychiatric damage as a result of the events. The claimant alleged the health authority was negligent in failing to diagnose that there was a real risk of Armstrong committing serious sexual offences against children. Further, it was alleged that the health authority failed to provide adequate treatment for Armstrong or to prevent him being released from the hospital. Mr Justice Gage struck out the claim as failing to show a cause of action.

1.5.43 The Court of Appeal found that, following the decision in *Barrett* v. *London Borough of Enfield*, it was not correct to strike out the claim on the basis that it was not just, fair and reasonable to impose a duty of care. However, the claim could be struck out on the basis that proximity was not established. On the facts of the case, Gage J. was correct to find that proximity could not be established and the claim rightly struck out in accordance with the decision of the House of Lords in *Hill* v. *Chief Constable of West Yorkshire* [1989] AC 53.

G v. *Berrow Wood School and others* (CA, 17 October 1999, unreported)

1.5.44 The claimant in this case was never in local authority care but his placement at Berrow Wood School (an independent school for boys with behavioural problems) was organised by a local authority. The claimant alleged that while at this independent school he was violently assaulted by members of staff employed at the school. Initially a claim was brought against Berrow Wood School Limited, the individuals alleged to be responsible for assaulting him at the school and Hereford and Worcester County Council. The local authority had been responsible for the claimant's placement at the school, they had paid the fees in the first instance but then recovered them from the claimant's stepfather. The school went into liquidation and apparently the insurance policy did not cover the position. The individual abusers had no funds to meet a judgment. The claimant therefore pursued the claim against the local authority and made an application to join the Secretary of State for Education and Employment.

1.5.45 The claimant was refused leave to join the Department of Education and the claim against the local authority was struck out. Mr Justice Jackson found that the claimant would not be able to establish proximity or that it was just fair and reasonable to impose a duty of care on the Department in the circumstances of this case. The judge struck out the claim against the local authority applying the principles laid down by the House of Lords in *X (Minors)* v. *Bedfordshire County Council*. Following the House of Lords decision in *Barrett* v. *Enfield London Borough Council,* the claimant applied for permission to appeal. The Court of Appeal refused permission to appeal and confirmed that the judge was right to find there was not the requisite proximity between the claimant and the Department of

Education and that the case against the local authority was 'quite hopeless' in circumstances where the claimant had never been in care and the local authority had no control over the independent school.

S v. *Gloucestershire County Council* [2001] Fam 313, [2000] 3 All ER 346

1.5.46   The two cases of *S* v. *Gloucestershire County Council* and *L* v. *London Borough of Tower Hamlets and London Borough of Havering* were heard consecutively and a combined judgment given. In that judgment, the Court of Appeal held that following the House of Lords decision in *Barrett* v *London Borough of Enfield,* a damages claim by a victim of sexual abuse against a local authority which had placed the victim in the abuser's home might be capable of being formulated as a viable cause of action in negligence. In the case of L, the court found that all the facts that were likely to be relevant were already before the court in respect of the strike-out application. On the basis of those facts, the court found the case had no prospect of succeeding.

1.5.47   Lord Justice May in the leading judgment set out the development of the law. The judgment analysed in detail the cases of *X (Minors)* v. *Bedfordshire County Council* and *Barrett* v. *London Borough of Enfield.* Having summarised the strands of the relevant law May LJ stated:

> It is clear from these principles that in an ordinary case a local authority defendant is unlikely to establish a defence which relies on a blanket immunity. There would be a blanket immunity for this purpose if it were decided without reference to particular facts that all cases which have certain basic characteristics were not justiciable, or that in every case with certain characteristics it was not just or reasonable to impose a duty of care. Thus it seems to me it would be incorrect to say, as counsel for the local authorities were inclined to submit in appeals before this court, that cases that may be labelled child abuse cases are bound to fail as a class. The 'child abuse cases' was no more than a convenient label under which *X and ors (minors)* v. *Bedfordshire County Council* and *M (a minor)* v. *Newham London Borough Council* travelled. *Remembering always that the critical question is a composite one which embraces the alleged duty of care and its breach in the context of the damage alleged to have been caused, the court has to consider the nature of the actions and decisions of the local authority which are said to have been negligent.* From this it may be said that the decision whether or not to take a child said to have been abused away from its natural parents and into care may often be acutely difficult. But many of the decisions about the care and upbringing of a child once he or she has been taken into care, difficult though they may be, may not have the acute complications, strains and conflicts identified in *X and ors (minors)* v. *Bedfordshire County Council.* For this reason I am inclined to think that the House of Lords' decision in *Barrett* v. *London Borough of Enfield* requires this court to say that *H* v. *Norfolk County Council* was wrongly decided. [*Emphasis added*]

1.5.48 The Court of Appeal in this case also considered the implications of Article 6 of the European Convention on Human Rights and the procedural overlap between strike-out applications and summary judgment applications under the Civil Procedure Rules 1998.

Various claimants v. *Flintshire County Council (the former Clwyd County Council)* (Mr Justice Scott Baker, 26 July 2000, unreported)

1.5.49 This was the first tranche of contested claims in the North Wales Children's Homes litigation arising from the Inquiry into Child Abuse in North Wales by Sir Ronald Waterhouse, *Lost in Care*. Liability was not in issue in most of the cases except in respect of isolated discrete issues. Limitation was only in issue in one case. In that case Mr Justice Scott Baker exercised his discretion to allow the claimant's claim to proceed.

1.5.50 The main issue for the judge's determination was the level of damages and the judge analysed the principles on which the claimants should be awarded damages for pain, suffering and loss of amenity and the basis of calculating past and future loss of earnings. Awards of damages between £2,000 and £94,000 including special damages were made, as set out in Chapter 4, para. 4.5.11 onward.

C v. *Flintshire County Council* ([2001] EWCA Civ 302)

1.5.51 The defendant in the *Flintshire* cases appealed one award of damages. C had been awarded a total of £70,719: £35,000 for pain, suffering and loss of amenity; £20,000 past loss of earnings; £5,000 future loss of earnings and £7,919 therapy costs. The Court of Appeal dismissed the appeal and confirmed that the award of damages for pain, suffering and loss of amenity, loss of earnings and costs of therapy were acceptable. The court stated that the Judicial Studies Board *Guidelines* did not encompass cases of this type (JSB (2000) *Guidelines for the Assessment of General Damages in Personal Injury Cases*, 5th edn, Blackstone Press). Claimants suffering sexual, physical and emotional abuse from those employed to look after them came into a wholly different category from that covered by psychiatric damage in the JSB *Guidelines*. Further, the bands set out in the *Guidelines* did not reflect compensation for the painful events themselves.

Lister v. *Hesley Hall Ltd* [2001] UKHL 22, [2001] 2 WLR 1311 HL

1.5.52 The claimants were pupils at a privately owned residential school and alleged they were subjected to sexual abuse by a warden at the school. The warden was convicted of sexual abuse and sentenced to seven years' imprisonment. In a claim against the school for damages, HH Judge Walker held that the school could not be vicariously liable for the sexual abuse of an employee but could be liable for the employee's failure to report the abuse.

1.5.53 The Court of Appeal allowed the defendant's appeal and held that the failure to report was so closely connected to the sexual abuse itself that it was outside the course of the employee's employment and the defendant could not be vicariously liable. The House of Lords reversed the decision of the Court of Appeal, overruled the case of *T* v. *North Yorkshire County Council* (see para. 1.5.38 above) and found that the defendant was vicariously liable for the warden's acts of abuse. The House of Lords found that the warden of the school had such close contact with pupils at the school that there was sufficient connection between the work he was employed to do and the acts of abuse he had committed for those acts to be committed within the scope of his employment. The defendant could therefore be vicariously liable for those acts.

1.5.54 Lord Hobhouse described the position as follows:

> What these cases and Trotman's case in truth illustrate is a situation where the employer has assumed a relationship to the plaintiff which imposes specific duties in tort upon the employer and the role of the employee (or servant) is that he is the person to whom the employer has entrusted the performance of that duty. These cases are examples of that class where the employer, by reason of assuming a relationship to the plaintiff, owes to the plaintiff duties which are more extensive than those owed by the public at large and, accordingly, are to be contrasted with the situation where a defendant is simply in proximity to the plaintiff so that it is foreseeable that his acts may injure the plaintiff or his property and a reasonable person would have taken care to avoid causing such injury . . .
>
> The fact that sexual abuse was involved does not distinguish this case from any other involving the care of the young and vulnerable and the duty to protect them from the risk of harm.
>
> *Lister* v. *Hesley Hall Ltd* (at para. 54)

1.5.55 This claim against the owners and managers of a private school had failed in negligence as the judge found it could not be shown that the defendants had been negligent in their care, selection and control of the warden. The claim succeeded on the basis the defendant was held vicariously liable for the abuse perpetrated by the warden. The speeches of Lord Steyn (with whom Lord Hutton agreed), Lord Clyde and Lord Hobhouse describe the vicarious liability of the defendant in terms of breach of duty. Lord Clyde describes how:

> It appears that the [defendants] gave the warden a quite general authority in the supervision and running of the house as well as some particular responsibilities. His general duty was to look after and to care for, among others, the [claimants]. That function was one which the [defendants] had delegated to him. That he performed that function in a way that was an abuse of his position and an abnegation of his duty does not sever the connection with his employment. The particular acts that he carried out upon the boys have to be viewed not in isolation but in the context and the circumstances in which they occurred. Given that he had a general management of the house and in the care and supervision of the boys in it, the employers should be liable for the way in which he behaved towards them in his capacity as warden of the house. The [defendants] should then be vicariously liable to the [claimants] for the injury that they suffered at the hands of the warden.
>
> *Lister* v. *Hesley Hall Ltd* (at para. 50)

1.5.56 Lord Millett however described the liability of the defendants as vicarious liability 'for the warden's intentional assaults, not (as was suggested in argument) for his failure to perform his duty to take care of the boys'. This leaves open the important issue as to whether the vicarious liability of the defendants in *Lister* v. *Hesley Hall Ltd* gives rise to a cause of action for breach of duty with a three-year limitation period (and the extension provisions of ss.11, 14 and 33 of the Limitation Act 1980) or whether it gives rise to a cause of action in trespass with a non-extendable six-year limitation period.

1.5.57 In the case of *Various claimants* v. *Bryn Alyn Community Homes Ltd and another* (Connell J., 26 June 2001, unreported) (see para. 1.5.61 and Chapter 3) Connell J. found that the claim for deliberate acts of abuse for which the defendant was vicariously liable was subject to a non-extendable six-year limitation period. However, this case is due to be heard in the Court of Appeal in 2002 and therefore this decision may not finally determine this issue.

Z and Others v. *UK* Report of European Commission Application No. 29392/95, 10 September 1999 (ECHR 10 May 2001; [2001] 2 FLR 612)

1.5.58 The social services cases in the *X (Minors)* v. *Bedfordshire County Council* litigation have subsequently been considered by the European Commission of Human Rights and the European Court of Human Rights (ECHR). The European Commission of Human Rights found breaches of Articles 3 and 6 of the European Convention on Human Rights. In *Z and others* v. *UK* (the *X (Minors)* v. *Bedfordshire County Council case*) the European Commission of Human Rights stated:

The Commission is aware that social services face difficult and delicate decisions when intervening in family situations . . . it also recognises that neglect manifests itself in more insidious and invisible effects than some types of physical abuse and may have a cumulative effect the seriousness of which is not readily apparent. The Commission is nonetheless satisfied in the present case that the authorities were aware of the serious ill-treatment and neglect suffered by the applicants over a number of years at the hands of their parents and failed, despite the means reasonably available to them, to take any effective steps to bring it to an end. It finds therefore that the State failed in its positive obligation under Article 3 of the Convention to provide the applicants with adequate protection against inhuman and degrading treatment.

1.5.59 The European Commission applied the case of *Osman* v. *UK* [1993] 1 FLR 193, and found that the striking out of the children's claims in *X (Minors)* v. *Bedfordshire County Council* was a breach of Article 6 as it prevented them having the facts of their cases heard by a court and was a disproportionate restriction to their right of access to court.

1.5.60 The European Court in *Z* v. *UK* [2001] confirmed the decision of the European Commission in part. It confirmed that the applicants had suffered a breach of Article 3 of the European Convention on Human Rights and that there was a failure to provide a remedy and a breach of Article 13 of the Convention. However, the Court (by a majority) did not find a breach of Article 6 (see Chapter 3: paras. 3.7.18–3.7.22).

Various claimants v. *Bryn Alyn Community Homes Ltd* and the *Royal and Sun Alliance plc* (Connell J. 26 June 2001) unreported

1.5.61 This case involved 14 cases from the third tranche of claims arising out of the physical and sexual abuse of children in children's homes in North Wales. The claims concerned the Bryn Alyn Community, a collection of five homes privately run from November 1972 by the company Bryn Alyn Community Ltd. Until 1990 the managing director of this company was John Allen. In 1995 John Allen was convicted of six offences of indecent assault on residents in the community and sentenced to six years' imprisonment. In 1997 the company managing the Bryn Alyn Community went into liquidation and the liquidator took no part in the proceedings brought against it by the claimants. The company's insurers, the Royal and Sun Alliance plc gave notice to the claimants that there was a potential conflict of interest arising out of an exemption clause in the insurance for the company. The insurers were joined as second defendant and were the effective defendants at the trial. The insurers required each of the claimants to prove their case and to establish that they had suffered physical or sexual abuse through a breach of duty of care on the part of the company or its employees acting within the course of their employment. Further, the second defendant argued that the claims were limitation barred.

1.5.62 Mr Justice Connell heard the claims over five weeks and made awards of damages in 13 of the cases. The judge exercised his discretion to allow all the claims to proceed pursuant to s.33 Limitation Act 1980. The judge found the majority of individual allegations proved to the requisite standard having regard to the speech of Lord Nicholls in *re H Minors* [1996] AC 563 at 586C–H (see Chapter 7). The judge found that judged by the standards of the time (1973–91) the staff employed at Bryn Alyn were not trained or experienced in dealing with damaged children, the homes were overcrowded with too many difficult children and the staff failed to heed obvious warning signs about the principal and paedophile John Allen. The staff failed to prevent other staff from resorting to violence as a matter of course. The judge found overall that the Community was neither adequately nor properly organised or supervised. The company was proved to have been directly negligent and vicariously liable for the negligent acts of its employees. In individual cases the judge found that some abuse, while deliberately caused could not be said to have been negligently caused and that any claim for vicarious liability for this abuse was statute barred by reason of the non-extendable six-year limitation period.

1.5.63 The judge awarded general damages for pain, suffering and loss of amenity of between £35,000 and £2,000 to claimants who had suffered severe sexual abuse including repeated acts of buggery leading to permanent psychiatric damage and/or physical abuse including very severe beatings. Further, the judge awarded therapy costs of up to £10,000 and in four cases some past or future damages for vulnerability on the labour market. These awards varied between £2,500 and £10,000.

1.5.64 This decision has been appealed by both the insurance defendant and the claimants and is due to be considered by the Court of Appeal in 2002. The appeal raises issues in respect of limitation, liability and quantum.

1.6 CONCLUSION

The issues in civil claims

1.6.1 The common law duty of a public authority to protect children from abuse was considered by the House of Lords on three occasions in the 1990s. The European Convention on Human Rights and the implementation of the Human Rights Act 1998 have led to further scrutiny of the public policy considerations in this area. There are many issues still to be determined but the cases set out in this introduction demonstrate the variety of situations already examined by the courts.

1.6.2 The civil claims for compensation for child abuse now proceeding through the litigation system raise complex and novel issues of fact, law and practice, as follows:

- the scope of the direct duty of care owed by any public authority or institution;
- the scope of the vicarious duty owed by any public authority or institution for its employees and the extent to which such employees were acting within the scope of their employment;
- the identity of the authorities, institutions or individuals owing a duty of care at the time of the allegations;
- the identity of the correct defendant to any proceedings, that is authorities, institutions or individuals who may have taken over responsibility for outstanding torts from preceding bodies or institutions;
- the professional standards of teachers, social workers, inspectors at the relevant time;
- the appropriate experts to identify the standards acceptable at the time;
- the extent of any breach of duty measured by the standards of care acceptable at the time;
- the relevant statutory framework governing the authority or institution against which complaint is made;
- the provisions for inspection of schools and homes by the Home Office and Department of Education at the relevant time;
- causation of damage to the claimant in a particular regime or by a particular abuser;
- the apportionment of responsibility between institutions, public authorities and/or other individuals who are alleged to have caused injury to the claimant;
- the extent of the damage suffered: physical, emotional and psychiatric;
- the appropriate experts to identify and substantiate such damage;
- the quantification of the damage for pain, suffering and loss of amenity, particularly where there is a lack of comparable cases and the JSB *Guidelines* do not encompass such cases;
- the extent of past and future losses and in particular loss of earnings that can be attributable to the injury sustained (see *Various claimants* v. *Flintshire County Council* (Scott Baker J. 26 July 2000) and *C* v. *Flintshire County Council* (CA 26 July 2000)).

30

- limitation;
- disclosure of documents; identifying the relevant documents and where they are now stored;
- identifying witnesses and other evidence;
- case management, particularly in relation to generic actions.

The statutory framework

2.1   INTRODUCTION

2.1.1   Although child abuse compensation claims are personal injury claims, the lawyer dealing with them needs to have some knowledge of family, administrative and criminal law. This chapter will examine the development of the modern child care system from 1933 to date. It covers the various systems of protection for children in: homes, foster care, adoption, schools, hospitals, prisons and other scenarios e.g. nurseries, youth clubs. It will also examine the concept of children's rights, the international treaties which influence domestic law, and the way in which the criminal law deals with children.

2.1.2   The developments in childcare law have been examined in various reports commissioned by government, local authorities and private organisations, for example:

- The *Report of the North Wales Child Abuse Tribunal of Inquiry* by Sir Ronald Waterhouse (*Lost in Care*) – see para. 1.2.11 – contains an encyclopaedia which summarises the relevant law from 1974 to 1991.

- The *Report of the Review of the Safeguards for Children Living away from Home* commissioned by the Department of Health and the Welsh Office 1997 by Sir William Utting (*People Like Us*) is a comprehensive review of the procedures and codes of practice available to various child protection agencies, schools, mental health institutions, and so on, mainly under the Children Act 1989.

2.1.3 Obviously, such reports are invaluable sources of information for the practitioner, as they show the state of the law and childcare practice at particular periods in the past. Further detail can be obtained from family law textbooks such as *Children Law and Practice* (Hershman and McFarlane) published by Jordans; and Clarke, Hall and Morrison's textbook on children published by Butterworths.

2.1.4 When bringing a compensation claim, it is important to understand the statutory framework governing the childcare system at the material time (see Chapter 3). The primary source of legislation is statute followed by statutory regulations. Local authorities must act within the terms of their powers prescribed by Acts of Parliament and the regulations prescribed thereunder. If they do not, then their actions can be challenged by way of judicial review. In addition, central government departments such as the Home Office or the Department of Health are able to issue orders, circulars, guidance documents and reports to local authorities and other organisations involved in the care of children. Finally, it is quite common for local authorities and voluntary organisations to produce their own childcare guidelines. These are all documents which may be relevant on disclosure.

2.1.5 The powers and duties of public authorities are also affected by the Human Rights Act 1998, which incorporates the European Convention on Human Rights into domestic law (see Chapter 3).

2.1.6 The original power of the Secretary of State to give guidance to local authorities on the subject of childcare was contained in s.42 of the Children Act 1948. Section 7 of the Local Authority Social Services Act 1970 is now the mechanism whereby the Secretary of State for the relevant central government department, e.g. the Department of Health provides guidance, directions and orders to each local authority in the field of childcare. These powers were expanded by the National Health Service and Community Care Act 1990. A local authority is bound to act under the general guidance of the Secretary of State and again may be subject to judicial review if it fails to do so. The Secretary of State may arrange for an inquiry to be held into the childcare functions of a local authority and other agencies under s.81 of the Children Act 1989. He may also make an order declaring the local authority to be in default of its duties (s.84(1) Children Act 1989). The latter power may again be subject to judicial review.

2.1.7   Practice Guidance from the Department of Health which is not issued under s.7 is nevertheless 'something to which regard must be had in carrying out the statutory functions' (*R.* v. *Islington London Borough Council* ex parte Rixon (1996) 32 BMLR 136). The circulars issued by the Department for Education and Employment to local education authorities are of similar status.

2.2   CHILDCARE LEGISLATION FROM 1933 TO 2001

The Children and Young Persons Act 1933

2.2.1   The Children and Young Persons Act 1933 (the 1933 Act) introduced the concept of care proceedings in respect of children and set out the conditions under which such proceedings could be brought. These conditions were extended under the Children and Young Persons (Amendment) Act 1952, the Children and Young Persons Act 1963 and 1969. The 1933 Act also sought to bring together the criminal law and the law relating to the protection of the children.

2.2.2   A local authority was permitted (where parents were prosecuted for mistreatment) to remove a child from the care of those parents. The Children and Young Persons (Amendment) Act 1952 later removed the need for a criminal prosecution against the parents.

2.2.3   The 1933 Act is still important today since parts of it are still in force. The Act imposed a liability on a local authority to contribute towards the maintenance of a child in its care (ss.86–88). This liability is repeated in ss.23–26 of the Children Act 1948 and s.62 of the Children and Young Persons Act 1969. Section 1 places a duty on parents (including foster parents) to protect a child under 16 from unnecessary suffering or injury to health. Under s.11, there is a specific duty to a child under 12, to protect the child from burning and scalding. These duties were amended by the Children Act 1989 Schedule 13, paras. 2–5.

2.2.4   The 1933 Act made provision for local authorities to provide remand homes, approved schools and persons to whose care children and young persons might be committed. A remand home was effectively a prison for children accused of certain crimes. Approved schools replaced the old industrial schools and reformatories, and were intended for child offenders, children taken into care and children in need of education. Section 92 of the 1933 Act defined voluntary homes as meaning 'any home or other institution for the boarding care, and maintenance of poor children or young persons, being a home or other institution supported wholly or partly by voluntary contributions'. The 1933 Act also dealt with the treatment of children by the criminal courts.

The Children Act 1948

2.2.5 The Children Act 1948 (the 1948 Act) provided for a local authority to set up specialist children departments. The Home Secretary exercised general guidance as the central authority for the care of children (with some concurrent responsibilities vesting in the Ministers of Health and Pensions).

2.2.6 Under s.1 of the 1948 Act, the local authority had a duty to keep a child 'received' into its care for so long as the child appeared to require care, although the circumstances under which a local authority could act to protect a child were fairly restrictive (see para. 2.2.8 for discussion of s.2). Section 12 of the 1948 Act set out the general duties of a local authority in relation to children in its care:

> (a) To exercise their powers with respect to him so as to further his best interests and to afford him opportunity for the proper development of his character and abilities.
>
> (b) To make such use of facilities and services available for children in the care of their own parents as appeared to the local authority reasonable in each child's case.

2.2.7 In addition, a Home Office Memorandum was published in November 1948 which stated that the 1948 Act was designed to ensure that 'all deprived children shall have an upbringing likely to make them sound and happy citizens and shall have all the chances, educational and vocational, of making a good start in life which are open to children in normal homes'. The general duty of local authorities towards children in their care was amended by the Children and Young Persons Act 1969 (s.24) and the Children Act 1975 (Part IV), which were re-enacted and amended in the Child Care Act 1980 (ss.1 and 18).

2.2.8 Section 2 of the 1948 Act empowered local authorities to assume the rights and powers of parents with respect to children in care if:

> (a) the child's parents were dead and the child had no parent or guardian; or
> (b) if a parent or guardian suffered from permanent disability which made him incapable of caring for the child;
> (c) if a parent or guardian was 'of such habits or mode of life as to be unfit to have the care of the child'.

2.2.9 The 1948 Act was aimed at the situation of a particular child in need, rather than the family unit. It did not cover every social work situation, and consequently child care officers found themselves having to deal with cases outside of the existing legislation. At that time, there was an emphasis in social work to try to keep the family unit together, and this became known as 'preventive social work'.

2.2.10   Under s.13 of the 1948 Act, the local authority was obliged to discharge its duty to accommodate and maintain the child by:

    (a)   boarding the child out (i.e. state approved fostering);

    (b)   maintaining the child in a home;

    (c)   making such other arrangements as might be appropriate, i.e. placing the child with a guardian, relative or friend

Boarding-out

2.2.11   The concept of boarding-out generally took priority over placing a child in a home before the Children and Young Persons Act 1969. Voluntary child care organisations with parental responsibility for children could also board children out to foster parents. Local authorities and voluntary organisations were under certain duties towards children who were boarded out. The Home Office published a guidance document, the Memorandum on the Boarding-Out of Children Regulations 1955. The relevant regulations were the Boarding-Out of Children Regulations 1955 (SI 1955 No. 1377) as amended by the London Government Order 1965 (SI 1965 No. 654) and The Boarding-Out of Children (Amendment) Regulations 1982 (SI 1982 No. 447). From 1 June 1989, the 1955 Regulations were replaced by the Boarding-Out of Children (Foster Placement) Regulations 1988 (SI 1988 No. 2184). The Department of Health and Welsh Office issued a handbook of guidance; Department of Health/Welsh Office The Boarding-Out of Children (Foster Placement) Regulations 1988: *Handbook of Guidance 1989*.

Homes

2.2.12   In addition, regulations were made for the provision of homes whether under the care of a local authority or a voluntary organisation. Voluntary homes were homes or institutions (not being nursing, mental nursing and certain residential care homes for mentally disordered children), which were supported wholly or partly by voluntary contributions or endowments but not being a school. Voluntary homes had to register with the Secretary of State and could be removed from the register in certain circumstances.

2.2.13   Private sector profit-making homes were not voluntary homes and children in those homes were not covered by any statutory legislation. The Children Homes Act 1982 would have placed them under a system of regulation, but it was never brought into force. Local authorities were quite entitled to place children at such homes. Consequently, children in such homes were covered by the local authority's general duties of care towards children in its area. However, the Memorandum on the Boarding-Out of

Children Regulations 1955 comments on local authority placements where no regulations apply (this would by analogy apply to private children's homes). The regulations state that this:

> does not mean that there is no need for supervision by the local authority . . . As will be realised, there is undoubted need for adequate supervision of children . . . This supervision may call for particular care and discretion for the reason that it has to be exercised as part of a general responsibility, with no statutory provisions which specifically require it or prescribe, for example, the frequency of visits.

2.2.14 The relevant regulations for voluntary and local authority homes were the Administration of Children's Homes Regulations 1951 (SI 1951 No. 1217). These regulations remained in force until 1991. In 1951 the Home Office circulated a memorandum to local authorities entitled the Memorandum on the Conduct of Children Homes. Voluntary homes were subject to further regulations under the Voluntary Homes (Return of Particulars) Regulations 1949 (SI 1949 No. 2092) and Voluntary Homes (Registration) Regulations 1948 (SI 1948 No. 2408). In addition Home Office Circulars issued in October 1964 to local authorities and voluntary organisations stressed the importance of taking up references before appointing staff and asked local authorities to inform the Home Office of anyone they ceased to employ on work with children because of a criminal offence.

2.2.15 These Regulations were partly replaced by the Children's Homes (Control and Discipline) Regulations 1990, which *inter alia* provided:

    (a)   Those responsible for the control of homes are required to maintain the homes in accordance with good professional practice

    (b)   The use of certain sanctions such as punishment, in particular corporal punishment, deprivation of food and the restriction of visits is prohibited.

    (c)   Permanent records are to be kept of any sanctions used.

2.2.16 The Secretary of State had power to inspect any voluntary home unless the home was subject to inspection by a government department. That power could be delegated by consent to a relevant local authority. The Registered Homes Act 1984 consolidated certain enactments relating to residential care homes, nursing homes and registered homes tribunals. Local authority-run homes were also open to Home Office inspection.

Approved schools

2.2.17 Approved schools before the 1969 leglislation were part of a residential system, quite separate from the local authority service and subject to different management and inspection by the Home Office. They came under the provisions of the Criminal Justice Act 1948, and they were used for young offenders. In 1971 they were consolidated in the new community homes system (see para. 2.2.33) by implementation of the Children and Young Persons Act 1969.

2.2.18 Children were placed at an approved school under what was known as an approved school order. The court did not specify the particular approved school the child was to attend. On leaving the court, the child was usually placed at an assessment centre for a few weeks or sometimes months. The child was assessed and then allocated to a particular approved school by order of the Secretary of State at the Home Office pursuant to the powers contained in ss.23 and 24 Children and Young Persons Act 1933. The period of detention of children in an approved school was not determined by the court but was governed by the provisions of the Children and Young Persons Act 1933. The maximum period of detention was three years. From 1 January 1971, when the Children and Young Persons Act 1969 came into force, the care order replaced the approved school order. Children were then placed at an approved school while in the care of the local authority.

2.2.19 The Children and Young Persons Act 1933 and the Education Act 1944 provided for children to be placed at approved schools in a variety of circumstances including:

(a) Where they were found guilty of a criminal offence which would in the case of an adult be punishable with a term of imprisonment; (s.57 1933 Act).

(b) Where they were found to be in need of care or protection; (s.62(1) 1933 Act).

(c) When they were not attending school regularly (s.40 Education Act 1944).

2.2.20 *The Handbook for Managers of Approved Schools* published by the Home Office in 1961 described the nature and purpose of approved schools as follows:

The schools provide care and training under residential conditions. They give a general education with considerable attention to craft training for the older groups, but their primary objects are the readjustment and social re-education of the boys in preparation for their return to the community. The aim is to base this process of rehabilitation on understanding of the personality, history, abilities and aptitudes of each boy, and on knowledge of the family situation and to promote it by stable environment in the school enabling remedial influences to be brought to bear and progressive training to be given, by contact with the home and by help and supervision after the boy leaves the school. The main ingredients of approved school training are education (in the more formal sense) religious education and guidance, practical or vocational training, attention to health and to the use of recreation and leisure, social training (how to live with others) and personal casework (help with personal problems).

2.2.21   *The Handbook for Managers* further described to managers how:

> The school managers are in *loco parentis* to the boys; and the statutory
> Approved School Rules 1933 as amended by the Approved School Rules
> 1949 specify certain requirements regarding the managing body, the
> treatment and discipline of the boys and other matters designed to safe-
> guard the welfare of those who have been deprived of their full liberty by
> order of a court.

2.2.22   Pursuant to Rule 14 Approved School Rules 1933 the managers of an approved school were responsible for the appointment, suspension and dismissal of all staff at the school. The *Handbook for Managers* described
how the headmaster, deputy headmaster, matron, teachers, housemasters
and instructors should all be employed under a written agreement. Other
staff could be appointed without a written agreement. The *Handbook for
Managers* described the duties of Managers as follows:

> The managers are required to maintain an efficient standard throughout the
> school, and for this purpose to take into consideration any report communi-
> cated to them by or on behalf of the Secretary of State. It is their duty to en-
> sure that the condition of the school and the training and welfare and
> education of the boys under their care are satisfactory, and for this purpose
> to pay frequent visits to the school (Rule 10(1) and (2)). To do their work
> effectively, managers should know the school and should be known to the
> staff and to the boys.

The Children and Young Persons Act 1963

2.2.23   The Children and Young Persons Act 1963 added new grounds on which
parental rights could be assumed by a local authority. These were (a)
where the parent or guardian suffered from a mental disorder; and (b)
where the parent or guardian had so persistently failed without reasonable
cause to discharge parental obligations as to be unfit to care for the child.
These powers applied to children who had already been taken into local
authority care (s.48). In addition, juvenile delinquency (i.e. children committing criminal offences) became the responsibility of social services
whereas before it had been handled by probation officers.

The London Authorities (Children) Order 1965 (SI 1965 No. 554)

2.2.24   This Order provided for people taken into care under the Children Act
1948 in the Greater London area to be transferred to a 'successor authority' from the London County Council.

The Children and Young Persons Act 1969

2.2.25   The Children and Young Persons Act 1969 (the 1969 Act) created a new childcare scheme for local authorities. The 1969 Act came into force at the same time as a general reorganisation of local authority social services under the Local Authority Social Services Act 1970. On 18 March 1969 the office of the Secretary of State of Social Services was created as the central authority for the care of children in England. On the 1 April 1969 responsibility for social services in Wales was transferred to the Secretary of State for Wales. On the 1 January 1971, the remaining Home Office responsibilities for children in Wales were transferred to the Welsh Office. The Local Government Act 1972 brought about the reorganisation of local authorities in England and Wales on the 1 April 1974.

2.2.26   The Local Authority Social Services Act 1970 consolidated local authority children's departments, welfare departments and certain functions of public health departments. Thereafter, local authorities no longer had specialist departments responsible for children. The 1970 Act further established local authority social services committees and the office of director of social services.

2.2.27   The 1969 Act provided that where a child or young person was being ill-treated, neglected or had committed an offence and was in need of care and control, a juvenile court could make an order for his care, parental control, supervision, hospital admission or health authority guardianship.

2.2.28   In addition, the 1969 Act created a wider duty than previous towards children in a local authority's area. Section 2 of the 1969 Act (which included 14 subsections) set out the circumstances in which a local authority should bring care proceedings. The section provided that:

(a)   A local authority which received information suggesting that there were grounds for bringing care proceedings in respect of a child should make enquiries unless it was satisfied that such enquiries were unnecessary.

(b)   In circumstances where enquiries provided grounds for bringing care proceedings, a local authority was under a duty to bring proceedings unless it was satisfied that it was not in the interests of the child or the public interest to do so.

2.2.29   From 1 January 1971, and under s.24(1) of the 1969 Act, the local authority powers and duties were further enlarged so as to add an obligation to receive a child committed into its care. In addition, s.24(2) of the 1969 Act gave a local authority the same powers and duties as the parent and guardian would have had but for the order, including the power to restrict the child's liberty (s.24(2)). The local authority also came under a duty to hold six-monthly reviews of children in care (s.27(4)). The 1969 Act gave more discretion to social workers as to where a young offender might be placed. Provisions were made for the abolition of approved schools and the setting up of community homes with education on the premises.

2.2.30 The discontinuance of approved schools was provided for in s.46 of the 1969 Act. This section provided for the Secretary of State to order that an approved school should 'cease to be an approved institution' in consequence of the establishment of a community home in the area. A series of Cessation of Approved Institutions Orders was made pursuant to s.46 of the 1969 Act. Schedule 3 to the 1969 Act sets out the provisions that the Secretary of State could make in respect of such cessation orders. Section 39 of the 1969 Act provided for the Secretary of State to make Instruments of Management in respect of former approved schools that would become designated as controlled community homes.

2.2.31 Paragraph 10(2) of Schedule 3 to the 1969 Act makes provisions in respect of such controlled community homes and provides:

> (a) the Secretary of State may by the section 46 order, make such provision as he considers appropriate for the transfer to the responsible authority of any rights, liabilities and obligations which immediately before the specified date, were rights, liabilities and obligations of the managers of, or the society or person carrying on, the former approved institution; and
>
> (b) except in so far as the section 46 order otherwise provides, any legal proceedings pending immediately before the specified date by or against those managers or that society or that person shall be continued on and after that date, with the substitution of the responsible authority for those managers or that society or person as a party to the proceedings.

2.2.32 Care orders were introduced in place of the old 'approved school' and 'fit person' orders which had been used under the 1933 and 1948 Acts. Observation and assessment centres were substituted for remand homes and the concept of intermediate treatment was introduced.

Children's homes under the Children and Young Persons Act 1969

2.2.33 The 1969 Act introduced a planned and controlled approach to the provision of accommodation in homes for children in care. Voluntary sector homes were brought into the coordinated planning system, in so far as they were described as controlled or assisted community homes, i.e. the local authority was to participate in their management. Community homes were homes for the accommodation and maintenance of children in the care of local authorities. They could be provided by local authorities or voluntary organisations.

2.2.34 The Community Homes Regulations 1972 (SI 1972 No. 319) laid down the relevant provisions. Controlled community homes were homes where the management, equipment and maintenance were the responsibility of a local authority. The local authority acted through the managers of the home and the managers acted as agents of the local authority. Furthermore the employment of staff in a controlled home was the responsibility of the local authority.

2.2.35 Assisted community homes were homes where the management, equipment and maintenance were the responsibility of a voluntary organisation. However, employment or termination of employment without notice was to be done in consultation with the local authority. These regulations remained in force until 1991.

2.2.36 The Secretary of State had the power to direct that, premises in use as a community homes should cease to be used for that purpose if it appeared to him that they were unsuitable or the conduct of the community home was not in accordance with the regulations. He could inspect, and it was the local authority's duty to appoint an independent visitor: Children and Young Persons (Definition of Independent Persons) Regulations 1971 (SI 1971 No. 486).

2.2.37 In 1969 the Home Office Children's Department adopted residential care guidelines for local authorities and voluntary organisations which set out standards of good practice and the staffing needed to achieve it. These guidelines supplemented and developed the recommendations of the Williams Committee on staffing and training that were first published in 1967. In 1971 the Department of Health and Social Security set up a single advisory consultative and policy planning body, known as the Social Work Service. In the late 1980s, this became the Social Services Inspectorate.

The Children Act 1975

2.2.38 Section 59 of the Children Act 1975 (the 1975 Act) substituted new subsections in s.12 of the 1948 Act so that the 1948 Act thereafter provided that a local authority had a duty:

(a) to give first consideration to the need to safeguard and promote the child's welfare throughout his childhood; and

(b) so far as was practicable to ascertain the wishes and feelings of the child regarding the decision and give due consideration to them having regard to the child's age and understanding;

(c) to make such use of facilities and services available for children in the care of their own parents as appears to the local authority reasonable in each child's case.

2.2.39   Section 60 of the 1975 Act also allowed the local authority to vest parental rights in a voluntary organisation. Section 61 of the 1975 Act extended the circumstances under which a local authority might assume parental rights and duties.

Wardship

2.2.40   The High Court can exercise wardship which is in effect the inherent power of the Family Division of High Court to make orders relating to the protection of children as supplemented by the Family Law Reform Act 1969, the Guardianship of Minors Act 1971 and the Guardianship Act 1973. In the 1970s, local authorities began to make increasing use of wardship proceedings, where it was felt that the existing powers given by statute were too narrow or inflexible. Section 7 of the Family Law Reform Act 1969 gave the High Court the power to place a ward of court in the care or under the supervision of a local authority. Section 100 of the Children Act 1989 provides that this section has now ceased to have effect and has now restricted the use of the court's wardship jurisdiction in public law cases.

The Child Care Act 1980

2.2.41   The Child Care Act 1980 consolidated enactments relating to the care of children by local authorities and voluntary organisations. It also included enactments relating to the care and welfare of children. It came into force on 1 April 1981 and repealed the Children Act 1948 together with the Children and Young Persons Act 1969.

The Children Act 1989 (see Chapter 1)

2.2.42   The preceding childcare legislation had created a complex and somewhat unwieldy system, which produced numerous methods of taking children into care. The 1980s saw an impetus towards a complete reform of the law relating to childcare, which culminated in the Children Act 1989 (the 1989 Act). This came into force on 14 October 1991. In 1991, a series of publications were issued by HMSO under s.7 of the Local Authority Social Services Act 1970 entitled *The Children Act 1989: Guidance and Regulations*. They set out detailed advice and guidance on the standards of care which are expected in various childcare scenarios.

2.2.43 The Children Act 1989 is now the basis of our present childcare system. The Act covers both private and public childcare law. It widens the statutory duties on local authorities in relation to children in its area, from the duties applicable under the Children and Young Person Act 1969. The procedure for assuming parental rights and duties was discontinued, and the single available process is now an application for a care order.

2.2.44 Each local authority has a specific duty to take reasonable steps through the provision of services under the Children Act 1989 Part III (ss.17–30) to prevent children in its area from suffering ill-treatment and neglect. It should in accordance with various circulars check with local police forces the possible criminal background of those who apply to work with children, including staff, volunteers, childminders, those providing day care and foster parents. (See Children (Protection from Offenders) (Miscellaneous Amendments) Regulations 1997 (SI 1997 No. 2308).

2.2.45 Furthermore, under s.47 of the 1989 Act a local authority has a duty to investigate any case where it has reasonable cause to believe that a child is at risk of significant harm; where the authority has been informed that a child is the subject of an emergency protection order; where the child has been taken into police protection; or where the child has contravened a curfew notice under the Crime and Disorder Act 1998 (s.14). Further duties to investigate lie in the context of family proceedings and education supervision orders.

2.2.46 The 1989 Act also states (Sched. 2, para 1(1)) that a local authority must take reasonable steps to identify children in need in its area as defined by s.17(5)(b). It is the general duty of the local authority to provide a range and level of services appropriate to the needs of children who are in need in its area in order to safeguard their welfare and to promote their upbringing by their family (Sched. 2, Part 1, paras. 1–11).

2.2.47 When a care order is made with respect to a child, it is the duty of the local authority designated by the order to receive the child into its care and to keep him in its care while the order remains in force (s.33). The local authority must provide accommodation and maintenance for the child while he is in care (s.23(1)), and the local authority has a duty to safeguard and promote the child's welfare (s.22(3)). Whilst the care order is in force the local authority will have parental responsibility for the child.

Corporate liability

2.2.48 The 1989 Act provides for a number of offences against children. Under s.103 of the Act, if the offence is proved to have been committed with the consent or connivance of or to be attributable to any neglect on the part of any director, manager, secretary or other similar officer of the body corporate, or any person purporting to act in any such capacity, he (as well as the body corporate) shall be guilty of the offence.

Guidelines for local authorities exercising their powers under the Children Act 1989

2.2.49 From around 1985 onwards, a number of important guidelines have been issued by central government which affect the way in which local authorities act in childcare cases. The following are the most important examples, but this is not an exhaustive list: see, for example, appendix to *People Like Us, The Report of the Review of the Safeguards for Children Living away from Home*, by Sir William Utting (HMSO, 1997):

1. *Social Work Decisions in Child Care* (HMSO, 1985; published by DHSS (now Department of Health)).

2. *Protecting Children* (HMSO, 1988). 'The Orange Book' is published by the Department of Health. It is a guide to the comprehensive assessment of the children and family which occurs after the completion of the initial investigation. It attempts to set out a clear practice framework for assessment.

3. *Working Together under the Children Act 1989* (HMSO, 1991). This is the authoritative guide to arrangements for inter-agency cooperation for the protection of children from abuse. It has no legal status *(Re G (A minor)* [1996] 2 All ER 65–8).

4. *Working Together to Safeguard Children*, Department of Health, Home Office, Department for Education and Employment (HMSO, 1999). This sets out how all agencies and professionals should work together to promote children's welfare and protect them from abuse and neglect. It is addressed to those who work in the health and education services, the police, social services, the probation service, and others whose work brings them into contact with children and families. It also replaces (3) above.

5. *Framework for the Assessment of Children in Need and their Families* (HMSO, 2000). This guidance builds on the Orange Book in (2) and is intended to be used when an assessment of a child and family is undertaken.

2.2.50 Good social work practice has also been defined in caselaw. *See Re E (Care Proceedings: Social Work Practice)* [2000] 2 FLR 254.

2.2.51 Local authority social workers are required by Department of Health guidelines to attempt to work in partnership with parents and others with parental responsibility, and in partnership with other agencies of government – see the Social Services Inspectorate *The Challenge of Partnership in Child Protection* (HMSO, 1995); *Working in Partnership* (HMSO, 1991); *Working in Partnership under the Children Act 1989*. See also the *Handbook of Best Practice in Children Act Cases* (published by LCD, 1997) and Local Authority Circular (LAC) (99)29 for guidance on care plans for children under the 1989 Act.

2.2.52   In any child abuse investigation, whether it be undertaken by the police for the purpose of criminal proceedings, or by social workers for the purposes of proceedings under Children Act 1989, the *Memorandum of Good Practice on Video Recorded Interviews with Child Witnesses for Criminal Proceedings* (DoH, HMSO, 1992) should be used. (See *Re A and B (Minors) (No.1) (Investigation of Alleged Abuse)* [1995] 3 FCR 389).

Police powers

2.2.53   The police are also empowered under s.46 of the Children Act 1989 to remove a child to suitable accommodation if they have reasonable cause to believe that the child would otherwise be likely to suffer significant harm.

Child protection registers and conferences

2.2.54   Child Protection Registers and Conferences have been in use by local authorities since the early 1970s, although the basis of their operation was prescribed by a series of departmental circulars which were consolidated in 1991 in the handbook, *Working Together under the Children Act 1989* (as amended by the 1999 Handbook *Working Together*). Briefly, the register provides a record of those children whom professionals from various agencies believe are in need of protection, and must be reviewed by all health and child care agencies. However, there is still no legal duty on any health professional to report suspicions of abuse (*D* v. *National Society for the Prevention of Cruelty to Children* [1978] AC 171). The register has four categories of abuse: neglect, physical injury, sexual abuse and emotional abuse. Local authorities use the following guidelines when deciding whether to place a child on the register.

1.   There must be one or more identifiable incidents which can be described as having adversely affected the child.
2.   Significant harm is expected on the basis of professional judgment of findings of the investigation in this particular case or on research evidence.

2.2.55   A child protection conference is essentially a multi-disciplinary meeting between various professionals and family members to discuss the case of a particular child, convened at the request of either the local authority or any other agency involved. The decision of the conference is not binding on the local authority but is a recommendation to a particular agency for action.

The Crime and Disorder Act 1998

2.2.56 The Crime and Disorder Act 1998 allows a 'relevant authority' to apply to a magistrates' court for an antisocial behaviour order against children. This can include an application for a parenting order or a child safety order.

The duty to provide accommodation

2.2.57 A local authority has a duty to provide accommodation for a child in its care (s.23 1989 Act). Furthermore, it is under a duty to provide accommodation for a child in need who appears to require accommodation (s.20 1989 Act). It must also provide accommodation whether or not the child is in need in certain other circumstances, for instance where the child has been taken into police protection under s.46(3)(f) 1989 Act.

2.2.58 Before the local authority provides accommodation for the child, it is under a series of duties under the Children Act 1989 and the Arrangements for Placement of Children (General) Regulations 1991 (SI 1991 No. 890). Once the child is taken into care, the authority must consult the child, the parents and anyone else with parental responsibility for the child before making major decisions about the child, including where the child is placed and what school he or she attends. Within four weeks of a child being accommodated by an authority, that authority must hold a review of the child's position. Another review must be held within three months; thereafter, review must be held at six-monthly intervals (Review of Children's Cases Regulations 1991 (SI 1991 No. 895).

2.2.59 There are a number of options open to a local authority when accommodating a child.

1. private fostering arrangement (see paras. 2.3.1–2.3.15)
2. local authority foster parents (see paras. 2.3.1–2.3.15)
3. accommodation with a voluntary organisation;
4. accommodation in a registered children's home;
5. accommodation in a community home;
6. secure accommodation (see paras. 2.2.52, 2.2.56 and 2.12.6);
7. being placed in a home provided in accordance with arrangements made by the Secretary of State;
8. such other arrangements as the local authority may consider appropriate.

Children's homes

2.2.60 Volume 4 of the *Children Act 1989: Guidance and Regulations* deals with the subject of residential care. It should also be noted that the Secretary of State has the right in certain cases to inspect homes or make regulations regarding local authority inspection. See also LAC (93)13 for guidance on permissible forms of control in children's residential care (including secure accommodation).

2.2.61 Voluntary homes and voluntary organisations are regulated in accordance with the 1989 Act Part VII (ss.59–62), Schedule 5 to the Children Act 1989 and the Children's Homes Regulations 1991 (SI 1991 No. 1506). A voluntary organisation may accommodate a child in a voluntary home, with foster parents, in a registered children's home and in a community home. A voluntary home is any home or institution providing care and accommodation for children which is carried on by a voluntary organisation (see 2.2.56–2.2.58 for definition of voluntary organisations). Where the child is accommodated in a voluntary home by a voluntary organisation, the voluntary organisation will be subject to the Arrangement for Placement of Children (General) Regulations 1991, the Review of Children's Cases Regulations 1991 and the Representations Procedure (Children) Regulations 1991 (SI 1991 No. 894). If the child is placed in a voluntary home by a local authority, those duties fall on the local authority. In either case, the local authority is subject to duties to that child under ss.20–23 of the 1989 Act together with s.62.

2.2.62 A registered home is a children's home registered under the 1989 Act Part VIII (ss.63–65). It is an offence to set up a children's home which is not registered and a local authority will set up an annual review of each home. The person or body running the registered home is under certain duties under s.64 of the 1989 Act, together with the Arrangement for Placement of Children (General) Regulations 1991, the Review of Children's Cases Regulations 1991 and the Representations Procedure (Children) Regulations 1991. The local authority will be subject to its general duties under ss.22–24, and specific duties under the Children's Homes Regulations 1991 (SI 1991 No. 1506).

2.2.63 Community homes are defined by s.53 of the 1989 Act. If a home is run by a voluntary organisation, it may be either a controlled or assisted community home (see ss.53 and 60 of the 1989 Act). Essentially, the local authority is generally responsible for the management, equipment and maintenance of a controlled community home, while with an assisted home, the voluntary organisation undertakes those tasks. A 'maintained' community home is one provided, equipped and maintained by the local authority but it may be run by some other person or body under the Contracting Out (Management Functions in Relation to Certain Community Homes) Order 1996. If a child is accommodated in a community home, the local authority has duties as detailed in ss.22–24, ss.53–58 of, and Schedule 4 to, the 1989 Act and the Children's Homes Regulations 1991.

2.2.64 In addition, a local authority can place a child in a residential care home, a nursing home and a mental nursing home (ss.85–86 Children Act 1989) although responsibility for such placements would then fall to the area health authority or the local education authority.

2.2.65 Children's refuges are governed by the Refuges (Children's Homes and Foster Placements) Regulations 1991 (SI 1991 No. 1507). Those persons providing a refuge must notify the designated office of the local authority of the fact that the child is being cared for at the refuge.

Voluntary organisations

2.2.66 The term 'voluntary organisation' is defined under s.105(1) of the Children Act 1989 as a body (other than a public or local authority) whose activities are not carried on for profit. Voluntary organisations can arrange foster care or place the child in a home. Their main responsibilities are defined under s.61(1) of the 1989 Act. Secure accommodation is not available to a voluntary organisation (s.25 1989 Act).

2.2.67 A voluntary organisation is subject to the provisions of the Arrangement for Placement of Children (General) Regulations 1991 and the Foster Placement (Children) Regulations 1991 (SI 1991 No. 910) as well as the Representations Procedure (Children) Regulations 1991.

2.2.68 A local authority has a number of responsibilities in relation to a voluntary organisation which is providing accommodation for a child. It must satisfy itself that the organisation is satisfactorily safeguarding and promoting the child's welfare; visit the child; and intervene if necessary (s.62 1989 Act).

The latest childcare legislation

2.2.69 In 1997, the government announced a thorough review of childcare policies under the heading 'Quality Protects'. This promises extra resources aimed at improving the situation of those placed in care.

2.2.70 The Care Standards Act 2000 makes provision for the registration and regulation of children's homes, independent hospitals, independent clinics, care homes, residential family centres, independent medical agencies, domiciliary care agencies, fostering agencies, nurses agencies and voluntary adoption agencies. It also makes provision for the regulation and inspection of local authority fostering and adoption services. The provisions of the 1989 Act in relation to childminding and day care are amended. The Protection of Children (Access to Lists) (Prescribed Individuals) Regulations 2000 (SI 2000 No. 2537) provides a list of certain individuals who will be subject to checks.

2.2.71 The Sexual Offences (Amendment) Act 2000 creates a specific and new offence of sexual activity by a person in a position of trust. That is, the offence will be committed where a person over the age of 18 engages in sexual activity with a person under that age, if the older person is in a position of trust in relation to the younger person. A position of trust arises where a person under 18 is looked after in a number of different circumstances including:

- detention in an institution by virtue of a court order;
- placement in a home or accommodation under the 1989 Act;
- placement in accommodation provided by a voluntary organisation;
- care in hospital;
- care in a residential care home, nursing home, mental nursing home or private hospital;
- care in a community home, voluntary home, children's home or residential establishment;
- receipt of full-time education in an educational institution.

2.2.72 A person is described as looking after a person under 18 for the purposes of this offence if:

> he is regularly involved in caring for, training, supervising or being in sole charge of such persons.

A hospital is described as having the meaning given by s.128(1) National Health Service Act 1977 and a nursing home and mental nursing home have the meanings given by ss.21(1) and 22(1) respectively of the Registered Homes Act 1984.

2.2.73 The Care Standards Act 2000 creates a new National Care Standards Commission which will be responsible for the regulation of social care and private and voluntary healthcare services in England. The National Assembly for Wales will be the regulatory body for such services in Wales. It also creates a General Social Care Council and a Care Council for Wales, which will oversee standards and training through social services. The Council will draw up codes of practice and conduct for workers and employers and establish a register of staff, ensuring those who have record of abuse will not be able to work in residential care. At the time of writing, only parts of the Act have come into force.

2.3   FOSTER CARE UNDER THE CHILDREN ACT 1989

2.3.1   Until the 1989 Act, a parent had the right to place a child with foster parents without any interference by the state. The local authority's rights were limited to visiting together with the power to inspect and remove in accordance with the relevant child protection provisions. The obligation to notify the local authority regarding a placement rested with the foster carer. Private fostering was covered by the Children Act 1958, which provided for the protection of such children, later amended by the Children and Young Persons Act 1969 and the Children Act 1975, and replaced by the Foster Children Act 1980. Essentially, a local authority was under a duty to satisfy itself as to the well-being of foster children within its area, and to make visits from time to time.

2.3.2   Most children in local authority care are now placed with foster parents. Fostering may be described as the accommodation of a child by a person who is neither the parent of, nor a person with parental responsibility for, the child.

2.3.3   Fostering may take the form of:

1. A private fostering arrangement.
2. The placement of a child by a local authority with local authority foster parents.
3. A placement under wardship proceedings.

Each of these situations places different statutory duties on the person with parental responsibility and the foster parent.

2.3.4   In addition, a local authority has the power to place a child who is in its care with a person who is a parent, or with parental responsibility or a residence order. Such a placement is not a fostering placement and is covered by the Placement of Children with Parents, etc. Regulations 1991 (SI 1991 No. 893). There are particular private arrangements, i.e. placement of children with certain relatives which fall outside the terms of the Children Act 1989. See also LAC 98(2) for regulations guidance relating to delegation of local authority statutory fostering duties.

51

Private foster care

2.3.5   Private fostering is now defined by s.66 of the Children Act 1989. Any person (including a local authority) who has parental responsibility for a child may arrange for some or all of the responsibility to be met by one or more persons acting on his behalf. Such an arrangement cannot amount to a surrender or transfer of any part of the parental responsibility to the foster parent, who acts as the agent for the holder of the parental responsibility (Children Act 1989, Sched. 8, para.10). Schedule 7 paras. 2–5 to the Children Act 1989 sets out certain restrictions on foster parents (including the situation of private fostering) taking more than three children without the approval of the authority in whose area they reside. Any person who exceeds this limit is treated as running a children's home and so falls under the relevant provisions. See also the Foster Placement (Children) Regulations 1991 (SI 1991 No. 910) as amended by the Children (Protection from Offenders) (Miscellaneous Amendments) Regulations 1997 (SI 1997 No. 2308).

2.3.6   The Disqualification for Caring for Children Regulations 1991 (SI 1991 No. 2094) as amended by the Children (Protection from Offenders) (Miscellaneous Amendments) Regulations 1997 (SI 1997 No. 2308) disqualify from private fostering, childminding or providing day care services people whose children have been the subject of a care order, or who have been convicted of any offence involving children or involving violence against children or others, or have been involved in a voluntary or registered children's home which has been deregistered. They do not apply to local authority foster parents or community homes.

2.3.7   A local authority has certain specific duties with respect to children who are privately fostered. These are described in s.67 of the Children Act 1989. The local authority has a general duty (s.67(1) 1989 Act) to satisfy itself that the welfare of children who are privately fostered in its area is being satisfactorily safeguarded and promoted. Certain persons are disqualified from being foster parents under s.68 of the Children Act 1989 and the Disqualification for Caring for Children Regulations 1991 (SI 1991 No. 2094). See also the Children (Protection from Offenders) (Miscellaneous Amendment) Regulations 1997 (SI 1997 No. 2308) which prohibit local authorities from placing children with foster carers who have been convicted of child abuse. The Children Act 1989 gives responsibility to the Home Office to inspect any premises in which a child who is being looked after by a local authority is living (s.80 Children Act 1989). The Department of Health has issued *Signposts* [2000] (FL 526), an information pack with briefing sheets and examples of forms and procedures. The Secretary of State also has a number of powers relating to private foster placements under s.80 of the Children Act 1989.

2.3.8   A private foster parent is under a number of statutory duties. First, there is the general duty described in s.1 of the Children and Young Persons Act 1933 (as amended by the Children Act 1989, Sched. 13, paras. 2–5) to protect the child from physical harm. Second, the foster parent may be under certain duties described in the Children Act 1989 to notify the local authority of the foster placement or comply with certain requirements demanded by that local authority. Third, the foster parent will be required by the Education Act 1996 to carry out certain duties with regard to the child's education. For these reasons, private foster parents are encouraged to take out insurance by the National Foster Care Association.

2.3.9   A person who proposes to foster a child must notify the local authority within a certain period (volume 8 *Children Act 1989: Guidance and Regulations*). Similar requirements are placed on those who propose to be involved, either directly or indirectly, in arranging for a child to be fostered privately, or those who are a parent or hold parental responsibility. See also the Children (Private Arrangements for Fostering) Regulations 1991 (SI 1991 No. 2050).

Local authority foster care

2.3.10   The Children Act 1989 distinguishes between children looked after by local authority foster parents (as defined in s.23(2)(a) and s.23(3)) and private arrangements for fostering under s.66 of the 1989 Act. The relevant regulations are contained in volume 3 of the *Children Act 1989: Guidance and Regulations*. A local authority foster parent must be approved by the local authority and registered under the Foster Placement (Children) Regulations 1991 (SI 1991 No. 910) before a child may be placed in his care. The approval process involves a detailed system of checks and training.

2.3.11   A local authority will be the 'responsible authority' in relation to any placement made by it under the Arrangement for Placement of Children (General Regulations) 1991 (SI 1991 No. 890) or the Family Proceedings Courts (Children Act 1989) Rules 1991 (SI 1991 No. 1395). The local authority has various duties relating to the placing of the child in care under ss.22–24 of, and Sched. 7 to, the Children Act 1989, the Arrangement for Placement of Children (General Regulations) 1991 and the Foster Placement (Children) Regulations 1991.

2.3.12   Once the child has been placed in care, the local authority's duties are to be found under ss.22–26 and Sched. 2 to the Children Act 1989 together with the Arrangement for Placement of Children (General Regulations) 1991 and the Foster Placement (Children) Regulations 1991. Volume 3 of the *Children Act 1989: Guidance and Regulations* stresses the importance of each child being the subject of a detailed plan for his immediate and long-term needs.

2.3.13 A local authority may not place a child with a foster parent, other than as an emergency or immediate placement, unless the foster parent has, before or at the time of placement, signed two separate agreements. This is a written foster care agreement and a foster placement agreement. These are important because they set out the rights and duties of the foster parents, and the nature of their relationship with the local authority. Local authority foster parents are covered by the general duty described by s.1 of the Children and Young Persons Act 1933 as amended.

2.3.14 The same limitations with regard to the number of children placed with private foster parents apply to local authority foster parents. Also, the local authority must under the Foster Placement (Children) Regulations 1991 make arrangements for inspection of the foster home.

Fostering by a voluntary organisation

2.3.15 A voluntary organisation may place a child with foster parents in accordance with the provisions of Arrangement for Placement of Children (General Regulations) 1991 and the Foster Placement (Children) Regulations 1991 as the 'responsible authority'. The same limitation for the number of children placed with a foster parents relevant to local authorities, applies equally to voluntary organisations. A child placed at a foster home will be subject to visits not only from the voluntary organisation but also the local authority. The voluntary organisation must also carry out reviews in accordance with the Review of Children's Cases Regulations 1991 and is subject to duties under s.61 of the Children Act 1989 and the regulations cited in this paragraph.

2.4   DUTIES TO YOUNG PEOPLE LEAVING CARE

2.4.1 Prior to the Children Act 1989, there was little effective statutory provision for children leaving care (ss.20 and 34 of the Children Act 1948, s.58 of the Children and Young Persons Act 1963, ss.27–29 of the Child Care Act 1980). Now under s.24 of the Children Act 1989, local authorities do owe certain limited duties to young people under the age of 21 who have been in their care, or the care of other organisations. However, this is limited to a duty to 'advise, assist and befriend' a person qualifying for assistance. (See the *Children Act 1989: Guidance and Regulations*, volume 2: *Family Support, Day Care and Education Provision for Young Children*). They may also continue to assist a person after his twenty-first birthday in certain circumstances.

2.4.2   The *Children Act 1989: Guidance and Regulations*, volume 3: *Family Placements* para. 9.19 and volume 4: *Residential Care* para. 7.19 sets out the principles underlying preparing a young person for leaving care. See also the *Children Act 1989: Guidance and Regulations*, volume 6: *Children with Disabilities*. Each social services department should provide a written statement of its philosophy and practice on the preparation of young people for leaving care and the provision of aftercare support.

2.4.3   The Children (Leaving Care) Act 2000 replaces s.24 of the Children Act 1989. The Act sets out a range of local authority powers and duties in relation to care leavers up to the age of 21 and, exceptionally, beyond. In essence, it places a duty on a local authority to act more like normal parents in that they are required to continue providing support after the age of 16. Local authorities will have a duty to assess and meet the care needs of children who have been in care for at least 13 weeks since the age of 14 until they reach the age of 18. Children in receipt of education and training should be further assisted until 21.

2.5   COMPLAINTS PROCEDURES AND THE RIGHTS OF THE CHILD

Complaints procedures

2.5.1   Up until 1990, there was no statutory provision for complaints procedures for children in care. The National Health Services and Community Care Act 1990 inserted s.7B(1) into the Local Authority Social Services Act 1970. The Local Authority Social Services (Complaints Procedure) Order 1990 (SI 1990 No. 2244) and the Complaints Procedure Directions 1990 introduced a complaints procedure for matters outside the provisions of the Children Act 1989. This procedure applies to a 'qualifying individual', i.e. a person for whom the authority has a power or duty to provide a service and his need or possible need for the service has come to the attention of the local authority.

2.5.2   As regards matters within the scope of the Children Act 1989, under s.26(3) of the Act all local authorities are under a duty to establish procedures for consideration of complaints from children or parents who believe those bodies have not complied with their duties under the Children Act 1989. See the Representations Procedure (Children) Regulations 1991 (SI 1991 No. 894). This duty also applies to registered children's homes and voluntary organisations.

2.5.3   The ombudsman is an independent and impartial officer appointed by Parliament to investigate complaints of injustice through maladministration by a local authority, i.e. failing to follow procedures. The relevant statute is the Local Government Act 1974 (s.23). The ombudsman can generally only investigate the process of the decision making, rather than the merits and quality of the decision itself. The local authority must first be given the opportunity to deal with the complaint. If this does not provide a satisfactory result, the complainant can go direct to the ombudsman or to a local councillor.

2.5.4   A court can also make a specific issue order under s.8 of the Children Act 1989, if it is felt that a local authority is not carrying out its duties to a child in need, but this power is limited.

The rights of a child

2.5.5   A 'child' is a person who has not reached his or her eighteenth birthday, although various statutes in the past have used the words 'infant' or 'minor'. Prior to the Family Law Reform Act 1969, the age of majority was 21.

2.5.6   A child cannot bring or defend a civil claim in court, but can only do so through a 'litigation friend'. A child between the ages of 10 and 14 are presumed unable to form the specific intent to commit a crime, although this can be rebutted by the prosecution. A child under 14 cannot enter a public house. Those between the ages of 14 and 17 may enter a public house, but cannot buy alcoholic beverages. A child from the age of 16 can leave school, claim income support, have intercourse with either sex, marry with the consent of their parents or the leave of the court.

2.5.7   The Children Act 1989 specifically states that the child's wishes must be put before the court, if the child can communicate those wishes. It is also provided that there will be instances where the child's interests will conflict with those of its parents or legal guardian and, consequently, a guardian will be appointed by the court. Any child of sufficient understanding can actually make an application under the 1989 Act (section 10(8)) against either parents or the local authority.

Parental chastisement

2.5.8   In *A* v. *United Kingdom* [1999] 27 EHRR 611 a child was awarded £10,000 by the European Court of Human Rights after being severely beaten by his stepfather. The domestic courts of the United Kingdom had rejected A's claim on the grounds that the stepfather was entitled to employ 'reasonable chastisement'. The ECHR held that this was a breach of Article 3 of the Convention.

56

Right to refuse medical treatment

2.5.9   In certain circumstances, courts will allow a child to exercise the rights of an adult citizen. In the case of *Gillick* v. *West Norfolk and Wisbech Area Health Authority and Another* [1986] AC 112 it was held by the House of Lords that a child of sufficient understanding could, in some circumstances, consent to medical treatment despite being under the age of 16. However, the courts have said that they would deal with such situations on a case-by-case basis, and it is clear that courts will limit *Gillick* to its facts. The point is important where a medical practitioner has been asked by a parent to treat a child, and the child refuses treatment. The medical practitioner would require some protection from the child later suing him/her for assault, if the treatment is to go ahead. It is now the case that a parent or someone with parental responsibility can consent to treatment on behalf of a child aged less than 16: *Re R (A minor) (Wardship: Medical Treatment)* [1992] 1 FLR 190 and *Nielsen* v. *Denmark* (1989) 11 EHRR 175). The High Court might also use its inherent jurisdiction to order override the refusal of a child to accept treatment: *Re W (A minor) (Consent to Medical Treatment)* [1993] 1 FLR 1 CA. The position is less clear with children in the 16- to 17-year-old bracket. Whilst a competent adult can refuse medical treatment, it is far harder for a competent 16 to 17 year old to do so: *Re C (Adult – Refusal of Medical Treatment)* [1994] 1 FLR 31. See also s.8 of the Family Law Reform Act 1969.

Right to privacy

2.5.10   Children do not have any rights to 'privacy', but some protection is afforded to them by the courts and statute. Section 39 of the Children and Young Persons Act 1933 provides that in relation to any proceedings in any court, the court may direct that no newspaper report of the proceedings shall reveal the name, address or school or include particulars calculated to lead to identification of any child or young person concerned with the proceedings. Section 49 prohibits reporting on any child before a youth court, which is now confirmed by the Criminal Justice and Public Order Act 1994. The Children and Young Persons Act 1963 prohibits identification of children involved in appeals to the Crown Court or High Court. Section 12 of the Administration of Justice Act 1980 prohibits as a contempt of court any publication of information relating to proceedings before a court sitting in private where the inherent jurisdiction of the High Court with respect to children, or Children Act 1989 proceedings are concerned. However, it does not prohibit the reporting by the media of an order of judgment of the court, unless the court specifically makes an order to that effect.

2.5.11 It is also a fundamental rule in legal proceedings involving children that documents produced to the court in the proceedings might not be disclosed to those not parties to the case (Family Proceedings Rules 1991 (SI 1991 No. 1247) and Family Proceedings Courts (Children Act 1989) Rules (SI 1991 No. 1395)). Under s.12 of the Administration of Justice Act 1960 as amended by s.108(5) of the Children Act 1989, it is a contempt of court to publish information relating to proceedings in childcare cases.

2.5.12 Sections 1 and 2 of the Sexual Offences (Amendment) Act 1992 prohibit identification in any written publication or broadcast programme to be published in England and Wales of a complainant who alleges that a sexual offence has been committed against him or her.

Employment rights

2.5.13 Section 18 of the Children and Young Persons Act 1933 restricts and in certain cases prohibits the employment of children. Under s.558 of the Education Act 1996 any person, who is not for the purposes of that Act over compulsory school age (normally 16), shall be deemed to be a child within the meaning of any enactment relating to the prohibition or regulation of the employment of children or young persons. See also s.559 of the Education Act 1996.

2.5.14 Up until the Employment Act 1989, local authorities could make byelaws requiring all employers to notify a local authority of the hours and conditions of the employment of a child under 18. Section 20 of the 1933 Act covers street trading by children; s.23 children's entertainment and performances; and s.24 restricts training for performances of dangerous nature. The Children and Young Persons Act 1963 lays down restriction on persons under 16 taking part in public performances.

2.6 DUTIES OF COURT-APPOINTED CHILDCARE OFFICERS

2.6.1 The most important type of officer in present-day childcare proceedings is the guardian *ad litem* who provides the experience of social work while being independent of local authorities, the probation service and the courts. Each local authority is responsible for providing GALRO (the guardian *ad litem* and reporting officers panel) services. The panel was established in 1984. In circumstances where the child's interests will conflict with those of its parents or legal guardian, a guardian will be appointed by the court. A guardian *ad litem* is subject to certain duties towards the child under the Children Act 1989, s.41(2)(b).

2.6.2 It is also possible for the Official Solicitor to be appointed to act, but this is rare in Children Act proceedings. Generally, the Official Solicitor is involved in health and medical issues, or conflicts of older children with parents. The duties of the Official Solicitor are explained in *Re M (Official Solicitor's Role)* [1998] 2 FLR 815.

2.6.3 The court welfare officer is a person requested by the court to report to the court on matters relating to the welfare of a child. This is either a probation officer, or an employee of the local authority. Unlike the guardian *ad litem* and the Official Solicitor, they cannot be a party to proceedings. There are now basic standards applicable to the work of court welfare officers: the National Standards for Probation Service Family Court Welfare Work, 1 January 1995).

2.7 INTERNATIONAL TREATIES ON CHILDREN

2.7.1 The first international treaty on children was the Declaration of Rights of the Child adopted by the League of Nations in 1924. This was followed in 1948 by the Universal Declaration of Human Rights produced by the United Nations and the Declaration of Rights of the Child in 1959. Whilst the statements have been adopted throughout the world, they carry no obligations.

2.7.2 The above declarations did however lead to the ratification of the United Nations Convention on the Rights of the Child which was brought into force in England and Wales in January 1992. There are no direct mechanisms available for enforcement of any right by individuals, but all signatories to the Convention are required to submit to an international committee a periodic report on their progress in implementing the Convention. The European Social Charter came into force on 26 February 1965, and is mainly concerned with the protection of social and economic rights, i.e. welfare benefits. Again, it relies on a system of international supervision by the contracting parties.

2.7.3 The European Convention for the Protection of Human Rights and Fundamental Freedoms 1950 was incorporated into domestic law with the coming into force of the Human Rights Act 1998 on 2 October 2000. The Convention had already led to changes in childcare law such as the amendment to the Child Care Act 1980 in 1983 (Part 1A Child Care Act 1980) which gave greater rights to the parents of children in care. The main provisions of the Convention relating to children are Article 2, the right to basic education; Article 3, the right to be free from oppression or torture; Article 8, the right to respect for private and family life.

2.7.4   The European Convention for the Prevention of Torture and Inhuman or Degrading Treatment or Punishment was signed by the United Kingdom Government in 1987 and came into force on 1 January 1989.

2.8   CHILDREN'S EDUCATION

The duty to educate

2.8.1   All education legislation from 1944 onwards has now been codified by the Education Act 1996. The state is under a legal duty to provide education to children from the age of 5 up to the age of 16. The statutory school-leaving age has not always been the same. Under the Education Act 1944, it was 15 and was only raised to 16 by the Raising of the School Leaving Age Order 1972 (SI 1972 No. 444). Beyond the age of 16, there is no duty to educate, but local education authorities and Further Education Funding Councils are empowered to provide educational facilities for 16 to 19 year olds.

2.8.2   The United Nations Convention on the Rights of the Child and the Universal Declaration of Human Rights referred to above, also provide statements relating to the child's rights to basic education, and various obligations on signatory states to provide that education. Article 2 to the first protocol of the European Convention on Human Rights has various implications for children's and parents' rights with regard to education.

2.8.3   Parents have been under a statutory duty to educate their children since the Education Act 1944 (s.36). This duty is now found in s.7 of the Education Act 1996. A breach of this duty is a criminal offence leading to a fine. Conversely, a child is under no statutory duty to attend school. Under the present law, if a local education authority determines that a child is not receiving a suitable education, it must serve a notice on the parent requiring that the parent demonstrate that the child's education is in fact suitable. If the parent cannot comply, then the authority must serve upon the parent a school attendance order (s.437 Education Act 1996). A local education authority can apply to the court under s.36(1) and (2) of the Children Act 1989 for an education supervision order which puts the child under the supervision of a designated local education authority. See also *The Children Act 1989: Guidance and Regulations*, volume 7.

2.8.4   Prior to the Children Act 1989, the only method of forcing a child into education was to take out care proceedings, and this was certainly done under the Children and Young Persons Act 1969. Now, s.36 of the Children Act 1989 provides that a local education authority may apply for an education supervision order in respect of a child. The Act provides that a supervisor will be appointed who advises the child and his parents in a manner calculated to ensure that the child is properly educated. The parents are placed under a duty to obey the supervisor or face criminal prosecution. Care proceedings can of course still be taken out by the local authority.

Educational discipline

2.8.5   Corporal punishment has remained a feature of British schools up until relatively recently. Section 1(7) of the Children and Young Persons Act 1933 provided that any parent, teacher or other person having the lawful control or charge of a child or young person could administer punishment to him. However, children were not to be punished immoderately or unreasonably: *R* v. *Hopley* [1860] 2 F & F 202.

2.8.6   Article 3 of the European Convention on Human Rights prohibits punishment which amounts to inhuman or degrading treatment. As a result of applications submitted to the European Court of Human Rights: *Y* v. *United Kingdom* (1994) 17 EHRR 238, the Education (No. 2) Act 1986 outlawed corporal punishment in schools maintained by local education authorities and certain other schools. This was extended to certain independent schools under the Education (Abolition of Corporal Punishment) (Independent Schools) Regulations 1987 (SI 1987 No. 1183) and Education (Abolition of Corporal Punishment) (Independent Schools) (Prescribed Categories of Persons) Regulations 1989 (SI 1989 No. 1825). Section 293 of the Education Act 1993 provided that corporal punishment in independent schools could not be justified if it was 'inhuman or degrading'.

2.8.7   The School Standards and Framework Act 1998 has now abolished the use of corporal punishment in all schools (both maintained schools and those in the independent sector). It is also proscribed in respect of children for whom education is provided, otherwise than at school, under any arrangements made by a local education authority, or for whom specified nursery education is provided otherwise than at school. Section 154 of the Education Act 1996 sets out guidelines for the enforcement of discipline in state schools.

2.8.8   Detention is also used as a means of discipline. Prior to the Education Act 1996, the position regarding detention was governed by the common law. Detention might be false imprisonment unless it was 'just and reasonable': *Mansell* v. *Griffin* [1908] 1 KB 947, 72 JP 179, CA. Section 550B of the Education Act 1996 amends the position with regard to local education authority maintained schools and certain other schools (s.4). As regards independent and other types of schools, it should be remembered that 'secure accommodation' is regulated by s.25 of the Children Act 1989. Consequently, locking a child in a room with the intention of preventing him leaving voluntarily is unlikely to be appropriate.

2.8.9 The use of force to restrain a child is now covered (for certain schools) by s.550A of the Education Act 1996. In addition, a number of circulars have been published on the subject of discipline. These are Department for Education and Employment Circular No.10/98, No.10/99 and DES Circular No.9/94 LAC 94(9) for children with emotional and behavioural difficulties.

2.8.10 The governing body of a maintained school has a statutory duty (Education Act 1997 ss.2 and 3) to ensure that policies designed to promote good behaviour and discipline are pursued at the school.

2.8.11 The local authority is under a duty to monitor the welfare of children accommodated in independent schools. In addition, the Children Act 1989 (s.87) imposes a duty on the proprietor of any independent school to safeguard and promote the child's welfare and provides that where a local authority is of the opinion that there has been a failure to comply with that duty by the independent school, the local authority must notify the Secretary of State and take steps for the child's welfare (volume 5 of *The Children Act 1989: Guidance and Regulations* deals with independent schools). See also the Inspection of Premises, Children and Records (Independent Schools) Regulations 1991 (SI 1991 No. 975) and *The Children Act 1989: The Welfare of Children in Boarding Schools: A Practice Guide* (DoH, HMSO, 1991). The Independent Schools Joint Council has produced general advice for independent schools. See also Department for Education and Employment (1995) Protecting Children from Abuse: The role of the Education Service (Circular 10/95).

Children with special educational needs and physical disabilities

2.8.12 The Education Act 1944 specifically provided for categories of pupils who would require special educational treatment, although the system was very much more basic than it is today, and a distinction was drawn between the handicapped and non-handicapped. The Warnock Report in 1978 recommended that children should (as far as possible) be educated in the mainstream system. A new definition was introduced, children with learning difficulties, which would encompass children formerly classified as educationally subnormal as well as children with emotional difficulties.

2.8.13 The Education Act 1996 fixes local education authorities with the duty to ensure adequate provisions for children in their area who have special educational needs. The Disability Discrimination Act 1995 requires each county, voluntary or grant maintained school to make proper provision for physically disabled pupils.

2.8.14 Local education authorities may have a duty to educate people with learning difficulties after the age of 16. *R* v. *Dorset County Council, ex parte Goddard* [1995] ELR 109.

2.9   CHILDREN IN THE HEALTH SYSTEM

The basic structure

2.9.1 The National Health Service Act 1977 amended the National Health Services Act 1946 to establish a duty of cooperation between health and social services. The Children Act 1989 also imposes a number of duties on local authorities regarding health.

Disabled children

2.9.2 In the case of local authority duties towards disabled children, initially s.29 of the National Assistance Act 1948 empowered authorities to promote the welfare of the disabled. Today, the main statutory authorities are found in the Chronically Sick and Disabled Persons Act 1970, the Disabled Persons (Services, Consultation and Representation) Act 1986. These Acts placed certain duties on local authorities relating to the provision of services to the disabled. This legislation was later enhanced by the National Health Service and Community Care Act 1990 (the 1990 Act) and s.17 of the Children Act 1989. The 1990 Act provided that a local authority had a duty to carry out an assessment of a disabled person's needs regardless of whether an assessment had been requested.

2.9.3 If a local authority decides that a child does have a medical need as defined by s.2 of the Chronically Sick and Disabled Persons Act 1970, or a need under the Mental Health Act 1983 (s.117) then it is under a duty to provide the child with certain services (see also s.28A Children Act 1989). If a carer is provided for a child in need, the Carers (Recognition and Services) Act 1995 imposes a duty on social services, if requested, to carry out a separate assessment of the carer at the same time it assesses anyone under any enactment. The object is to identify the potential carer's ability to provide and continue to provide care. It is not unknown for children to become carers of sick or disabled parents, in which case there may be grounds to call on services provided under s.17 of the Children Act 1989, as the child's development may be impaired by its role as carer. Volume 6 of *The Children Act 1989: Guidance and Regulations* deals with children with disabilities.

Schedule 2 to the 1989 Act requires local authorities to keep a register of disabled children.

2.9.4 See also the Department of Health (1994) Protection of Children: Disclosure to NHS Employers of Criminal Background of those with Access to Children (Health Service Guidelines (94) 43); Department of Health (1994) Occupational Health Services for NHS Staff (Health Service Guidelines (94) 51); *The Welfare of Children and Young People in Hospital* (HMSO, 1991).

Children with mental health problems

2.9.5 The National Health Service Act 1946 provided for arrangements to be made for children with mental health problems. Under the Mental Health Act 1959 as amended by the Mental Health (Amendment) Act 1982, a local authority might accommodate in a community home any child: not within its care within the meaning of Part II of the Children Act 1948; whose care or after care was being undertaken by that or any other local authority; and who was suffering or had suffered from a mental disorder (s.9 of the Mental Health Act 1959 as amended by the Local Government Act 1972). A court could also authorise the admission of such a child to hospital. The Children and Young Persons Act 1969 also provided that a local authority could apply for a hospital order for a child, although that power was removed by the Children Act 1989.

2.9.6 At present, a child may be detained under the Mental Health Act 1983 on a voluntary or compulsory basis. The Code of Practice annexed to the Mental Health Act 1983 also contains the way in which the health authority should deal with patients. In practice it was and is still rare for a child to be compulsorily detained under the 1983 Act, simply because the local authority can make use of its powers to take the child into care and then arrange for treatment (see s.27 Mental Health Act 1983 as substituted by s.108(5) Children Act 1989).

2.9.7 Where a local authority has parental rights or responsibility for a child and that child is in hospital for mental-health-related reasons, the local authority must arrange for the child to be visited in hospital and do whatever else is expected of a parent. A child kept in a hospital where their liberty is curtailed must be subject to a secure accommodation order. The Children Act 1989 (ss.85 and 86) requires notification to the local social services authority if any child is accommodated by a health or local education authority for more than three months, and local authority social services must make a determination of what services might be needed by the child, including education.

2.9.8   In addition s.25 of the Children Act 1989 and the Children (Secure Accommodation) Regulations 1991 (SI 1991 No. 1505) and (No. 2 Regs) (SI 1991 No. 2034) apply to children accommodated by health authorities and NHS trusts as well as by nursing or mental nursing homes.

2.10   ADOPTION

2.10.1   The state did not regulate adoption until the Adoption of Children Act 1926 which allowed adoption without parental consent on certain limited grounds. The Adoption of Children (Regulation) Act 1939 placed adoption societies under certain regulations, which were strengthened by the Adoption Act 1958. The 1958 Act allowed local authorities to arrange adoption for children who were not in care. The Children Act 1975 and the Adoption Act 1976 further limited the scope of adoption. The 1976 Act (which took effect on 1 January 1988) is now the main statute governing adoption although it has been modified by the Children Act 1989 and the Care Standards Act 2000. It lays the fundamental principle that the birth parents of the child must consent to the adoption of that child, unless certain grounds are laid out. Section 11 of that Act provides that no one other than an adoption agency shall make arrangements for the adoption of a child, or place a child for adoption, unless the proposed adopters are relatives of the child, or the person is acting in pursuance of an order of the High Court.

2.10.2   The Adoption Act 1976 places a duty on local authorities to provide an adoption service, either through its own offices or it might provide the service through an approved adoption society. Adoption agencies have certain duties under the 1976 Act; for instance they must attempt to identify children who might benefit from adoption; supervise the child's placement during adoption proceedings; and the agencies must provide post-adoption support. Further regulations dealing, *inter alia*, with checks on persons applying to adopt children, were set out by the Adoption Agencies Regulations 1983 (SI 1983 No. 1964) as amended by the Adoption Agencies and Children (Arrangements for Placement and Reviews) (Miscellaneous Amendments) Regulations 1997 (SI 1997 No. 649) and the Children (Protection from Offenders) (Miscellaneous Amendments) Regulations 1997 (SI 1997 No. 2308). See also the Guidance document to those regulations, LAC (97)17.

2.10.3   Where a person gives notice to the local authority pursuant to the Adoption Act 1976 that a child in the authority's area will be the subject of an adoption application, that child becomes a 'protected child' under s.32

of the Act and certain duties are owed by the local authority to the child to take care for that child's welfare.

2.10.4 The 1976 Act also ratified the Hague Convention on Adoption 1965 at s.17(1).

2.10.5 The Children Act 1989 gives to the court the power in adoption proceedings to make a s.8 order allowing for contact between the child and the birth family. The Adoption Agencies Regulations 1983 (SI 1983 No. 1964) governs placements by a local authority of a child with foster parents for adoption.

2.11 CHILDMINDING, DAY CARE AND CLUBS

2.11.1 Childminding was originally dealt with by the Nurseries and Child-Minders Regulation Act 1948, as amended by the Health Services and Public Health Act 1968. The law was updated by Part X of the Children Act 1989 and by the Care Standards Act 2000. The 1989 Act replaced the term 'nursery' with the new and wider concept of 'day care'. This new term could include day nurseries, playgroups, out-of-school clubs, holiday schemes, and other children's activities (see volume 2 of *The Children Act 1989: Guidance and Regulations*). The Children Act 1989 requires the local authority to keep a register of persons who act as childminders on domestic premises and persons who provide day care for children under the age of 8 on premises (other than domestic premises).

2.11.2 A local authority can refuse to register applicants if they are 'not fit' to look after children. The Home Office has issued a circular on child-minders entitled 'The Children Act and Day Care for Young Children: Registration'. This lists the factors which local authorities should use in assessing childminders, and indicates that corporal punishment should not be used by any childminder. Certain conditions may be placed on the childminder, such as the number of children he or she is allowed to foster. See the Child Minding and Day Care (Applications for Registration) Regulations 1991 (SI 1991 No. 1689).

2.11.3 Many childcare organisations (such as sports clubs) have their own internal guidelines for the protection of children. If a particular club, such as a youth club, is not covered by the specific provisions of the Children Act 1989, then the general provisions relating to children in the local authority's area would apply to the children in that club.

2.12   CHILDREN IN DETENTION AND SECURE ACCOMMODATION

The penal system for children

2.12.1   The Children and Young Persons Act 1933 expanded the penal system for children and the Criminal Justice Act 1948 raised the minimum age for imprisonment to 15. In 1963 the criminal age of responsibility was raised to 10. The Criminal Justice Act 1948 also included a number of methods of detaining children, namely remand homes, Borstals, detention centres, attendance centres, approved schools and prison. The Children and Young Persons Act 1969 gave to the courts the power to consider whether to make a care order or a supervision order to the local authority.

2.12.2   The relevant Acts are the Criminal Justice Act 1948, the Prison Act 1952 and the Criminal Justice Act 1961. The rules for the management of such places were:

(a) The Prison Rules 1964 (SI 1964 No. 388) (as amended).

(b) The Borstal Rules 1964 (SI 1964 No. 387).

(c) The Detention Centre Rules 1952 (SI 1952 No. 1432).

(d) The Attendance Centre Rules 1958 (SI 1958 No. 1990).

2.12.3   The Criminal Justice Act 1982 abolished the Borstal system, and replaced it with sentences of 'youth custody'. The Criminal Justice Act 1988 made it more difficult to impose custodial sentences on young offenders. The Criminal Justice Act 1991 excluded 14 year olds from youth custody. The Children Act 1989 removed from the juvenile court the power to order a young offender into local authority care.

2.12.4   Prisoners between the ages of 15 and 21 are now held in Young Offender Institutions. These institutions are governed by the Young Offender Institution Rules 1988 (SI 1988 No. 1422) as amended. However, where a defendant is below the age of 17, he will normally be remanded in secure accommodation provided by a local authority designated by the court.

2.12.5   Under s.5(9) of the Children and Young Persons Act 1969, the police were under a duty to the local authority social services department for the area where the child lived (or the social services area where the police are located) of any decision to commence criminal proceedings against a person under the age of 18. The relevant provisions are now contained in s.46(3) of the Children Act 1989. A local authority may also have other duties to the young person under s.47 of the 1989 Act.

Secure accommodation provided by local authorities

2.12.6 Secure accommodation is the means by which social workers place children in care under lock and key. Under the Children and Young Persons Act 1969 (s.24(2)), a local authority was given the power to restrict the child's liberty to such extent as was thought appropriate. This was known as providing 'secure accommodation' and essentially it replaced the former means of detaining children by placing them in approved schools, etc. Section 43(2)(c) of the 1969 Act allowed the Secretary of State to make regulations with respect to the conduct of community homes, and these are found in the Community Homes Regulations 1972, Regulations 10–14. A local authority could seek the Secretary of State's approval for the use of secure accommodation in community homes. DHSS Circular No. 78/1972 gave guidance to local authorities in relation to the control provisions in Regulation 10. See also LAC 1/1975.

2.12.7 This scheme was replaced on 1 January 1984 by section 21A of the Child Care Act 1980 which introduced a new scheme for the restriction of a child's liberty. This consisted of:

- the Secure Accommodation Regulations 1983 (SI 1983 No. 652) which came into effect from 24 May 1983;
- the Secure Accommodation (No. 2) Regulations 1983 (SI 1983 No. 1808) with effect from 1 January 1984; and
- the Secure Accommodation (No. 2) (Amendment) Regulations 1986 (SI 1986 No. 1591) with effect from 15 October 1986.

2.12.8 Guidance on the use of secure accommodation was given in LAC (83) 18 dated 9 December 1983: Restriction of Children in Care.

2.12.9 At present, secure accommodation for children is covered by s.25 of the Children Act 1989 and the Children (Secure Accommodation) Regulations 1991 (SI 1991 No. 1505) and (No. 2 Regs) (SI 1991 No. 2034). A child may be kept in secure accommodation in a community home when the home has been approved by the Secretary of State for such use. (See also *The Children Act 1989: Guidance and Regulations*, volume 4: *Residential Care* together with the Children (Homes and Secure Accommodation) (Miscellaneous Amendments) Regulations 1996 (SI 1996 No. 692).

2.12.10 An application to the court to place a child in secure accommodation is not restricted to local authorities. It can also be made by a health authority, an NHS trust, a local education authority and a person carrying on a residential care home, nursing home or mental nursing home.

2.13 THE VOLUNTARY SECTOR, ASYLUM CHILDREN AND CHILDREN IN THE ARMED FORCES

The voluntary sector

2.13.1 Local authorities are encouraged to use and monitor the voluntary sector: *The Children Act 1989: Guidance and Regulations*, volume 2 (HMSO, 1991). One of the best-known organisations in this area is the National Society for the Prevention of Cruelty to Children (NSPCC). The NSPCC now has a nationwide network of 60 child protection teams, staffed by fully trained social workers. It now concentrates on the prevention of child abuse by the provision of support and services to children. The NSPCC has also produced reports on child protection issues.

2.13.2 Other organisations are the Children's Society, the National Children's Homes, the National Children's Bureau, Barnardo's, Boys' and Girls' Welfare Society, Family Service Units, the National Association of Young People in Care, the Children's Legal Centre and Childline.

Asylum children

2.13.3 Asylum children will generally be covered by the local authority's general powers and duties towards children in their area. However, there is a document published by the Social Services Inspectorate (1995) Un-accompanied Asylum Seeker Children (Chief Inspector Letter CI (95) 17) which deals specifically with this issue.

Armed forces

2.13.4 All child protection matters within the Royal Navy are managed by the Naval Personal and Family Service, the Royal Navy's social work department. There is a social services department for the Royal Marines, the Royal Marines Welfare Service, the Army (the Army Welfare Service) and the Royal Air Force. See also the Armed Forces Act 1991 for protection of children in the armed forces.

2.14 CHILDREN AND THE MEDIA

2.14.1 Children enjoy certain rights of protection from the media (see also para. 2.5.10). The Video Recordings Act 1984 (as amended by the Criminal Justice and Public Order Act 1994) provides that the Home Secretary might designate a person as the authority responsible for the classification of video films. That power has been handed to the British Board of Film Classification, which classifies films for general release and sets age limits for each film.

2.14.2 The current regulatory framework for cinema is set out in the Cinemas Act 1985. All cinemas are subject to a local authority franchise, which require cinemas to enforce age restrictions. Television and radio is governed by the Broadcasting Act 1996 which established the Broadcasting Standards Commission. The Commission is responsible for monitoring material, drawing up codes for broadcasters and investigating complaints.

2.14.3 As regards satellite broadcasts, the Broadcasting Act 1996 allows the Secretary of State to make orders preventing the reception of unacceptable foreign satellite services. The European Court of Justice has said (*Commission of the European Communities* v. *United Kingdom* C222/94 (1996) *The Times* 3 September) that only the country from which the transmission emanates can regulate that transmission.

2.14.4 Finally, the Internet is not only a source of child pornography but also a means for potential abusers to approach children. The new technology has been held to be covered by the Protection of Children Act 1978 and the Obscene Publications Acts 1959 and 1964 (*R* v. *Fellows* [1997] 2 All ER 548). The 1978 Act covers the taking, distribution and possession with a view to distributing any indecent photograph or film of a child. Section 160 of the Criminal Justice Act 1988 makes it an offence for a person to have in his possession an indecent photograph of a child.

2.14.5 The Children and Young Persons (Harmful Publications) Act 1955 makes it a criminal offence to publish or sell or loan any magazine or other work portraying the commission of crimes, acts of violence or cruelty or instances of a repulsive or horrible nature in such a way as the work would tend to corrupt a child or young person, where that magazine or other work is likely to fall into the hands of a child or young person. Child pornography is also covered by the Protection of Children Act 1978 (s.1) and the Criminal Justice Act 1988 (s.160).

2.15 CHILDREN, THE CRIMINAL LAW AND REGISTRATION OF OFFENDERS

Punishment of children

2.15.1 The common law principle that parents could punish their child was codified into the Children and Young Persons Act 1933. Cases arose where parents claimed that they had simply been attempting to punish their child, but had ended up killing them. In this way, a charge of murder could be reduced to manslaughter: *R* v. *Griffin* (1865) 11 Cox CC 402. Likewise a parent who wilfully neglects a child leading to the child's death may also be convicted of manslaughter: *R* v. *Sheppard* [1980] 3 WLR 960.

Abortion, infanticide and child cruelty

2.15.2 The offence of abortion is still a part of the Offences Against the Person Act 1861 (s.58). It is also an offence to supply or procure the means for abortion, or to attempt to conceal the birth of a child. However, these offences are rarely prosecuted, and courts will take into account the fact that a person might procure a legal abortion either privately or under the NHS. The relevant statute governing terminations is the Abortion Act 1967, which requires that the medical procedure takes place in an approved place, i.e. a hospital approved by the Minister of Health or the Secretary of State under the National Health Service Act 1946.

2.15.3 The crime of infanticide comes under the Infanticide Act 1938, and is aimed at mothers whose minds are disturbed after giving birth. The defence has the burden of showing diminished responsibility, while the prosecution has the burden of showing that the crime is not infanticide, if it wishes to allege murder.

2.15.4 The present law on cruelty to children is found under s.1 of the Children and Young Persons Act 1933 (as amended by the Children and Young Persons Act 1963, Children Act 1975, Criminal Justice Act 1988, Children Act 1989 and the Magistrates' Courts Act 1980). Where a person over 16 years of age having the control of a child under 16 years of age

(a) assaults the child

(b) ill-treats the child

(c) neglects the child

(d) abandons the child

(e) exposes the child or causes or procures the child to be assaulted, ill-treated, neglected, abandoned or exposed

that person commits an offence, if those actions are likely to cause the child unnecessary suffering or injury to health.

2.15.5 The Children and Young Persons Act 1933, Sched. 1 also created a list of offences against children from which we derive the term 'Schedule 1 Offence'.

Sexual offences against children

2.15.6 The Sexual Offences Act 1956 (as amended by subsequent legislation) deals with male–female intercourse, and sets out a list of sexual offences against children. The Sexual Offences Act 1956 also introduced the offence of indecent assault although no definition is provided for that term. See also s.1 of the Indecency with Children Act 1960, s.54 of the Criminal Law Act 1977 (inciting girl under 16 to incest) and Sexual Offences (Amendment) Act 2000 (abuse of trust); see para. 2.2.63.

2.15.7 The Vagrancy Act 1824 makes it an offence for any man to 'wilfully, openly, lewdly and obscenely expose [his] person with intent to insult a female'. The Indecency with Children Act 1960 created the crime of gross indecency with a child under 16 years of age. The Sex Offenders Act 1997 has made unlawful certain sexual offences committed against children abroad by UK citizens, although the acts must be unlawful both in the host country and in the UK. The Sexual Offences (Conspiracy and Incitement) Act 1996 makes unlawful the organisation and sale of holidays to UK residents for the purpose of committing sexual offences abroad.

Other offences against children

2.15.8 It is a criminal offence to give any child under the age of 5 any intoxicating liquor (Children and Young Persons Act 1933 (amended by Criminal Justice Act 1967 and Criminal Justice Act 1982)). It is also an offence to supply to persons under the age of 18 certain substances which may cause intoxication if inhaled (Intoxicating Substances (Supply) Act 1985, s.1).

2.15.9 The Children and Young Persons Act 1969 (as amended) also makes it an offence for any person to procure any child under the age of 16 years of age for the purpose of begging or receiving alms. See also Children Act 1989, Sched. 13, para. 3(b).

2.15.10 The Prohibition of Female Circumcision Act 1985 makes female circumcision, excision or infibulation an offence, except on specific physical and mental health grounds.

Disqualification and registration of offenders working with Children

2.15.11 Arrangements have existed since 1965 under which prison authorities have notified local authority social services departments of the release of men convicted of incest. In 1975 these arrangements were extended to the release of persons convicted of offences against children in the home (see LAC No. 3/1975 and No. 22/1978).

2.15.12 Social services and certain other statutory agencies (such as the probation service) have also had the ability to check with the police for a person's criminal record since 1982. Police checks for childminders were instituted in 1982 (Home Office Circular (HOC) 195/1982), and later widened to other categories of persons working with children. See HOC 45/1986, 22/1991, 47/1993, 42/1994, 46/1994. Access to this information has been extended by the Police Act 1997.

2.15.13 The Sex Offenders Act 1997, which came into force on 1 September 1997 set up a National Register of convicted child sex offenders (including those who deal in child pornography) who will be under a duty to give their names and addresses to the local police. It only applies to offenders convicted in the Crown Court, not those found to have abused children in Children Act proceedings.

2.15.14 The Criminal Justice and Courts Services Act 2000 Part II (the 2000 Act) provides a mechanism whereby a criminal court can order the disqualification of certain offenders from working with children. An individual who applies for employment working with children commits an offence under s.35 of the 2000 Act. Similarly, an employer may also be guilty of an offence under s.35(2) of the 2000 Act if he 'knowingly' offers employment to an offender who is disqualified from working with children.

2.15.15 In addition, there are several national sources of information which social services can access. This information is governed by the Data Protection Acts, employment protection legislation, the laws on defamation and the threat of judicial review. See Part IV, Chapter 14 of *People Like Us* (*The Report of the Review of the Safeguards for Children living away from Home*, by Sir William Utting, HMSO, 1997) for a discussion of the various sources of information available to statutory authorities and other organisations.

2.15.16 List 99 is a list prepared by the Department for Education and Employment. It lists people barred or restricted from teaching or working in schools, and operates under s.218 of the Education Reform Act 1988. Regulations under that Act give the Secretary of State power to make directions barring or restricting the conditions of employment of unsuitable people from employment by local education authorities, grant-maintained schools, non-maintained schools and proprietors of independent schools. The grounds for inclusion on the list are misconduct whether or not they are evidenced by a conviction for a criminal offence. The standard of proof is the balance of probabilities. List 99 is sent to local education authorities and the associations representing independent schools annually.

2.15.17 Local authorities and voluntary organisations can also check with the Department of Health Consultancy Index. This provides information on a register of persons compiled from police reports, local authority and voluntary organisation reports and List 99 reports.

2.15.18 The Protection of Children Act 1999 (the 1999 Act) amends s.218 of the Education Reform Act 1988 and creates a framework for identifying people unsuitable to work with children and compels or allows employers to access a single point for checking the names of people they propose to employ in a post involving the care of children. This involves permitting checks against criminal records, List 99 and the Consultancy Index. The 1999 Act also requires childcare organisations not to offer work to anyone so listed for any posts involving regular contact with children in a childcare capacity. See also the Protection of Children (Child Care Organisations) Regulations 2000 (SI 2000 No. 2432).

2.15.19 Other organisations involved in childcare have produced their own information. The General Medical Council has produced guidance entitled *Confidentiality* (1995). The United Kingdom Central Council for Nursing Midwifery and Health Visiting (UKCC) has produced *Guidelines for Professional Practice* (1996).

2.15.20 Gwent Constabulary has created a national database of care workers against whom allegations have been made. This is known as the Historical Abuse Database. It is compiled using reports from all the major abuse inquiries across the country. It will only contain names together with basic information such as aliases, date of birth and last-known address. Investigating police officers will only be told about connections once two separate forces have filed the same name. Only senior investigating officers or their deputies will have access to the information.

CHAPTER 3

Causes of action

3.1   THE IMPORTANCE OF IDENTIFYING THE CAUSE OF ACTION

3.1.1   The importance of identifying the correct cause of action when considering a potential child abuse compensation claim is obvious. The position may however be complex. The choice of cause of action may involve considerable preliminary investigation.

3.1.2   It is significant that the cause of action may dictate the applicable limitation period. Most notably a trespass claim will be subject to a six-year period of limitation and cannot be extended pursuant to ss.11, 14 or 33 Limitation Act 1980 (see Chapter 5). However, consideration will need to be given to the possibility of relying on s.32 Limitation Act 1980 and the concealment provisions. On the other hand, a negligence action will have a three-year primary limitation period, which may be extended for a later date of knowledge.

3.1.3   The choice of cause of action is also significant in identifying the correct defendant to the action. If there is a claim in trespass, the individual abuser may need to be a defendant. If the individual is unlikely to be able to pay compensation, then it will be necessary to ascertain whether any other individual or organisation could be vicariously liable for the abuser's actions (see para. 3.3).

3.1.4   It is common for alternative causes of action to be pleaded but this approach carries with it significant risks. If the claimant ultimately succeeds with the claim based on one cause of action but fails in respect of other causes of action there may be considerable costs penalties. Likewise a defendant who has a good defence to one cause of action but no defence to another cause of action may ultimately gain little benefit from fighting all aspects of the claim.

3.1.5   Under Rule 44.3 Civil Procedure Rules (CPR), specific provision is made for costs to be awarded to reflect that a party has succeeded on part of his claim but not been wholly successful. Further, in considering the conduct of the parties to the litigation, the court will consider whether it was reasonable for the parties to pursue particular points. Costs may therefore be awarded to reflect the proportion of court time spent on arguing any particular cause of action rather than on the basis of which party has won or lost the claim as a whole. For either party losing one point may offset the benefit of winning another. For a claimant there is the further risk of joining unnecessary defendants to the action if attempting to pursue every theoretical cause of action.

3.2   THE STEPS REQUIRED TO IDENTIFY THE CAUSE OF ACTION

3.2.1   Identifying the cause of action which the claimant is ultimately likely to succeed in proving may be difficult. A number of steps will be necessary in order to do this competently.

Step 1: identifying the allegations of abuse

3.2.2   The first task for the claimant's lawyer is to ascertain the nature and scope of the complaints made by the lay client. This in itself may be complex. In all but straightforward cases this step is best achieved by obtaining a psychiatric report. A psychiatrist with experience of abuse cases will be able to take a very detailed history from the client. The psychiatrist can then assess the weight and significance to be given to the various allegations that are made in terms of their long-term effect on the claimant. For example, in some circumstances, sexual abuse may be the most obvious complaint but emotional abuse may ultimately be the more damaging.

3.2.3   A psychiatrist should be specifically instructed on behalf of the claimant to assess the extent to which ascertainable psychiatric damage has been caused by:

- sexual abuse by individuals;
- physical abuse by individuals;
- emotional abuse by individuals;
- a harsh or uncaring institutional regime;
- a failure to believe and deal with the claimant's earlier complaints of abuse;
- a combination of these factors.

Step 2: identifying the responsible person or institution

3.2.4 In cases that involve sexual or physical abuse by individuals there will be a potential claim in trespass against the abuser himself/herself. However, the six-year unextendable time limit may rule out such a claim. Further, the abuser may be serving a prison sentence and be unlikely to be able to meet a substantial claim for damages. The task will then be to ascertain whether any other potential defendant might be either: (a) vicariously liable for the abuse; or (b) liable in negligence for allowing the abuse to occur.

3.2.5 Examples of possible persons or institutions who may be either vicariously liable for the actions of abusers or liable in negligence for allowing the abuse to occur are:

- a public authority responsible for running an institution (e.g. a children's home, a school, an approved school, a detention centre, an assessment centre, a secure unit) in which the claimant has been placed;
- a public authority who has been responsible for the claimant as a child in its care through a care order;
- an institution such as a private school or children's home run by a religious order, a charity or other organisation;
- a health authority or NHS trust responsible for supervising doctors and nurses in a hospital;
- individuals or a company running a private children's home or a private school;
- individuals caring for a child including a natural parent, a step-parent, a foster parent, a childminder, a friend or a relative;
- institutions or individuals running a sports club, a holiday club or other youth clubs.

Step 3: identifying the potential defendant

3.2.6 Once a possible candidate for liability is identified, the next step is to ascertain the correct defendant to sue. The public authority or institution responsible for supervising the claimant's welfare at the date the abuse occurred may have ceased to exist or may have passed responsibility to a different authority or institution.

3.2.7 For example until 1973 the Home Office and approved school managers were responsible for running approved schools. In 1973 a series of specific statutory instruments made cessation orders which passed responsibility for particular approved schools from the managers to particular local authorities. The precise terms of the cessation order for each approved school will determine whether responsibility for past torts has passed to a local authority (see paras. 2.2.30–2.2.31).

3.2.8 Local government reorganisation has altered the identity and responsibilities of many local authorities. A series of changes has passed responsibility between different county councils in neighbouring areas and between metropolitan borough councils and county councils. It is necessary to trace the statutory provisions that apply in a particular geographical area in order to ascertain the identity of the authority responsible for the acts of an earlier authority.

3.2.9 Health authorities have also undergone reorganisation and the relationship between previous health authorities and new NHS trusts is governed by specific contractual terms that need to be ascertained in order to identify correctly the defendant to sue.

3.2.10 Charities, trusts and other institutional organisations may also have undergone significant changes in organisation and responsibility. These too can be difficult to trace. The starting point is to ask the potential defendant to confirm the position. If the potential defendant will not confirm it is the correct organisation to sue for the relevant period of abuse, it should be asked to disclose the relevant documents to enable the correct identity of relevant defendant to be traced.

Step 4: identifying the sources of documents for disclosure

3.2.11 Identifying the correct defendant to sue is one step in seeking to obtain disclosure of the necessary documents from which to assess the prospects of success in respect of a claim. Other public authorities or institutions which no longer have legal liability for past torts against the claimant may still hold documents. Other relevant documents may be held by hospitals, general practitioners, schools and assessment centres that had some responsibility for the claimant during his/her childhood. All these documents should be requested in order that a proper assessment of the merits of any potential cause of action can be made (see Chapter 7).

Step 5: assessing the merits of the possible causes of action

3.2.12 Once all of these documents have been obtained it will be necessary to seek expert opinion in respect of a possible claim in negligence (see para. 3.5). Claims for breach of statutory duty and misfeasance in public office should also be considered, although these will be rarer and likely to arise out of exceptional circumstances. The Human Rights Act 1998 may also be relevant.

One possibility will be a free-standing claim under the Act. Another possibility will be that the claimant can rely on convention rights in support of a claim for negligence, breach of statutory duty or misfeasance in public office.

3.3   TRESPASS/BREACH OF DUTY

3.3.1   Trespass to the person is a description in civil proceedings used to cover acts which in criminal proceedings would be an assault, grievous bodily harm, rape or buggery. It will include deliberate acts that caused the claimant to apprehend immediate unlawful violence. In civil proceedings, trespass to the person will include deliberate sexual and physical abuse and unlawful imprisonment.

Vicarious liability for trespass/breach of duty

3.3.2   The issue of whether an employer can be vicariously liable for an assault by an employee has become an important one in child abuse claims. The following cases demonstrate the development of the law in this area culminating in the decision in *Lister* v. *Hesley Hall Ltd* [2001] UKHL 22, [2001] 2 WLR 311. From this decision it appears that the distinction between a deliberate assault by a stranger and one committed by a person with a duty of care to the victim may be an important one, particularly in the context of vicarious liability.

3.3.3   In *Racz* v. *Home Office* [1994] 2 AC 45 a prisoner who claimed he had been taken to a strip cell where his clothes were forcibly removed brought a claim against the Home Office in assault, battery, negligence and misfeasance in public office. The defendant applied to strike out the claim in misfeasance in public office. It was held by the House of Lords that the Home Office may be vicariously liable for the ill-treatment of prisoners by prison officers if they were engaged in a misguided and unauthorised method of performing their authorised duties but not if the unauthorised duties were so unconnected with the authorised duties so as to be independent of and outside those duties. Prison officers are employed to discipline prisoners but if they overdiscipline prisoners the Home Office could arguably be liable.

3.3.4   The *Racz* case concerned a preliminary point in respect of misfeasance in public office but similar arguments apply in respect of trespass. In cases involving physical abuse of children in care or institutions there is a potential claim for vicarious liability. That is, if the complaint is that those perpetrating the abuse were disciplining the claimant but in implementing punishment they used excessive force there may be a claim for vicarious liability.

3.3.5   In the case of *T* v. *North Yorkshire County Council* [1999] IRLR 98 (see
para. 1.5.38), the Court of Appeal held that an employer could not be held
vicariously liable for sexual abuse perpetrated by an employee. In that
case the claimant was a child with head injuries and learning difficulties.
The claimant alleged he had been sexually abused by a teacher. The
teacher was employed by the defendant local authority. The claimant was
abused by the teacher while on a school holiday. At the time he was in the
care of the teacher who was employed to take the school trip. The claimant
claimed damages for assault alleging the local authority was vicariously
liable for the sexual assault by its employee. In the Court of Appeal, Lady
Justice Butler-Sloss described how:

> the classic test for vicarious liability is to be found in *Salmond on Torts*
> (now *Salmond and Heuston*, 21st edition). The statement in the 9th edition
> at page 95 was expressly approved by the Privy Council in *Canadian
> Pacific Railway Company* v. *Lockhart* [1942] AC 591 in the speech of Lord
> Thankerton at page 599:
>
>> It is clear that the master is responsible for acts actually authorised by
>> him: for liability would exist in this case, even if the relation between
>> the parties was merely one of agency, and not one of service at all. But a
>> master, as opposed to the employer of an independent contractor, is
>> liable even for acts which he has not authorized, provided they are so
>> connected with acts which he has authorized that they may rightly be re-
>> garded as modes – although improper modes – of doing them. In other
>> words, a master is responsible not merely for what he authorizes his ser-
>> vant to do, but also for the way in which he does it . . . On the other
>> hand, if the unauthorized and wrongful act of the servant is not so con-
>> nected with the authorized act as to be a mode of doing it, but is an inde-
>> pendent act, the master is not responsible: for in such a case, the servant
>> is not acting in the course of his employment but has gone outside of it.

3.3.6   Applying the test set out in *Salmond on Torts* to the facts in *T* v. *North
Yorkshire County Council*, Butler-Sloss LJ concluded:

> it is useful to stand back and ask: applying general principles, in which cat-
> egory in the *Salmond* test would one expect these facts to fall? A deputy
> headmaster of a special school, charged with the responsibility of caring for
> a handicapped teenager on a foreign holiday, sexually assaults him. Is that
> in principle an improper mode of carrying out an authorised act on behalf of
> his employer, the Council, or an independent act outside the course of his
> employment? His position of caring for the plaintiff by sharing a bedroom
> with him gave him the opportunity to carry out the sexual assaults. But
> availing himself of that opportunity seems to me to be far removed from an
> unauthorised mode of carrying out a teacher's duties on behalf of his em-
> ployer. Rather it is a negation of the duty of the Council to look after chil-
> dren for whom it was responsible. Acts of physical assault may not be so
> easy to categorise, since they may range, for instance, from a brutal and un-
> provoked assault by a teacher to forceful attempts to defend another pupil
> or the teacher himself. But in the field of serious sexual misconduct, I find

it difficult to visualise circumstances in which an act of the teacher can be an unauthorised mode of carrying out an authorised act, although I would not wish to close the door on the possibility.

In my judgment the judge was wrong in principle to find the Council capable of being liable for the sexual assaults committed by its employee on the plaintiff.

3.3.7   Lord Justice Chadwick in coming to the same conclusion analysed the position as follows:

> It is essential to keep in mind that it is not alleged that the Council itself was in breach of any duty which it may have owed to the plaintiff. The only basis of the claim advanced against the Council is vicarious liability for the acts of its employee.
>
> I am satisfied that the claim cannot succeed on that basis. I find it impossible to hold that the commission of acts of indecent assault can be regarded as a mode – albeit, an improper and unauthorised mode – of doing what, on the case advanced, the deputy headmaster was employed by the Council to do. In the circumstances alleged, [the teacher] was employed to supervise the plaintiff's welfare while on the holiday in Spain. The commission by him of acts of indecent assault on a pupil in his charge cannot be regarded as a way of doing that. Rather, it must be regarded as an independent act of self-indulgence or self-gratification. It is that element which distinguishes the facts alleged in this case from those in *Poland* v. *John Parr and Sons* [1927] 1 KB 236, *Rose* v. *Plenty* [1976] 1 WLR 141 and *Vasey* v. *Surrey Free Inns Plc* (Court of Appeal, 5 May 1995) – to which we were referred in argument. It is not sufficient to found vicarious liability in the employer that the employment provided the opportunity for the employee to commit the act if the act itself was outside the scope of the employment – see *Heasmans* v. *Charity Cleaning Co Ltd* [1987] IRLR 286.

3.3.8   In the case of *Fennelly* v. *Connex South Eastern Ltd* (CA Schiemann LJ, Buxton LJ, 11 December 2000) the Court of Appeal considered a claim brought by a rail traveller against a rail company for damages for assault by a ticket collector. The ticket collector challenged the claimant over his fare and in the course of doing so took the claimant's head into a head lock. The issue was whether such an assault could be carried out in the course of the ticket collector's employment so as to render the rail company vicariously liable for his actions. Lord Justice Buxton took as a starting point the passage from *Salmond on Torts* cited in the case of *T* v. *North Yorkshire County Council*. Buxton LJ then considered the *Salmond* test as discussed by the editor of *Clark & Lindsell on Torts* in paragraph 5-24 of the eighteenth edition. He stated:

> Having noted that the test, as indicated by *Salmond*, is in terms of the acts authorised by the master the learned editor then goes on to say this:
>
> > Lord Wilberforce in *Kooragang Investment Pty Ltd* v. *Richardson and Wrench Ltd* [1982] AC 62 noted that in recent years the tendency has

been toward more liberal protection of third parties. So, in establishing a particular employee's 'course of employment', the court should not dissect the employee's tasks into component parts but should ask in a general sense: 'what was the job at which he was engaged for his employer?' . . . Sometimes the court will use the phrase 'was the employee on a frolic of his own?', to conclude that the tort was not committed during the course of employment. This involves a finding that the employee has so clearly departed from the scope of his employment that the employer will not be liable for his acts.

In support of that formulation the learned editor refers to a case decided by Comyn J., *Harrison* v. *Michelin Tyre Co* [1985] 1 All ER 918. In that case, with the assistance of distinguished counsel, Comyn J. went in very considerable detail into the true understanding of the test of course of employment. He formulated the matter thus:

'Was it so divergent from the employment as to be plainly alien to and wholly distinguishable from the employment?'

3.3.9   In *Fennelly* v. *Connex South Eastern Ltd* the rail employee was employed to collect fares. The Court of Appeal found that a challenge to a passenger that involved placing the passenger's head in a head lock was not so far removed from the course of his employment to be outside it. The Court of Appeal reversed the trial judge's decision and allowed the claimant's claim to succeed. Lord Justice Schiemann specifically considered the defendant's argument that a criminal act such as an assault could not be committed in the course of an employee's employment. Schiemann LJ stated:

[The defendant] submitted that, where you have a criminal act the client has a remedy against the Criminal Injuries Compensation Scheme. In those circumstances it will be wrong to give a judgment in his favour under the civil law generally. For my part I see no force in this distinction at all. The rationale behind the imposing liability for torts committed by an employee in these circumstances seems to me to remain exactly the same whether the tort is also a crime or whether it is not. As I have said I agree this appeal ought to be allowed.

3.3.10   The law in this area has now finally been reviewed by the House of Lords. The decision in *T* v. *North Yorkshire County Council* has been specifically overruled by the House of Lords in the case of *Lister* v. *Hesley Hall Ltd* [2001] UKHL 22, [2001] 2 WLR 1311. In that case Lord Steyn stated at para. 25:

In my view the approach of the Court of Appeal [in *Trotman* v. *North Yorkshire County Council* [1999] BLGR 584] was wrong. It resulted in the case being treated as one of the employment furnishing a mere opportunity to commit the sexual abuse. The reality was that the county council were responsible for the care of vulnerable children and employed the headmaster to carry out that duty on its behalf. And the sexual abuse took place while the employee was engaged in duties at the very time and place demanded by his employment. The connection between the employment and the torts was very close. I would overrule *Trotman* v. *North Yorkshire County Council*.

3.3.11   At para. 28 Lord Steyn stated:

> I am satisfied that in the cases of the appeals under consideration the evidence showed that the employers entrusted the care of the children in Axeholme House to the warden. The question is whether the warden's torts were so closely connected with his employment that it would be fair and just to hold the employers vicariously liable. On the facts of the case the answer is yes. After all, the sexual abuse is inextricably interwoven with the carrying out by the warden of his duties in Axeholme House.

3.3.12   The case of *Lister* v. *Hesley Hall Ltd* was a claim for damages arising from sexual abuse perpetrated by the warden of a boarding annex to a school for children with emotional and behavioural difficulties. The school was privately run but children were sent to the school by local authorities. Lord Clyde described the duties in respect of those running and managing the school as follows at para. 50:

> It appears that the care and safekeeping of the boys had been entrusted to the respondents and they in turn had entrusted their care and safekeeping, so far as the running of the boarding house was concerned, to the warden. That gave him access to the premises, but the opportunity to be at the premises would not in itself constitute a sufficient connection between his wrongful actings and his employment. In addition to the opportunity which access gave him, his position as warden and the close contact with the boys which that work involved created a sufficient connection between the acts of abuse which he committed and the work which he had been employed to do. It appears that the respondents gave the warden a quite general authority in the supervision and running of the house as well as some particular responsibilities. His general duty was to look after and to care for, among others, the appellants. That function was one which the respondents had delegated to him. That he performed that function in a way which was an abuse of his position and an abnegation of his duty does not sever the connection with his employment. The particular acts which he carried out upon the boys have to be viewed not in isolation but in the context and the circumstances in which they occurred. Given that he had a general authority in the management of the house and in the care and supervision of the boys in it, the employers should be liable for the way in which he behaved towards them in his capacity as warden of the house. The respondents should then be vicariously liable to the appellants for the injury and damage which they suffered at the hands of the warden.

3.3.13   Lord Hobhouse described the duty of the employer in respect of his employee as follows at para. 54:

> What these cases and *Trotman*'s case in truth illustrate is a situation where the employer has assumed a relationship to the plaintiff which imposes specific duties in tort upon the employer and the role of the employee (or servant) is that he is the person to whom the employer has entrusted the performance of that duty. These cases are examples of that class where the employer, by reason of assuming a relationship to the plaintiff, owes to

the plaintiff duties which are more extensive than those owed by the public at large and, accordingly, are to be contrasted with the situation where a defendant is simply in proximity to the plaintiff so that it is foreseeable that his acts may injure the plaintiff or his property and a reasonable person would have taken care to avoid causing such injury [. . .]

The fact that sexual abuse was involved does not distinguish this case from any other involving the care of the young and vulnerable and the duty to protect them from the risk of harm.

3.3.14 Lord Hobhouse, Lord Steyn (with whom Lord Hutton agreed) and Lord Clyde described the position of the employer as one in which there was a duty imposed on the employer through a specific assumption of responsibility by the employer towards the claimant. This employer's duty and responsibility was then entrusted to the employee and the employer is in breach of duty if the employee abused the claimant. This is illustrated by the following passage at para. 55:

> The classes of persons or institutions that are in this type of special relationship to another human being include schools, prisons, hospitals and even, in relation to their visitors, occupiers of land. They are liable if they themselves fail to perform the duty which they consequently owe. If they entrust the performance of that duty to an employee and that employee fails to perform the duty, they are still liable. The employee, because he has, through his obligations to his employers, adopted the same relationship towards and come under the same duties to the plaintiff, is also liable to the plaintiff for his own breach of duty. The liability of the employers is a vicarious liability because the actual breach of duty is that of the employee. The employee is a tortfeasor. The employers are liable for the employee's tortious act or omission because it is to him that the employers have entrusted the performance of their duty. The employers' liability to the plaintiff is also that of a tortfeasor. I use the word 'entrusted' in preference to the word 'delegated' which is commonly, but perhaps less accurately, used. Vicarious liability is sometimes described as a 'strict' liability. The use of this term is misleading unless it is used just to explain that there has been no actual fault on the part of the employers. The liability of the employers derives from their voluntary assumption of the relationship towards the plaintiff and the duties that arise from that relationship and their choosing to entrust the performance of those duties to their servant. Where these conditions are satisfied, the motive of the employee and the fact that he is doing something expressly forbidden and is serving only his own ends does not negative the vicarious liability for his breach of the 'delegated' duty.

3.3.15 The concept that the employer is in breach of duty suggests that a claim for breach of duty would come within the provisions of ss.11, 14 and 33 of the Limitation Act 1980. Sections 11 and 14 specifically apply to actions for 'negligence, nuisance or breach of duty' (see Chapter 5). There was no suggestion in the House of Lords' speeches that the claim in the *Lister* case would be limitation barred because it was subject to an unextendable six-year limitation period as this point appears not to have been argued or considered.

3.3.16 However, the speech of Lord Millett suggests that the liability of the employer is not a liability for breach of duty but is vicarious liability for the tort of the employee. The implication being that, if the tort of the employee is an assault or trespass, then the responsibility of the employer is for that assault or trespass. A six-year unextendable time limit would then apply together with a possible claim for aggravated damages. Lord Millett concluded in para. 84:

> I would hold the school vicariously liable for the warden's intentional assaults, not (as was suggested in argument) for his failure to perform his duty to take care of the boys. That is an artificial approach based on a misreading of *Morris* v. *Martin*. The cleaners were vicariously liable for their employee's conversion of the fur, not for his negligence in failing to look after it. Similarly in *Photo Production* v. *Securicor Transport Ltd* the security firm was vicariously liable for the patrolman's arson, not for his negligence. The law is mature enough to hold an employer vicariously liable for deliberate, criminal wrongdoing on the part of an employee without indulging in sophistry of this kind. I would also not base liability on the warden's failure to report his own wrongdoing to his employer, an approach which I regard as both artificial and unrealistic. Even if such a duty did exist, on which I prefer to express no opinion, I am inclined to think that it would be a duty owed exclusively to the employer and not a duty for breach of which the employer could be vicariously liable. The same reasoning would not, of course, necessarily apply to the duty to report the wrongdoing of fellow employees, but it is not necessary to decide this.

3.3.17 The decision is clearly a very important one in bringing deliberate acts of child abuse within the sphere of responsibility of employers. It does not address the difficulty arising from the limitation position in *Stubbings* v. *Webb* [1993] AC 498. If it is right that the employer and/or employee in *Lister* v. *Hesley Hall Ltd* is in breach of duty when the employee committed a deliberate act, then it could also be argued that a parent (as in *Stubbings* v. *Webb*) is also in breach of duty as a parent clearly falls into the class of persons who has assumed a relationship to the claimant and thus owes to the claimant 'duties which are more extensive than those owed by the public at large' (see speech of Lord Hobhouse in *Lister* v. *Hesley Hall Ltd* para. 54).

3.3.18 A claim for trespass has the advantage over a claim in breach of duty/negligence negligence in that it can include a claim for aggravated damages (see Chapter 4).

3.4   BREACH OF STATUTORY DUTY

3.4.1 The important elements required to be established in respect of a claim for breach of statutory duty are analysed in detail by Lord Browne-

Wilkinson in *X (Minors)* v. *Bedfordshire County Council* [1995] 2 AC 640. In the context of claims against a public authority for child abuse Lord Browne-Wilkinson summarised the causes of action that might be considered as follows:

> The question is whether, if Parliament has imposed a statutory duty on an authority to carry out a particular function, a plaintiff who has suffered damage in consequence of the authority's performance or non-performance of that function has a right of action in damages against the authority. It is important to distinguish such actions to recover damages, based on a private law cause of action, from actions in public law to enforce the due performance of statutory duties, now brought by way of judicial review. The breach of a public law right by itself gives rise to no claim for damages. A claim for damages must be based on a private law cause of action. The distinction is important because a number of earlier cases (particularly in the field of education) were concerned with the enforcement by declaration and injunction of what would now be called public law duties. They were relied on in argument as authorities supporting the plaintiffs' claim for damages in this case: I will consider them in a little more detail later.
>
> Private law claims for damages can be classified into four different categories, viz.:
>
> (A) Actions for breach of statutory duty *simpliciter* (i.e. irrespective of carelessness).
>
> (B) Actions based solely on the careless performance of a statutory duty in the absence of any other common law right of action.
>
> (C) Actions based on a common law duty of care arising either from the imposition of the statutory duty or from the performance of it.
>
> (D) Misfeasance in public office, i.e. the failure to exercise, or the exercise of, statutory powers either with the intention to injure the plaintiff or in the knowledge that the conduct is unlawful.
>
> *X (Minors)* v. *Bedfordshire CC*, pages 730F–731A,
> Lord Browne-Wilkinson

3.4.2   Categories (C) and (D) are discussed in paras. 3.5 and 3.6. Categories (A) and (B) were further analysed by Lord Browne-Wilkinson.

3.4.3   Category (A) describes the limited group of cases where the claim can be brought because a public authority governed by statutory provisions fails to comply with the strict terms of the statutory provisions. In these cases there is no need to prove negligence by reference to the comparable standards of others, the failure to comply with the statute alone is sufficient. However, this class of action is only available to a limited group of people in limited circumstances. The claimant must be one of a class of persons that the statute in terms is intended specifically to protect. Further, the statute must in terms provide that compensation will be available in the event of a breach.

3.4.4   Lord Browne-Wilkinson described the limited circumstances in which a cause of action for breach of statutory duty *simpliciter* would exist in the context of social services as follows in *X (Minors)* v. *Bedfordshire CC* at pp. 731 B/C–732 B/C:

(A) Breach of statutory duty *simpliciter*.

This category comprises those cases where the statement of claim alleges simply (a) the statutory duty, (b) a breach of that duty, causing (c) damage to the plaintiff. The cause of action depends neither on proof of any breach of the plaintiffs' common law rights nor on any allegation of carelessness by the defendant.

The principles applicable in determining whether such statutory cause of action exists are now well established, although the application of those principles in any particular case remains difficult. The basic proposition is that in the ordinary case a breach of statutory duty does not, by itself, give rise to any private law cause of action. However a private law cause of action will arise if it can be shown, as a matter of construction of the statute, that the statutory duty was imposed for the protection of a limited class of the public and that Parliament intended to confer on members of that class a private right of action for breach of the duty. There is no general rule by reference to which it can be decided whether a statute does create such a right of action but there are a number of indicators. If the statute provides no other remedy for its breach and the Parliamentary intention to protect a limited class is shown, that indicates that there may be a private right of action since otherwise there is no method of securing the protection the statute was intended to confer. If the statute does provide some other means of enforcing the duty that will normally indicate that the statutory right was intended to be enforceable by those means and not by private right of action: *Cutler* v. *Wandsworth Stadium Ltd* [1949] AC 398; *Lonrho Ltd* v. *Shell Petroleum Co Ltd (No. 2)* [1982] AC 173. However, the mere existence of some other statutory remedy is not necessarily decisive. It is still possible to show that on the true construction of the statute the protected class was intended by Parliament to have a private remedy. Thus the specific duties imposed on employers in relation to factory premises are enforceable by an action for damages, notwithstanding the imposition by the statutes of criminal penalties for any breach: see *Groves* v. *Lord Wimborne* [1898] 2 QB 402.

Although the question is one of statutory construction and therefore each case turns on the provisions in the relevant statute, it is significant that your Lordships were not referred to any case where it had been held that statutory provisions establishing a regulatory system or a scheme of social welfare for the benefit of the public at large had been held to give rise to a private right of action for damages for breach of statutory duty. Although regulatory or welfare legislation affecting a particular area of activity does in fact provide protection to those individuals particularly affected by that activity, the legislation is not to be treated as being passed for the benefit of those individuals but for the benefit of society in general. Thus legislation regulating the conduct of betting or prisons did not give rise to a statutory right of action vested in those adversely affected by the breach of the statutory provisions, i.e. bookmakers and prisoners: see *Cutler* [1949] AC 398; *R* v. *Deputy Governor of Parkhurst Prison, ex parte Hague* [1992] 1 AC 58. The cases where a private right of action for breach of statutory duty have been held to arise are all cases in which the statutory duty has been very limited and specific as opposed to general administrative functions imposed on public bodies and involving the exercise of administrative discretions.

3.4.5 No case has yet succeeded in establishing that a statute in the area of child-care legislation gives rise to a specific right entitling individuals to sue in the event of a breach.

3.4.6 The second category (B) identified by Lord Browne-Wilkinson was that of careless performance of a statutory duty. After analysis, this did not survive as an independent category in which a claim could be brought. Lord Browne-Wilkinson concluded that only where there is a common law duty of care owed to the claimant could an action for negligent failure to act in accordance with the statute exist. He stated:

> this category comprises those cases in which the plaintiff alleges (a) the statutory duty and (b) the 'negligent' breach of that duty but does not allege that the defendant was under a common law duty of care to the plaintiff. It is the use of the word 'negligent' in this context which gives rise to confusion: it is sometimes used to connote mere carelessness (there being no common law duty of care) and sometimes to import the concept of a common law duty of care. In my judgment it is important in considering the authorities to distinguish between the two concepts: as will appear, in my view the careless performance of a statutory duty does not in itself give rise to any cause of action in the absence of either a statutory right of action (Category (A) above) or a common law duty of care (Category (C) below).

And Lord Browne-Wilkinson concluded in *X (Minors)* v. *Bedfordshire CC* at pp. 732C–E and 734H–735A:

> In my judgment the correct view is that in order to found a cause of action flowing from the careless exercise of statutory powers or duties, the plaintiff has to show that the circumstances are such as to raise a duty of care at common law. The mere assertion of the careless exercise of a statutory power or duty is not sufficient.

3.4.7 Lord Jauncey in *X (Minors)* v *Bedfordshire CC*, at pp. 728G–729A, summarised the position in respect of the overlap between statutory duty and common law duty as follows:

> Where a statute confers a private law right of action a breach of statutory duty howsoever caused will found the action. Where a statute authorises that to be done which will necessarily cause injury to someone no action will lie if the act is performed with reasonable care. If, on the other hand, the authorised act is performed carelessly whereby unnecessary damage is caused a common law action will lie. This is because the act would, but for the statute, be actionable at common law and the defence which the statute provides extends only to the careful performance of the act. The statute only authorises invasion of private rights to the extent that the statutory powers are exercised with reasonable and proper regard for the holders of such rights. Thus careless performance of an authorised act rather than amounting to breach of a new duty simply ceases to be a defence to a common law right of action.

3.4.8   On the present state of the authorities it is difficult to envisage circumstances where a claim for breach of statutory duty will succeed. However,
the statutory backdrop will usually be relevant to a claim for breach of
common law duty of care. The relevant statutory provisions should be set
out in the particulars of claim in order to illustrate the background in
which a common law duty of care is said to arise (see Chapter 2 for details
of the relevant statutory framework to child abuse claims).

3.4.9   The possibility of claims arising out of breach of the Human Rights Act
1998 is discussed in para. 3.7.

3.5   COMMON LAW DUTY OF CARE

The distinction between direct duty and vicarious liability

3.5.1   In *X (Minors)* v. *Bedfordshire County Council,* Lord Browne-Wilkinson
stressed how important it is, in respect of a claim against a public authority, to distinguish between:

- the direct duty owed by a public authority to the claimant; and
- the vicarious liability of the public authority for breach of its employees' duties.

3.5.2   If it is alleged that a public authority itself owed a duty of care to the
claimant, then it is necessary to identify and set out in the particulars of
claim the precise duties it is alleged are owed. If it is alleged that employees themselves owed duties to the claimant, then these too must be set out
specifically.

3.5.3   A public authority can only act through its servants or agents. The two
categories of common law duty of care can therefore be described and distinguished as follows:

- direct duties owed by the authority itself which it is alleged are
breached by the actions of servants or agents;
- duties owed by the employees of the public authority which it is
alleged are breached by the employees and the public authority is
vicariously liable for such breaches.

3.5.4   The distinction between direct and vicarious liability is clearly illustrated
in respect of claims against a hospital authority. The hospital authority
itself will owe a duty to provide a reasonable system for ensuring that

patients have access to doctors in a reasonable time. In the case of *Bull* v. *Devon Area Health Authority* [1993] 4 Med LR 117 a health authority was found liable when a consultant obstetrician took 68 minutes to attend to deliver a second twin and the baby suffered brain damage as a result of the delay. It was found the delay occurred because the hospital operated on two sites and the consultant obstetrician had to travel from one site to the other to attend to this emergency. The Court of Appeal confirmed that the health authority was liable, as the system should have been set up so that a consultant could always be available within 20 minutes.

3.5.5   The direct liability claim in *Bull* v. *Devon Area Health Authority* is to be distinguished from the more common situation where a health authority is vicariously liable for the negligence of a doctor employed by the health authority. Each doctor working for the health authority owes a duty of care to the patients that he/she treats. If a doctor negligently fails to treat the patient competently, the health authority is vicariously liable for the doctor's breach of duty.

3.5.6   A similar distinction requires to be made in respect of a local authority social services department between:

- the duties owed by the department of social services to individual claimants who are taken into care or placed in local authority institutions; and
- the duties owed by social workers or care workers themselves to those children allocated to them.

3.5.7   A child in care who is placed in a local authority children's home and is sexually abused by a care worker employed in the home may have:

- a claim against the local authority for breach of its direct duty in respect of the running of the home and its choice and supervision of staff; and/or
- a claim against the social worker allocated to him/her for failing to monitor his/her progress so as to identify and address the abuse; and/or
- a claim against other care workers in the same home who fail to keep the claimant safe from injury by the abuser;
- a claim against the local authority for vicarious liability arising out of the deliberate acts of the abuser either by way of trespass or breach of duty.

The first claim would be a direct liability claim, the second third and fourth vicarious liability claims.

3.5.8   Particulars of claim should set out the direct duties owed by the public authority to the claimant and the individual duties owed by employees of the local authority. The particulars should then identify the breach of duty by the authority through its employees separately from the breach of duties of the individual employees for whom the authority is vicariously liable.

The elements of common law duty of care

3.5.9   In order to establish either direct or vicarious liability it is necessary to establish:

- a duty of care exists;
- there has been a breach of duty;
- the claimant has suffered damage as a result of the breach of duty.

3.5.10   The starting point in examining whether a duty of care exists is to analyse the relationship between the claimant and the prospective defendant by reference to general principles. These can be summarised as follows:

- To establish that a duty of care arises it is necessary to show: foreseeability, proximity and that it is fair just and reasonable to impose a duty of care. See *Caparo Industries Plc v. Dickman* [1990] 2 AC 605 at 617D–F.

  However, these three elements are not distinct, they overlap and are really facets of the same thing. Where foreseeability and proximity are obvious it may follow as a matter of common sense that it is just fair and reasonable to impose a duty of care; see *Marc Rich & Co v. Bishop Rock Marine Co Ltd* [1996] 1 AC 211 at pp. 235F–236A.

- To establish a duty of care in novel circumstances it is necessary to look to analogous relationships from which to make an incremental extension. See *Caparo v. Dickman* at 617D–F and *Stovin v. Wise* [1996] AC 923 at 949A–C.

- Where there is foreseeability and proximity, a duty of care arises where there is an assumption of responsibility by the defendant and reliance on it by the claimant. See *Hedley Byrne & Co Ltd v. Heller & Partners Ltd* [1964] AC 465 and *Spring v. Guardian Assurance plc* [1995] 2 AC 296 at 318D.

- A duty of care will be more readily imposed to protect a claimant from personal injury than from economic loss. See *Hedley Byrne & Co Ltd v. Heller & Partners Ltd* at 536 and *Marc Rich & Co v. Bishop Rock Marine Co Ltd* at pp. 235F–236A.

3.5.11   In the context of child abuse claims there are broadly three main categories of claim for breach of common law duty of care:

1. Claims against a public authority, institution or individuals for failure to run, supervise or control a children's home, school or other institution so as to keep children safe from personal injury within the home. Examples include:

   - *Various Claimants* v. *Leicestershire County Council* (Mr Justice Potts, 2 April 1996, unreported) (see paras. 1.5.29–1.5.31).

   - *Various Claimants* v. *Flintshire County Council (the Former Clwyd County Council)* (Mr Justice Scott Baker, 26 July 2000, unreported) (see paras. 1.5.49–1.5.51).

2. Claims against a public authority for failure to look after a child who is the subject of a formal care order during the course of the period that that child is in care. This type of claim typically includes allegations of multiple moves, lack of medical treatment, lack of planning placements, etc. For example:

   - *Barrett* v. *London Borough of Enfield* [1999] 3 WLR 79 (see paras. 1.5.39–1.5.41).

3. Claims against individuals for failure to protect a child from an abuser. Examples include:

   - *S* v. *W (Child abuse: Damages)* [1995] 1 FLR 862.

3.5.12 In *S* v. *Gloucestershire County Council* [2001] 2 WLR 909 (see paras. 1.5.46–1.5.48) at 931F/G–H, Lord Justice May summarised the current state of the law in respect of negligence claims in the area of child abuse as follows:

> It is appropriate to draw together some strands of this developing area of the law. There have been attempts to promote as claims for breach of statutory duty cases in which it is said that local authorities have, by their failings in the care and upbringing of children, caused damage to the children. Claims of this kind have been successfully defended on the basis that the meaning of the relevant statute does not support such a claim. Where the failing alleged has related to a discretionary decision which is empowered by statute, the court has been hesitant to say that the exercise of the discretion was wrong so as to give rise to a cause of action unless it was plainly wrong. The intense intellectual analysis which questions of this kind engendered has been simplified by the now clear recognition that there may be circumstances in this acutely difficult area of human endeavour where an ordinary common law claim in negligence upon *Caparo* principles may be academically possible and, in an appropriate case, succeed in fact.

3.5.13 Lord Justice May at 932A–H described the claim in common law negligence as follows:

> A negligence claim is habitually analysed compartmentally by asking whether there was (a) a duty of care, (b) breach of that duty and (c) damage caused by

the breach of duty. But damage is the essence of a cause of action in negligence and the critical question in a particular case is the composite one, that is whether the scope of the duty of care in the circumstances of the case is such as to embrace damage of the kind which the plaintiff claims to have suffered. As Lord Bridge of Harwich said in the *Caparo* case at page 627C:

'It is never sufficient to ask simply whether A owes B a duty of care. It is always necessary to determine the scope of the duty by reference to the kind of damage from which A must take care to save B harmless.'

Lord Oliver of Aylmerton emphasised the same point in *Murphy* v. *Brentwood District Council* [1991] 1 AC 398 at 486A, when he said:

'The essential question which has to be asked in every case, given that damage which is the essential ingredient of the action has occurred, is whether the relationship between the plaintiff and the defendant is such . . . that it imposes upon the latter a duty to take care to avoid or prevent that loss which has in fact been sustained.

This question necessarily subsumes the question whether the acts or omissions of the defendant caused the damage relied on. It follows from this that, especially when relationships are complicated, it will often not be possible to determine by an abstract inquiry which does not address the detailed facts of a particular case that a claim in negligence is bound to fail. The opinions of the House of Lords in *Barrett* v. *Enfield* emphasise that this is particularly so in cases of the kind presently before this court.

In my view, a number of strands of the relevant law to be derived from *Barrett* v. *Enfield* and the cases which preceded it may be summarised as follows:

(a) Depending on the particular facts of the case, a claim in common law negligence may be available to a person who claims to have been damaged by failings of a local authority who were responsible under statutory powers for his care and upbringing. In each of the cases before this court, the claims were sensibly limited to common law negligence claims.

(b) The claim will not succeed if the failings alleged comprise actions or decisions by the local authority of a kind which are not justiciable. These may include, but will not necessarily be limited to, policy decisions and decisions about allocating public funds.

(c) The borderline between what is justiciable and what is not may in a particular case be unclear. Its demarcation may require a more extensive investigation than is capable of being made from material in traditional pleadings alone.

(d) There may be circumstances in which it will not be just and reasonable to impose a duty of care of the kind contended for. Here again, it may often be necessary to conduct a detailed investigation of the facts to determine this question.

(e) In considering whether a discretionary decision was negligent, the court will not substitute its view for that of the local authority upon whom the statute has placed the power to exercise the discretion, unless the discretionary decision was plainly wrong. But decisions of, for example, social workers are capable of being held to have been negligent by analogy with decisions of other professional people. Here again, it may well be necessary to conduct a detailed factual enquiry.'

3.5.14 Lord Justice May pointed out in *S* v. *Gloucestershire County Council*, at 933F that:

> The conclusion that cases of this kind may often be capable of being formulated as viable causes of action in negligence says little or nothing about whether they are likely to succeed on the facts.

3.5.15 The cases summarised in Chapter 1 explore the development of the law in this area on which the conclusion of May LJ in *S* v. *Gloucestershire CC* is based. The legal principles have been formulated through a series of cases in which the defendants sought to strike out claims for failure to disclose a cause of action. Now that it is established that viable causes of action may be brought in negligence by the victims of child abuse, the courts will need to determine the parameters of acceptable professional conduct in the realms of child care, social services and education.

3.5.16 Expert evidence from professionals in these areas will play an essential role in determining the level of competent care that could be expected at any particular date and the standards to be expected of those charged with protecting children from injury and abuse. The actions of professionals will be measured against the competent level of care accepted by contemporary professionals in similar posts, that is, the court will apply the test in *Bolam* v. *Frien Hospital Management Committee* [1957] 1 WLR 582 as confirmed by the House of Lords in *Barrett* v. *Enfield London Borough Council* [1999] 3 WLR 79 and set out in Chapter 1, para. 1.5.40.

3.6   MISFEASANCE IN PUBLIC OFFICE

3.6.1 The requirements for the tort of misfeasance in public office have been extensively analysed by the House of Lords in the case of *Three Rivers District Council* v. *Bank of England (No. 3)* [2000] 2 WLR 1220 and again in *Three Rivers District Council* v. *Bank of England (No. 3) (Summary Judgment)* [2001] UKHL 16.

3.6.2 The House of Lords has now identified the essential elements of the tort to be that:

1. The defendant must be a public officer.

2. The exercise of power complained of must occur in the course of the public officer's public functions.

3. There must be an abuse of power; the act or omission must be done with the required mental element. Either:

the public officer must specifically intend to injure the claimant (targeted malice); or

the act or omission must be done or made intentionally by the public officer:

(a) in the knowledge that it was beyond his powers and that it would probably cause the claimant to suffer injury, or

(b) recklessly, because although he was aware that there was a serious risk that the claimant would suffer loss due to an act or omission which he knew to be unlawful, he wilfully chose to disregard that risk.

That is, there must be an 'abuse of power' and at least 'reckless indifference to the illegality of the act';

4. The act or omission must have been carried out dishonestly or in bad faith.

5. Any claimant must have a sufficient interest to found a legal standing to sue.

6. The public officer must know the decision will probably damage the claimant.

7. The act or omission must have caused the claimant's loss or damage.

3.6.3 The tort of misfeasance in public office was considered by the Court of Appeal in the case of *W* v. *Essex County Council* [1998] 3 WLR 534 (see paras. 1.5.34–1.5.36). The only judgment dealing with misfeasance in public office was that of Lord Justice Stuart Smith. Lord Justice Judge and Lord Justice Mantell agreed with his judgment on this aspect of the case (Stuart Smith LJ gave a dissenting judgment on the issue of negligence). Stuart Smith LJ analysed the case in misfeasance as follows:

> Misfeasance in a public office –
>
> The tort of misfeasance in a public office can be committed in one of two ways, namely where a public officer has either (a) performed or omitted to perform an act with the object of injuring the plaintiff (i.e. where there was targeted malice); or (b) where he has performed an act which he knew he had no power to perform and which he knew would injure the plaintiff (*Three Rivers DC* v. *Bank of England* [1996] 3 All ER 558 approved in *R* v. *Chief Constable of North Wales Police Force, ex parte AB* [1997] 3 WLR 724 per Lord Bingham CJ at p. 735). Both limbs require an invalid, unauthorised or unlawful act (per Clarke J. in *Three Rivers* case at p. 578G). The plaintiffs accept that the first limb is not applicable.
>
> Like the judge I have been unable to detect what power it is that the plaintiffs allege has been exceeded. The plaintiffs sought to argue that if the second defendant had asked his immediate superior if he should answer the parents' question in the way he did, he would unquestionably have been given a negative

answer. But that is nothing to the point. It is plain in my view that the second defendant was acting pursuant to the statutory powers conferred upon the Council; the fact that while so acting he carelessly or even deliberately gives misleading information does not mean he is knowingly exceeding his powers. It should perhaps be noted in passing that the facts alleged do not constitute the peculiar tort exemplified by the case of *Wilkinson* v. *Downton* [1897] 2 QB 57.

3.6.4 In the case of *W* v. *Essex County Council* the social worker who failed to inform the foster family of the foster child's record of sexual abuse was carrying out an act he had power to perform in placing a child in a foster family. The fact that the social worker gave misleading information about the child did not in the view of the Court make the act 'unlawful'.

3.6.5 Examples of misfeasance claims are likely to continue to be rare. As was pointed out in *Three Rivers District Council* v. *Bank of England*, it was common ground that the claimants could not base their claim against the bank in negligence. Lord Justice Hirst in the Court of Appeal and Lord Hutton (at para. 54) in the House of Lords both described how:

> the immunity which the bank enjoys under section 1(4) of the Banking Act 1987 unless it is shown that the act or omission was in bad faith goes a long way to explaining why the claimants have undertaken the burden of seeking to prove misfeasance in public office.

3.6.6 In a dissenting speech in *Three Rivers District Council* v. *Bank of England,* Lord Millett at para. 179 further explained the reasons for the depositors bringing an action for misfeasance in public office:

> Unfortunately for the depositors, a regulatory authority cannot be held liable in English law for negligence, however gross, in the exercise of its supervisory functions. So the depositors have been forced to base their claim on a very different cause of action. They allege that the Bank has been guilty of misfeasance in public office. This is an intentional tort. It involves deliberate or reckless wrongdoing. It cannot be committed negligently or inadvertently. Accordingly it is not enough for the depositors to establish negligence, or even gross negligence, on the part of the Bank. They must establish some intentional or reckless impropriety. As your Lordships ruled unanimously at an earlier stage of these proceedings ([2000] 2 WLR 1220), and in the absence of what has been described as 'targeted malice' (which is not alleged), the tort has two elements. In the present case the depositors must prove (i) not merely that the Bank acted unlawfully, that is to say in excess of its powers or for an improper purpose, but that it did so knowingly (or recklessly not caring whether it had the necessary power or not); and (ii) that the Bank knew that its actions would probably cause loss to depositors (or was recklessly indifferent to the consequences of its actions). Such conduct in a public official is grossly improper and equates to dishonesty in a private individual.

3.6.7 Lord Hobhouse in *Three Rivers* v. *Bank of England* at para. 167, in a dissenting speech, also explained the significance of 'unlawful' conduct:

> The commission of the tort has two stages. The first is the act done by the defendant. The act must be an unlawful act, not in the sense that it is itself tortious but in the sense that it is contrary to the law for the defendant to have done what he did. In the case of a failure to act it must be a failure to do a specific act which it was the legal obligation of the defendant to do and which was therefore unlawful. In either case there must be unauthorised or forbidden conduct. The conduct must be accompanied by either actual or subjectively reckless, or 'blind eye', knowledge that it is unauthorised or forbidden. The second stage is that which relates to the defendants' appreciation of the consequences of his conduct. This may arise from his purpose in doing what he did (my first 'limb', Lord Steyn's first form of the tort) or from his appreciation that the plaintiff will in the ordinary course be caused loss or his consciously and wilfully turning a blind eye to the possibility of such loss (my second and third 'limbs', Lord Steyn's second form of the tort). Therefore, in making the assessment required by this appeal, one must apply this two stage test to the plaintiffs' case for the two periods.

3.6.8 The unlawful action alleged in the *Three Rivers* v. *Bank of England* case was the granting of a licence to BCCI (Bank of Credit and Commerce International SA) to accept deposits without carrying out any independent inquiry as to whether the criteria for authorisation were satisfied. The Banking Act 1979 required the Bank of England to carry out independent investigation as the BCCI's principal base of business was by then the UK. The Bank instead of carrying out this investigation relied on the fact that BCCI had obtained a banking licence from the Luxembourg Banking Commission (LBC). Because the Bank was not entitled to grant the licence in at least one respect it could be shown the Bank officials had acted unlawfully and outside the scope of the powers given to them. The question of whether they continued to act 'unlawfully' in their subsequent failure to supervise the activities of the bank was more controversial. In dissenting speeches Lords Millett and Hobhouse found this conduct could only be categorised as a negligent failure to exercise discretion. The majority, however, accepted for the purposes of the strike-out application that subsequent failures might also be categorised as 'unlawful'. Lord Hope in a majority speech explained in *Three Rivers* v. *Bank of England* at para. 104:

> the Bank knew that before the grant of the full licence to BCCI SA that it was not entitled to rely on the Luxembourg regulator. Given that starting point I cannot say that the claimants have no real prospect of proving that the Bank knew that their initial act in licensing BCCI SA was unlawful, that its licence and authorisation remained unlawful throughout the remaining three periods and that all subsequent omissions to revoke the licence and authorisation were affected by the same illegality.

3.6.9   It is now clear following *Barrett* v. *Enfield LBC* that there is no general immunity available to public authorities in respect of claims in negligence arising out of social services functions. The need to formulate claims in terms of misfeasance in public office is therefore less common. The difficulties in establishing this tort involving specific proof of unlawful conduct as explored in *Three Rivers* v. *Bank of England* and *W* v. *Essex CC* are likely to continue to deter claimants from bringing such claims. That is not to say that there will not be specific cases in the realm of child abuse which will justify a claim for misfeasance in public office being brought. Further, the decision of the House of Lords in *Racz* v. *Home Office* [1994] 2 AC 45 confirms that, in the right circumstances, it may be possible to claim vicarious liability for misfeasance in public office.

3.7   HUMAN RIGHTS ACT 1998

3.7.1   The Human Rights Act 1998, which came into force in October 2000, incorporates into English law the rights under the European Convention for the Protection of Human Rights and Fundamental Freedoms.

Sections 3–5

3.7.2   Sections 3–5 of the Act examine the position where there is a conflict between the implementation of Convention Rights and existing UK legislation. The position is that, where legislation leaves any room for ambiguity so that it can be interpreted in accordance with Convention rights, then the court has an obligation to interpret it in a way that is compatible. This of course may mean that a statutory provision that has previously been interpreted in one way may need to be interpreted differently in order to become compatible with the Convention.

3.7.3   Lord Steyn has pointed out how the Courts' approach will need to change and stated:

> Traditionally the search has been for the one true meaning of the statute. Now the search will be for a possible meaning that would prevent the need for a declaration of incompatibility. The question will be (1) What meanings are the words capable of yielding? (2) And critically can the words be made to yield a sense consistent with Convention rights? In practical effect there will be a rebuttable presumption in favour of an interpretation consistent with Convention rights.
> 'Current topic: incorporation and devolution' [1998] EHRLR 153: 155

3.7.4   If it is quite impossible to place an interpretation on a statute that is compatible with Convention rights then the Higher Courts (House of Lords,

Privy Council, Court of Appeal, High Court) may make a declaration of incompatibility but this does not for the time being affect the validity of the statute which will continue to be applied in a manner incompatible with the Convention rights.

Section 6

3.7.5 Section 6 of the Human Rights Act 1998 introduces the concept of a *public authority* for the purposes of the Act and provides that it is:

> Unlawful for a public authority to act in a way that is incompatible with a Convention right.

Section 7

3.7.6 Section 7 of the Act provides that a person who claims that a public authority has acted (or proposes to act) in a way made unlawful by s.6(1) has two separate remedies:

> (a) he/she can bring free-standing proceedings against the authority pursuant to the Act: i.e. effectively an action for breach of statutory duty in the sense of a violation of a Convention right which now has statutory force in respect of a public authority;

> (b) he/she can rely on the Convention right either in a claim brought on a conventional basis or as a defence or issue in proceedings brought against him/her by a public authority.

3.7.7 The practice direction made pursuant to the Act specifies that where a specific free-standing claim is made under s.7(1)(a) the claim form must state that this is the case and must give details of the Convention right which it is alleged has been infringed. If the claim is based on a finding of unlawfulness by another court details of that finding must be given. Where it is alleged that a judicial act constitutes a violation of the Convention then the Lord Chancellor should be joined in the proceedings.

3.7.8 Cases under s.7(1)(a) are envisaged to be brought in one of three ways:

> (a) using the existing judicial review procedures;

> (b) in the county court or High Court where a claim for damages is made;

> (c) in a county court or High Court following a finding of unlawfulness by another court which did not have the power to award damages, e.g. following a ruling in a criminal court that the prosecution had acted unlawfully. In these circumstances the claimant should be able to rely on the finding of unlawfulness as prima facie evidence that the defendant acted unlawfully in a similar way to convictions under s.11 Civil

99

Evidence Act 1968 although it would be open to the defendant to refute the findings.

Section 7(1)(b)

3.7.9   Section 7(1)(b) allows for Convention rights to be relied upon in the course of any other proceedings and it is probable that this will be the most frequent application of the Act. Most alleged breaches will occur in a situation where there is already an existing cause of action of some sort. The interesting point will be whether an application made directly under s.7(1)(a) of the Act will increase the damages otherwise available in any way.

3.7.10   A specific limitation period of one year (with discretionary extension) applies to a direct claim against a public authority but conventional existing limitation periods apply in respect of other proceedings in which a convention right might be raised. Section 22(4) provides that the right to rely on the Convention in existing proceedings only applies to alleged violations that occur after s.7(1)(b) comes into force except where the person claiming the right is responding to proceedings brought by a public authority (i.e. effectively is a criminal or civil defendant to proceedings).

3.7.11   The definition of public authority for the purposes of the Act is contained in s.6 and is a complex one. It includes a court of tribunal and any person carrying out public functions even if the person or organisation also carries out private functions.

3.7.12   There is no detailed definition of public authority in the Act and the precise scope of the concept will not become clear until there is a body of decisions construing s.6 of the Act. However, in the course of the Bill it was indicated by the Home Secretary that:

> The principle of bringing rights home suggested that liability in domestic proceedings should lie with bodies in respect of whose actions the United Kingdom Government was answerable in Strasbourg ... We could not directly replicate in the Bill the definition of public authorities used in Strasbourg because, of course, the respondent to any application in the Strasbourg court is the United Kingdom, as the state. We have therefore tried to do the best we can in terms of replication by taking into account whether a body is sufficiently public to engage the responsibility of the state.

3.7.13   The White Paper gave some examples of public bodies that were intended to come within the definition and the general guide is the test in judicial review proceedings that 'a body is performing public functions when it seeks to achieve some collective benefit for the public or a section of the public and is accepted by the public or that section of the public as having authority to do so' (de Smith, Woolf and Jowell, *Judicial Review of Administrative Action*, 5th edn, p. 167).

3.7.14 As the court is a public authority and has an obligation to apply the principles of the incorporated articles of the Convention, effectively once the Act came into force in proceedings between private individuals the Court has an obligation to decide private law disputes applying the Convention principles. This leads to the principle of horizontality.

3.7.15 The extent of the application of Convention rights between individuals by the courts stems from the court's obligation to apply Convention rights. There are therefore significant differences between acts carried out by public authorities against whom a direct action can be brought and those carried out by corporations or individuals who are not public authorities.

Section 8

3.7.16 Section 8 of the Act sets out the judicial remedies that can be applied for breach of the Act. It allows the court wide discretion to grant such relief or remedies as it considers fit and gives specific authority to a court to award damages, but only in civil proceedings. Damages will only be awarded where they are necessary 'to afford just satisfaction' to the person in whose favour an award is made. This is a Strasbourg concept contained in Article 41 of the Convention. The Strasbourg court allows damages to be awarded because a violation is established and because the domestic jurisdiction has not made full reparation. The concept is not equivalent to the principle of awarding damages as compensation so as to place the claimant in the position he would have been in the absence of a tort.

3.7.17 In section 8(4) the Act specifies that in determining whether to make an award the court must take into account the principles applied by the European Court of Human Rights – again there is a mixture of the mandatory and the discretionary. This provision will be particularly problematic to implement as it is difficult to discern any coherent principles by which the Strasbourg court has calculated damages. They have been calculated very much on a case-by-case basis to meet the fairness of any particular situation. Awards of damages in Strasbourg have also reflected the differing levels of damages in the many member states. The Strasbourg court has not awarded exemplary or aggravated damages. Further, in many cases the Strasbourg court has not awarded damages at all but has held that the finding of a violation is in itself 'just satisfaction'. The overlap between the award of damages in conventional claims and in claims for violation of the Convention will be a particularly interesting area in the development of case law now that the Act has been implemented.

3.7.18 In *Z and Others* v. *UK* [2001] 2 FLR 612 the European Court of Human Rights considered the applications by the children in *X* (*Minors*) v. *Bedfordshire County Council*. The applicants alleged that the local

101

authority had failed to protect them from inhuman and degrading treatment contrary to Article 3 of the Convention, which provides:

> *No one shall be subjected to torture or to inhuman or degrading treatment or punishment.*

3.7.19   The Commission in its report found unanimously that there had been a violation of Article 3 of the Convention. It considered that there was a positive obligation on the government to protect children from treatment contrary to this provision. The authorities had been aware of the serious ill-treatment and neglect suffered by the four children over a period of years at the hands of their parents and failed, despite the means reasonably available to them, to take any effective steps to bring it to an end. The applicants requested the court to confirm this finding of a violation. The government did not contest the Commission's finding that the treatment suffered by the four applicants reached the level of severity prohibited by Article 3 and that the state failed in its positive obligation under Article 3 of the Convention to provide the applicants with adequate protection against inhuman and degrading treatment.

3.7.20   In the judgment of the European Court of Human Rights it was said at paragraph 73:

> The Court re-iterates that Article 3 enshrines one of the most fundamental values of democratic society. It prohibits in absolute terms torture or inhuman or degrading treatment or punishment. The obligation on High Contracting Parties under Article 1 of the Convention to secure to everyone within their jurisdiction the rights and freedoms defined in the Convention, taken together with Article 3, requires States to take measures designed to ensure that individuals within their jurisdiction are not subjected to torture or inhuman or degrading treatment, including such ill-treatment administered by private individuals (see *A* v. *the United Kingdom*, judgment of 23 September 1998, Reports of Judgments and Decisions 1998-VI, § 22). These measures should provide effective protection, in particular, of children and other vulnerable persons and include reasonable steps to prevent ill-treatment of which the authorities had or ought to have had knowledge (*mutatis mutandis*, the *Osman* v. *the United Kingdom* judgment of 28 October 1998, Reports 1998-VIII, § 116).
>
> There is no dispute in the present case that the neglect and abuse suffered by the four child applicants reached the threshold of inhuman and degrading treatment (as recounted in paragraphs 11 to 36 above). This treatment was brought to the local authority's attention, at the earliest in October 1987. It was under a statutory duty to protect the children and had a range of powers available to them, including removal from their home. The children were however only taken into emergency care, at the insistence of the mother, in 30 April 1992. Over the intervening period of four and a half years, they had been subject in their home to what the child consultant psychiatrist who examined them referred to as horrific experiences (see para-

graph 40 above). The Criminal Injuries Compensation Board had also found that the children had been subject to appalling neglect over an extended period and suffered physical and psychological injury directly attributable to a crime of violence (see paragraph 49 above). The Court acknowledges the difficult and sensitive decisions facing social services and the important countervailing principle of respecting and preserving family life. The present case however leaves no doubt as to the failure of the system to protect these child applicants from serious, long-term neglect and abuse.

Accordingly, there has been a violation of Article 3 of the Convention.

3.7.21 The court further found that there had been a violation of Article 13 of the Convention and awarded damages to each of the four children with applications before the court (see para. 4.9.3). The court did not follow the Commission in finding a breach of Article 6 (failure to provide access to court).

3.7.22 The result of this decision is therefore that for claims that arise after the implementation of the Human Rights Act 1998 on 2 October 2000 a child in similar circumstances to a child in the *X* (*Minors*) v. *Bedfordshire County Council* litigation would have a free-standing claim for breach of Article 3 of the European Convention. However, as Article 13 has not been directly incorporated in the Human Rights Act 1998, the claimant would be dependent on the provisions of s.8 of the Human Rights Act 1998 for the Court to exercise its discretion in awarding damages.

CHAPTER 4

Causation and damage

4.1   INTRODUCTION

4.1.1   Child abuse compensation claims are personal injury claims. They will typically include claims for both general damages and special damages.

4.1.2   General damages: usually there are two elements to the injury suffered for which general damages for pain, suffering and loss of amenity will be claimed:

1. The pain, suffering and injury (if any) incurred at the time of the abuse and as an immediate result of it: e.g. bruising or broken bones from physical assaults, pain, suffering and bleeding from anal intercourse;

2. The long term psychiatric (and sometimes physical) damage suffered as a result of the abuse e.g. post-traumatic stress disorder, personality disorder, anxiety disorder, sexual problems, anal bleeding.

4.1.3   Special damages: the most common categories are:

- past loss of earnings;
- future loss of earnings/vulnerability on the labour market;
- cost of therapy/counselling;
- care costs.

4.1.4   This Chapter sets out the principles and case law applicable to the quantification of these heads of damage. Before doing so, it is necessary to consider causation of damage, i.e., how to separate out the damage caused by the defendant from other factors which may have contributed to the claimant's current condition. It is also relevant to consider any criminal record of the claimant.

4.2   CAUSATION OF DAMAGE

4.2.1   In child abuse cases, causation of damage poses special problems. Claimants have often suffered abuse in more than one setting, e.g. first in the birth family and then later in a care home (sometimes several care homes). It is not easy to determine the extent of a particular defendant's contribution to the problems suffered by the claimant as an adult. A physical injury may be easy to attribute to a specific defendant. By contrast, psychological illnesses may have many possible causes, including genetic predisposition. A typical case involves breaches of duty in an institutional setting, but the child's presence in the institution may result from a disrupted childhood and dysfunctional family background for which the institutional defendant bears no liability. The court has to assess which events have caused significant injury and to measure the proportion of damage caused by each defendant's particular breach of duty.

4.2.2   Even if the causes of damage are clear, the extent of damage suffered may be difficult to assess. Child abuse is inflicted before personality is fully formed, hence there is no 'pre-abuse adult' against whom the damage can be measured.

4.2.3   In a personal injury case the claimant's injuries must be substantiated by medical evidence. If the injuries are purely psychological, i.e., no physical injury, then the claimant must demonstrate that he or she is suffering from a recognised, diagnosable psychiatric illness (or a physical illness recognised to have psychological origins). Vexation, stress or upset will not be sufficient. There is no entitlement to damages unless the claimant has passed the threshold of an identifiable medical condition. As explained by Lord Lloyd in *Page* v. *Smith* [1996] AC 155:

> Shock by itself is not the subject of compensation, any more than fear or grief or any other human emotion occasioned by the defendant's negligent conduct. It is only when shock is followed by recognisable psychiatric illness that the defendant may be held liable.

4.2.4 A discussion of the identification of psychiatric illnesses is beyond the scope of this book. Currently, two diagnostic classificatory systems of mental disorders are in use: the American Diagnostic and Statistical Manual of Mental Disorders (DSM-IV) and the International Classification of Diseases and Related Health Problems (ICD-10), which also covers physical conditions. These classification systems identify the criteria for a diagnosis of post-traumatic stress disorder (PTSD). A prerequisite of a psychiatric injury claim is a diagnosis of one of these recognised illnesses. The diagnosis should be made by a suitably qualified medical practitioner, normally a consultant psychiatrist (see chapter 7 re choice of expert).

4.2.5 The legal principles regarding proof of causation of damage in a child abuse case are the same as those which apply in personal injury actions generally. The application of these principles in abuse cases may be more difficult. To succeed against the defendant, the claimant has to prove that a particular breach of duty is, as a matter of law, the cause of the relevant damage. If the damage would have occurred in any event, in the absence of the breach of duty, the claimant cannot recover. Causation is a matter of fact. There has to be clear evidence of how the breach caused the injury or illness. Proof of causation can be established if the claimant adduces sufficient evidence that the breach of duty made a 'material contribution' to the claimant developing a psychiatric illness: see *McGhee* v. *National Coal Board* [1973] 1 WLR 1.

4.2.6 The general principle in personal injury cases is that a claimant is required to prove his loss and damage on the balance of probabilities. If the claimant demonstrates that on the balance of probabilities the abuse made a material contribution to his psychiatric condition, then the defendant is liable for all the psychiatric damage suffered unless he can demonstrate (on the balance of probabilities) other factors caused or materially contributed to the claimant's psychiatric illness.

4.2.7 The causation of psychiatric illness following child abuse was considered in the judgment of Mr Justice Scott Baker in the case of *Various claimants* v. *Flintshire County Council* (26 July 2000, Scott Baker J., unreported). Scott Baker J. had to assess the extent to which the problems of the claimants in their adult life were caused by the abuse they suffered in care, as opposed to some other causative factor. He assessed the position as follows:

> I accept that it would be the wrong approach to discount any claimant's damages simply because there was a chance that he or she would have suffered from similar problems in later life, even if not abused in the defendants' children's homes. In each case, I have paused to consider the question whether it has been proved to the ordinary civil standard that matters other than the abuse have caused or contributed to the claimant's problems in later

life. That is an exercise I have, of course, conducted on the whole of the evidence . . . I must emphasise that in these cases, one is not dealing with certainties as to the cause or causes of the claimant's problems in later life. It is no more certain that the abuse is a cause than that absent the abuse, there would nevertheless have been problems of a similar nature. The court has to do its best in each individual case after weighing up all the evidence.

> (*Various claimants* v. *Flintshire CC* (26 July 2000) transcript p. 16)

4.2.8 At the trial in this litigation there were attempts by the medical experts to assess the contribution of particular causative factors in 'percentage terms'. Scott Baker J. commented as follows:

It is unhelpful, and indeed in my view, impossible, to express the defendants' degree of responsibility in percentage terms . . . There is an impossibility of making a precise apportionment between what the defendants' negligence has caused and what has been caused by other factors. Inevitably, I have taken a broad view and done my best to reach a fair conclusion on the whole of the evidence. It is very much a matter a matter of feel.

> *Various claimants* v. *Flintshire CC* (26 July 2000) transcript p. 17

4.2.9 Scott Baker J. adopted and cited the approach of Mustill J. in *Thompson* v. *Smiths Shiprepairers Ltd* [1984] 1 QB 405 at 443G (not a child abuse case) as follows:

In the end, notwithstanding all the care lavished on it by scientists and by counsel, I believe that this has to be regarded as a jury question and I propose to approach it as such.

> *Various claimants* v. *Flintshire CC* (26 July 2000) transcript p. 18

4.2.10 This approach was also followed in *Holtby* v. *Brigham & Cowan (Hull) Ltd* [2000] 3 All ER 421.

4.2.11 The Court of Appeal in *C* v. *Flintshire County Council* (CA 13 February 2001, unreported) dismissed the appeal brought by Flintshire County Council in one of the North Wales cases. Lord Justice Ward (with whom Lords Justices Buxton and Henry agreed) approved the approach of Scott Baker J. and stated at para. 57:

The Judge was, as is conceded, entitled to approach this case with a broad brush, as a jury question, and very much as a matter of feel.

4.2.12 In *C* v. *Flintshire County Council,* Lord Justice Buxton pointed out at para. 67 that:

[The judge] was also entitled to have well in mind when attributing the loss between various conflicting causes involved, that [C] was in the hands of the defendants precisely because of her initial vulnerability, in circumstances where they well knew of that vulnerability. He was entitled in that context to have well in mind Dr Abel's evidence . . . that in these circumstances the effect of mistreatment by carers would, or at least very well might, have a multiplying or compounding effect on [C's] initial vulnerability. To emphasise that point is not to say (as Mr Maskrey submitted that it was) that the defendants are being required to pay damages for not having cured [C's] problems. Rather, it is to say that this is a case where the usual process of attributing responsibility between various causes to a large extent breaks down, because the initial cause of [C's] vulnerability is the context in which the defendants have to take particular care. If they did not take that care, in circumstances where it was known and foreseeable what could be the outcome of abuse by persons of trust and in positions of responsibility, then they cannot complain if less weight than otherwise might be the case is given to that original cause. Those considerations therefore entitle – indeed oblige – the judge not to weigh too nicely arguments based on the respective causal effect of the various facts in the history.

4.2.13 Claimants often suffer from a multiplicity of technically distinct psychiatric conditions: e.g. PTSD, alcohol abuse, depression, personality disorder. These conditions may have multiple causes of which child abuse is only one factor. The abuse might have had made a greater contribution to one particular problem (e.g. PTSD) than to another (e.g. depression). These are issues which the psychiatrist should make some attempt to unravel, although it is extremely difficult to identify the precise psychological damage caused by any particular episode of abuse.

4.3   CRIMINAL OFFENCES

4.3.1 It is a controversial issue among psychiatrists/psychologists whether abuse in childhood is a risk factor for criminal behaviour in adult life. Those who argue that it is put forward the following points:

- abuse in childhood may affect a person's adult relationships and someone who cannot form attachments is more likely to offend;

- severe abuse may lead victims to become hostile and anti-authority, which in turn may have an effect on their education and their response to employment, giving rise to involvement in crime;

- those who have been abused may self-medicate against intrusive memories, which can take the form of using illegal drugs, and drug/alcohol abuse leads to a downward spiral into crime (Criminal Injuries Compensation Appeals Panel: Panel's policy on abuse in childhood, note by M. E. Lewer QC) (see para. 6.11.8).

4.3.2 Those who do not accept the connection argue that psychiatric research has not established clear cause-and-effect relationships between abuse in care and subsequent criminality.

4.3.3   A claimant who seeks to argue that abuse has been a cause of criminal offending in adult life may wish to recover damages for the consequences of his criminal convictions. In particular damages for periods of imprisonment (and consequential loss of earnings). It is therefore necessary to examine the court's approach to such claims. It should be noted that to date there is no reported case in which a causal link between sexual, emotional or physical abuse to a child in care and subsequent offending has been established. The point has however arisen in the context of other types of personal injury claims.

4.3.4   In *Meah* v. *McCreamer (No.1)* [1985] 1 All ER 367 the claimant sustained serious head injuries as a result of a road traffic accident. These head injuries resulted in him undergoing a marked personality change. Before the accident, the claimant had been convicted of various criminal offences such as theft and burglary and he had a poor employment record. However, the claimant had had a number of successful relationships with women and there was no evidence he had ever been violent towards women. Three years after the accident, the claimant sexually assaulted and maliciously wounded two women. A few months later he raped and maliciously wounded a third woman. He was sentenced to life imprisonment for these offences. The claimant claimed damages against the defendant on the grounds that but for the brain damage caused in the accident and the resulting personality change, he would not have committed the offences for which he was imprisoned. Woolf J. (as he then was) was satisfied on the medical evidence that the head injuries sustained in the accident had caused the claimant to commit the violent offences. In this action the defendant did not dispute, in principle, that the claimant was entitled to damages for imprisonment arising from crimes committed by reason of his head injuries. Woolf J. held that:

> Since but for the injuries received in the accident, and the resulting personality change, the claimant would not have committed the criminal acts for which he was serving a sentence of life imprisonment, he was entitled to damages to compensate him for being in prison . . . In assessing those damages, it was necessary to take into account the claimant's previous criminal tendencies, which would probably have resulted in him spending periods in prison, and the fact that, having regard to his previous poor employment record and the free board he would receive in prison, there would be no continuing financial loss.

4.3.5   Damages awarded to the claimant in *Meah* v. *McCreamer (No. 1)* were partly assessed by reference to awards for wrongful imprisonment.

4.3.6   Following this decision, the claimant's three victims, who had been raped/assaulted by him, claimed damages from him. In *Meah v. McCreamer (No. 2)* [1986] 1 All ER 943 the claimant sought an indemnity against the defendant for the amounts awarded to his victims. The claimant's claim was dismissed:

- on grounds of remoteness; and

- because it was considered contrary to public policy for the claimant to be indemnified by the defendant for the consequences of his crimes.

4.3.7 The public policy argument had not been raised by the defendant in the first action.

4.3.8 In *Clunis* v. *Camden and Islington Health Authority* [1998] QB 978 the claimant, who had a long history of mental disorder and seriously violent behaviour, stabbed a man to death at a tube station. The claimant was charged with murder, but at his trial pleaded guilty to manslaughter on the grounds of diminished responsibility. The 'diminished responsibility' verdict meant that although the claimant suffered from mental disorder, he none the less knew what he was doing and that it was wrong. He bore some degree of criminal responsibility, albeit a reduced one. The claimant was ordered to be detained in a secure hospital. Subsequently, he brought an action for damages against the Health Authority, alleging that it had negligently failed to treat him with reasonable professional care and skill. He claimed that the responsible medical officer had failed to ensure that he was properly assessed before he committed the act of manslaughter. If he had been properly assessed, he claimed, he would either have been detained or consented to become a patient, and would not have committed the manslaughter. The claimant sought damages for the consequences of the manslaughter. The Health Authority applied to strike out his claim as disclosing no cause of action. One ground of the application was that the claim arose from the claimant's own criminal act.

4.3.9 The Court of Appeal held that 'the public policy that the court will not lend its aid to the litigant who relies on his own criminal or immoral act (was) not confined to particular causes of action' ([1998] 3 All ER at p. 18). Public policy, therefore, precluded the court from entertaining his case because he had committed a serious criminal offence, he knew what he was doing and he knew that it was wrong. The decision of Woolf J. in *Meah v. McCreamer (No. 1)* was doubted. It was noted that the defendant in that case had not raised any public policy objection to Meah being awarded damages for the consequences of his criminal acts. A petition for leave to appeal to the House of Lords was refused ([1998] 1 WLR 1093). Therefore, since the decision in *Clunis* v. *Camden and Islington Health Authority*, it appears that *Meah* v. *McCreamer (No.1)* may no longer be good law. The position now appears to be that even if a claimant could demonstrate a causal link between abuse in care and subsequent offending, most such claims would be rejected on grounds of public policy.

4.3.10 In the Court of Appeal in *Clunis* v. *Camden and Islington Health Authority*, counsel for the claimant had argued that the court should look at the seriousness and circumstances of the offence in order to determine whether it was contrary to public policy that the claimant should be allowed to maintain a cause of action. The Court of Appeal in *Clunis* did not deal with this point directly. The same point was argued by the claimants in *Various claimants* v. *Flintshire County Council*. Scott Baker J. in that case observed that: 'Most crimes resulting in imprisonment would fall within the rule in *Clunis*'. However, he stated no concluded view as it was not necessary to do so when none of the claimants established the necessary facts for the point of law to arise. (*Various claimants* v. *Flintshire CC* (26 July 2000) transcript p. 22.)

4.3.11 The case of *Clunis* v. *Camden and Islington Health Authority* was also followed in the Court of Appeal in *Cooper* v. *Reed and another*. The claimant in that case claimed damages for negligence arising out of an accident which caused him to suffer PTSD. Some years after the accident the claimant spent nine months in prison. The judge at first instance found that it was more probable than not that the conduct leading to imprisonment would have been avoided but for the claimant's psychiatric condition (which was the fault of the defendants). The judge at first instance held that no deduction should be made from loss of earnings awarded to the claimant on account of his period of imprisonment. The judge found the imprisonment was a consequence of the defendants' breach of duty. In the Court of Appeal the Defendants argued that the judge should not have awarded the claimant damages for loss of earnings in relation to the nine month period of imprisonment.

4.3.12 Brooke LJ in the *Cooper* case found that:

> 'Although the judge (at first instance's) logic seems to me to have been impeccable, we are bound by the decision of this Court in *Clunis* v. *Camden and Islington Health Authority* to disallow this part of the award. Although the defendant's wrongdoing weakened Mr Cooper's resistance when provoked . . . the law as it now stands gives him no excuse for the criminal acts which he then committed or the sentence of imprisonment he served as a consequence of those acts. Nine months' loss of earnings at the relevant rate must therefore be deducted from his damages.

4.3.13 Brooke LJ further stated:

> I see no reason, in justice or in logic, why the award should be reduced any further on the basis that Mr Cooper's parlous condition, caused by the defendant's wrongdoing, gives rise to a risk, significant or otherwise, that he may re-offend or spend further time in prison.

4.3.14 It should be noted that this issue has recently been addressed by the Law Commission in its Consultation Paper 'The Illegality Defence in Tort' (Law Commission Consultation Paper 160, HMSO). The Law

Commission recommends retaining this aspect of the illegality defence so that cases where the claimant seeks to recover damages in respect of periods of imprisonment would continue to be barred.

4.4 AGGRAVATED DAMAGES

4.4.1 Intentional assault is actionable without proof of injury. In claims based on intentional assault aggravated damages may be sought simply for the *manner* of the assault. In *Appleton v. Garrett* [1997] 8 Med LR 75, Dyson J. in awarding aggravated damages against a dentist who had deliberately carried out unnecessary treatment to patients adopted the Law Commission summary:

> In *Rookes* v. *Barnard* ([1964] AC 1129) Lord Devlin said that aggravated awards were appropriate where the manner in which the wrong was committed was such as to injure the plaintiff's proper feelings of pride and dignity and give rise to humiliation, distress, insult or pain. Examples of the sort of conduct which would lead to these forms of intangible loss were conduct which was offensive or which was accompanied by malevolence, spite, malice, insolence or arrogance. In other words the type of conduct which has previously been regarded as capable of sustaining a punitive award. It would therefore seem that there are two elements to the availability of an aggravated award, first exceptional or contumelious conduct or motive on the part of the defendant in committing the wrong and second, intangible loss suffered as a result by the plaintiff, that is injury to personality.

4.4.2 This description is apt to cover many cases of child abuse. Commonly assaults are carried out by adults in positions of responsibility, trust and power in respect of the children in their charge.

4.4.3 In the case of *Griffiths* v. *Williams* (1995) *The Times*, 24 November, the Court of Appeal considered an award of damages by a jury to an adult who had been raped by her landlord. The Court of Appeal recognised that the award of damages made in the sum of £50,000 was a comparatively high award. However, the Court took into account the aggravating features which included the behaviour of the defendant after the claimant had reported the rape and the way in which the defendant had sought to defend the case by making allegations about the character of the claimant. Lord Justice Rose concluded that:

> In my judgment the circumstances and consequences of rape – or trespass to the person, as it is for the purposes of the civil law – place it, as I have already said, in a quite different category from personal injury cases in general. Furthermore, the present case, as it seems to me, is different from both the Criminal Injuries Compensation Board cases and from *W* v. *Meah*. In the case of *W* v. *Meah* the question of rape was not in issue and the victim

did not have to endure the subsequent events, including giving evidence in the circumstances referred to, which marked the present case.

4.4.4   In the *Griffiths* v. *Williams* case Millett LJ (as he then was) commented on the level of damages and the possible justification for it. He stated:

> the court ought to recognise that perceptions have changed since 1985 (when the case of *W* v. *Meah* was decided) of the gravity and seriousness of the outrage to a woman's feelings which is caused by the peculiarly intimate nature of this form of assault. I also consider that a jury is far better able than a judge to decide what sum is appropriate to compensate the victim of rape for the injury and outrage which she has suffered and for the ordeal of the jury trial itself in which serious allegations are made against her character.

Thorpe LJ in the same case stated:

> I have had greater misgivings than he on the quantum of the jury's award, and, applying the personal injuries scale, I doubt whether damages for the incident itself should be quantified at more than £15,000. The balance of £35,000 as aggravated damages compensating for subsequent happenings is at first sight out of due proportion, but I agree with my Lord that the manner in which she alleged that the defendant had subsequently treated her and the manner in which the defendant conducted the litigation are extreme. Indeed, the defendant's attack on the plaintiff's character and behaviour would amount to defamation unless justified. Accordingly my misgivings are not sufficient so as to lead me to dissent on the issue of damages.

4.4.5   Effectively, the Court of Appeal found the award of £50,000 higher than could be justified by the quantum of awards for personal injury claims. However, the Court was able to justify the award by adding a considerable additional sum by way of aggravated damages in the award made against the assailant himself.

4.4.6   In the subsequent case of *Marriott* v. *Parrington* (CA, Lord Woolf MR, Mummery LJ, Mantell LJ, 19 February 1999, unreported) the Court of Appeal again considered the proper level of damages for rape and sexual harassment. In this case an employee was claiming damages against her employer whom she alleged had raped her on two occasions at the office premises and had sexually harassed her at work for a period of 18 months. The judge awarded £25,000 general damages and £30,000 aggravated damages. The Court of Appeal dismissed the defendant's appeal against the quantum of damages. Lord Justice Mummery (with whom the other judges agreed) explained how the judge had found 'he would be doing less than [his] duty if [he] did not award a large element of aggravated damages in the circumstances of this case'. The judge had recognised that the award in *Griffiths* v. *Williams* was right at the top of the band or bracket. The Court of Appeal accepted, however, that the facts in *Marriott* v.

Parrington were worse both in terms of the conduct and the indignity to which the claimant was subjected.

Mummery LJ concluded:

> In my judgment, this court should not reduce the damages awarded to the plaintiff. There was no error of principle in the decision of the judge and it cannot be said, in the light of his clear findings of fact, that the sum was an entirely erroneous estimate or was plainly wrong. As was pointed out by Rose LJ in *Griffiths* v. *Williams* (supra) at 21 the circumstances of rape 'place it in quite a different category from personal injury cases in general'. He and Millett LJ also noted the change in attitudes to and perceptions of this kind of case since the decision in *W* v. *Meah*. This award is not out of all proportion to the circumstances of the case or so excessive as to justify the court's interference.

4.4.7 Awards of aggravated damages in cases where there is a cause of action in trespass can therefore significantly increase the overall level of damages awarded. An action in trespass should be carefully considered in preference to a claim in negligence in claims based on intentional assault.

4.5   QUANTIFICATION OF GENERAL DAMAGES

4.5.1 Since 1996, there have been three decisions in multi-party actions which have assessed the level of damages in child abuse cases. These now provide the main source of comparable awards for assessing general damages in child abuse compensation claims. The three cases are:

- *Various claimants* v. *Leicestershire County Council* (Potts J., 2 April 1996, unreported);

- *Various claimants* v. *Flintshire County Council* (Scott Baker J., 26 July 2000, unreported); and

- *Various claimants* v. *Bryn Alyn Community Homes Ltd* (Connell J., 26 June 2001, unreported).

4.5.2 Prior to these cases there was very little civil litigation relating to child abuse and the practitioner had to look to decisions of the Criminal Injuries Compensation Board (CICB) for guidance on general damages. Such decisions were not ideal for comparative purposes and usually only brief reports of the cases are available.

4.5.3 The highest CICB award of general damages for a sexual offence prior to 1996 was *Re G* (Kemp and Kemp Vol. 3 (4–201)). The applicant was a female aged 24 at the date of the CICB hearing. She had suffered sexual abuse and physical violence in a children's home at the hands of the male proprietor and a female teacher. The abuse and violence took place when she was aged between 15 and 19. The applicant was raped, buggered and had to engage in oral sex. Objects, including a broom-handle, were inserted into her vagina. She had to engage in group sexual activity with other children. She was urinated upon and tied up. In consequence, the applicant developed a number of urinary tract infections, a kidney infection and anal spasms. She had severe behavioural reaction, and attempted suicide by swallowing glass, self-electrocution and self-strangulation. The applicant became a psychiatric in-patient. The prognosis was guarded. She had no realistic hope of holding a job or of ever fulfilling early potential. The CICB awarded:

- general damages – £50,000;
- damages for lost earning capacity – £50,000.

4.5.4   In the small number of civil claims before 1996 there were a wide range of awards, partly reflecting judicial uncertainty about whether awards should include aggravated damages or should simply reflect the figures awarded in conventional personal injury cases. In *W* v. *Meah* and *S* v. *Meah*, two of Mr Meah's female victims brought claims for damages for assault against him. Woolf J. (as he then was) awarded the claimants £10,250 and £6,750 and stated, that despite the terrible circumstances in which the two claimants were injured:

> It is important that the court bears in mind that the award in this case must bear a proper relationship to the awards which the court makes in more conventional personal injury cases.

4.5.5   In 1992, the Judicial Studies Board (JSB) published the first edition of their *Guidelines*. The purpose of the guidelines was to 'provide a snap-shot' of what the courts were awarding for various categories of injuries.

4.5.6   The JSB *Guidelines* contained a section relating to 'psychiatric damage' and a separate section for 'Post-Traumatic Stress Disorder'. Psychiatric damage could, of course, include an element of PTSD, whereas PTSD is a specific reactive psychiatric disorder. In the first edition of the *Guidelines* the bracket for psychiatric damages ranged from £500 to £50,000. The bracket for damages for PTSD was £1,900 to £37,500. However, it was stressed that the JSB *Guidelines* were most relevant to 'the commoner categories of injury'. They were not intended to be exhaustive. Less common injuries were recognised as 'posing their own problems'.

4.5.7   In *C* v. *Flintshire County Council*, Ward LJ emphasised that the JSB brackets for psychiatric injury were not necessarily apt to cover child abuse claims. He stated at para. 54:

For my part, I am far from satisfied that the Judicial Studies Board categorisation applies to this kind of case at all. Physical, emotional and sexual abuse of children in care by those who are supposed to provide that care seems to me to fall into a wholly different category from psychiatric damage that follows other personal injuries. The injury is of a different character. The essential element of the damage is the extent to which the injury compounds and multiplies the effect of the pre-existing condition. The Judicial Studies Board guidelines do not include among the factors to take into account the duration of the suffering. In the nature of this kind of abuse, the victims are frequently unable to address the abuse until many years later. The claimant is an example of that unhappy state of affairs. She suffered from the age of 14 until 1995, five years before the judgment, or perhaps more accurately, until 1997 or 1998, when she first disclosed the harm she had suffered to the Waterhouse Tribunal and began to receive treatment for it. It is all very well to say that the prognosis today is optimistic but guarded, but today is 20 years after she began to suffer at the hands of the local authority. I am quite certain there is no easily definable bracket into which to place this case such as would enable the court to say that an award which fell outside the bracket must of necessity be so plainly wrong as to be set aside.

4.5.8 Comparison with cases not involving child abuse and reference to the JSB *Guidelines* are therefore of limited use in assessing general damages for a child abuse compensation claim. The *Leicestershire* and *North Wales* cases provide the most comprehensive comparables. These cases, however, in themselves illustrate a wide range of awards and the difficulty in making comparisons in such cases. It may be that awards of damages in this special class of case will always be more 'a matter of feel' than a matter of applying a relevant bracket. The awards made for general damages and under other heads in the *Leicestershire* and *North Wales* cases are summarised below. All claimants are referred to by their initials.

Various claimants v. *Leicestershire CC* (Potts J., 2 April 1996, unreported)

4.5.9 DB: Aged 15, was placed at Ratcliffe Road Children's Home where she was subjected to forced regression. This included her being accompanied by staff at all times, having no privacy even in the lavatory, being bathed (often by male staff) being fed by bottles or feeder cups, having her food cut up and fed to her, being read children's stories and having to carry a 'Honey Monster' toy. The claimant was violently treated and dragged upstairs by her hair. At times the claimant was confined to a room in pyjamas during the daytime for up to six weeks as a punishment. The claimant began to self-mutilate and attempted suicide by cutting her wrists and other parts of her body. At the date of trial the claimant was aged 31, she continued to suffer from depression, self-mutilation, difficulty with intimate relationships and affection even to her daughter, she continued behaviour as a child using cuddly toys and baby talk. The judge found that the claimant's most serious damage was her propensity to self-harm and that she would not have suffered this without the abuse.

General damages	£50,000
Therapy Costs (including in-patient treatment)	£20,000
Vulnerability on the labour market, past, present and future	£10,000

JL: Aged 15, was placed at Ratcliffe Road Children's Home where she was raped a number of times, buggered once by Frank Beck and subjected to numerous indecent assaults and brutal physical assaults. Beck was convicted of rape and buggery in respect of the claimant. Further, she was subjected to forced regression. The judge accepted that the claimant had been subjected to torture at the hands of the defendants' servants. At the date of the trial the claimant, aged 37, suffered from PTSD including flashbacks, depression, sexual difficulties and she had attempted suicide.

General damages	£80,000
Therapy costs	£25,000
Past vulnerability on the labour market	£40,000

Various claimants v. *Flintshire CC* (Scott Baker J., 26 July 2000, unreported)

4.5.10 AC: Physical assault by a care worker, indecent assault by a care worker, unlawful incarceration in a secure unit, significant psychiatric effect on later life.

General damages	£35,000
Therapy costs	£10,719
Past vulnerability on the labour market	£20,000
Future vulnerability on the labour market	£5,000
(award upheld on appeal to Court of Appeal)	

SC: Abused over a period of about 12 months by the officer in charge of the care home, consisting of leering at him while he was naked in the shower on about eight occasions, grabbing his penis on two or three occasions, pulling out pubic hair on other occasions. Minor effect on adult life; PTSD not established.

General damages	£7,500
Therapy costs	no award
Past vulnerability on the labour market	no award
Future vulnerability on the labour market	no award

EAD: Allegation of rape not established, damages for physical assault by other girls assisted by a member of staff placing her in a bath, cutting her hair and making her eat toast with unpleasant substances on. Defendants found not responsible for her considerable problems in later life.

General damages	£2,500
Therapy costs	no award
Past vulnerability on the labour market	no award
Future vulnerability on the labour market	no award

TD: Abused by the defendants' employees, including oral sex, sexual acts with a dog, masturbation, indecent assault in a shower, assault when sexual intercourse resisted, thrashing with a cane. The abuse was accepted as being severe and persistent. PTSD, major depressive disorder, sexual problems, personality disorder.

General damages	£50,000
Therapy costs	£6,525
Past vulnerability on the labour market	£20,000
Future vulnerability on the labour market	£17,500

GJ: Physical assaults including beatings, sexual assaults including touching in the genital area, significant effect on adult life.

General damages	£30,000
Therapy costs	no award
Past vulnerability on the labour market	£10,000
Future vulnerability on the labour market	no award

PJ: Repeated acts of sexual abuse, including touching in the genital area and oral sex; killing of the claimant's pet squirrels; boxing matches with older boys resulting in injury, psychological damage (not PTSD) and difficulty with relationships.

General damages	£25,000
Therapy costs	£5,000
Past vulnerability on the labour market	no award
Future vulnerability on the labour market	no award

IM: Subjected to a harsh, non-caring regime in a children's home and sexual abuse, including touching in the genital area, which caused difficulties in sex life and contributed to his personality disorder.

General damages	£24,000
Therapy costs	no award
Past vulnerability on the labour market	no award
Future vulnerability on the labour market	no award

DM: Subjected to a harsh, non-caring regime, psychological abuse, and sexual comments undermining his confidence and leading to psychological damage – other factors, however, contributed to this damage to a greater extent.

General damages	£15,000
Therapy costs	no award
Past vulnerability on the labour market	no award
Future vulnerability on the labour market	no award

MR: Sexual intercourse instigated by a female member of staff in a children's home when the claimant was $15\frac{1}{2}$, oral sex, causing confusion and upset to the claimant, and later difficulty with relationships.

General damages	£5,000
Therapy costs	no award
Past vulnerability on the labour market	no award
Future vulnerability on the labour market	no award

SW: Three incidents of sexual assaults, including one touching of the claimant's penis over his trousers, and two of rubbing his penis to ejaculation, both incidents when the claimant was 16 years of age.

General damages	£2,000
Therapy costs	no award
Past vulnerability on the labour market	no award
Future vulnerability on the labour market	no award

DW: Suffered physical abuse over a period of six months from male members of staff, including being made to strip naked and being kept in a secure unit, sexual intercourse instigated by a female member of staff. Some effect on adult life.

General damages	£14,000
Therapy costs	no award
Past vulnerability on the labour market	no award
Future vulnerability on the labour market	no award

Various claimants v. *Bryn Alyn Community Homes Ltd* (Connell J. 6 June 2001)

4.5.11   KR: One attempted buggery, one occasion of removing the claimant's clothes and trying to assault him, other physical assaults. Diagnosed as suffering PTSD caused by his experiences at Bryn Alyn, some adjustment to the disorder but the claimant continues to suffer significant symptoms affecting his relationships, his choices of employment and his mental state. He needs treatment with a combination of anti-depressant medication and psychotherapeutic intervention.

General damages	£35,000
Therapy costs	£2,000
Past vulnerability on the labour market	£5,000
Future vulnerability on the labour market	£5,000

DK: Subjected to a regime of persistent assaults by various members of staff including one occasion of nearly choking and numerous 'hammerings'. Suffered from cyclothymic disorder/personality (mood swings), judge found his experiences at Bryn Alyn made a significant contribution to his psychiatric and personality problems.

General damages	£25,000
Therapy costs	£1,250
Past vulnerability on the labour market	£3,000
Future vulnerability on the labour market	£5,000

CE: Suffered from the violent regime in which a number of members of staff violently assaulted him and one occasion when he was shaken, dragged out of a tent and repeatedly punched to the floor. Abuse exacerbated pre-existing psychological difficulties.

General damages	£17,500
Therapy	£1,000
Past vulnerability on the labour market	no award
Future vulnerability on the labour market	£2,500

RM: Subjected to violent regime, required to scrub floors with a toothbrush, punched, hair pulled and kicked, mock kidnap by staff when she was taken to woods and assaulted. Bryn Alyn was her twenty-sixth placement and she was significantly damaged in any event.

General damages	£5,000
Therapy costs	no award
Past vulnerability on the labour market	no award
Future vulnerability on the labour market	no award

GS: Allegation of significant violence on a daily basis rejected but violence still used inappropriately and more frequently than was justified. The claimant would have suffered significant problems in adulthood in any event but the experience at Gatewen was inappropriate and caused some additional material damage.

General damages	£5,000
Therapy costs	no award
Past vulnerability on the labour market	no award
Future vulnerability on the labour market	no award

MK: Sexual abuse on about six occasions when the claimant was asked to masturbate John Allen while he placed his hand down her trousers and on to her buttocks. The claimant cooperated to obtain extra pocket money, she did not find this particularly distressing at the time but has since felt alternating anger and guilt.

Claim dismissed as being assault and limitation barred and negligence not established. Damages assessed in any event. No recognisable psychiatric disorder but some damage from the experiences.

General damages	£5,000
Therapy costs	no award
Past vulnerability on the labour market	no award
Future vulnerability on the labour market	no award

DJ: Suffered sexual and physical abuse, which included allegations of buggery by John Allen and another man on several occasions. Allegations of physical abuse included cold showers, scrubbing floors and slapping, punching and beating. Judge found the claimant was suffering from PTSD 'that cannot be described as severe in light of the claimant's constructive manner and positive outlook for the future'.

General damages	£25,000
Therapy costs	£500
Past vulnerability on the labour market	no award
Future vulnerability on the labour market	no award

KM: Indecent assaults, alleged forced oral sex when John Allen pushed the claimant's head towards his groin, rubbing of the claimant's penis by Allen and the claimant was forced to rub Allen's penis.

Further serious allegations against two other employees were not found proved to the requisite standard.

Claimant would have suffered depression, anxiety and significant stress in daily life in any event; an element of PTSD but its overall effect on the daily life of the claimant comparatively modest.

General damages	£5,000
Therapy costs	£1,500
Past vulnerability on the labour market	no award
Future vulnerability on the labour market	no award

JS: Allegations proved included allegation that Patrick Bates invited her into his tent to sleep, kissed her, fondled her breasts and assumed a position above her with his penis out preparatory to sexual intercourse and then changed his mind. Judge found negligence against the defendant not proved.

An allegation of unlawful sexual intercourse was proved in a criminal trial in respect of the deputy head Ian Muir who had a sexual relationship with the claimant over a number of months.

Judge found the abuse at Bryn Alyn made a material contribution to her symptoms as did many other features disclosed in her unhappy history.

General damages	£15,000
Therapy costs	no award
Past vulnerability on the labour market	no award
Future vulnerability on the labour market	no award

GM: Allegations originally that John Allen touched the claimant's genitals and forced him to rub Allen's penis on about 30 occasions, shortly before trial the claimant alleged Allen had also buggered him. All allegations found proved and vicarious liability for negligence of other staff found proved. No additional damage found from scrubbing floors with a toothbrush and a regime of slapping from time to time.

Events sufficiently traumatic to contribute to diagnosis of PTSD but other factors also contributed.

General damages	£25,000
Therapy costs including in-patient treatment	£10,000
Past vulnerability on the labour market	no award
(90 criminal convictions and inability to work not attributable to the defendant)	
Future vulnerability on the labour market	£2,500

DHM: Allegations of sexual abuse by a care worker, David Stanley, including mutual masturbation leading to ejaculation, oral sex and attempted buggery, also buggery with another boy while masturbating the claimant. David Stanley convicted of offences relating to the claimant. Further allegations of masturbation and attempted buggery by John Allen also found proved by the judge. Physical abuse consisting of some assaults being 'over the top' proved. Vicarious liability for negligent supervision proved.

Judge found abusive experiences played a major part in delayed onset of PTSD and enduring personality change after major catastrophic experience.

General damages	£30,000
Therapy costs	£1,800
Vulnerability on the labour market	no award
Future vulnerability on the labour market	£10,000

PS: Allegations of physical abuse by John Allen hitting the claimant on the chest with the heel of his hand six times so as to frighten the claimant. Regime generally violent, top-dog system whereby older children were used to discipline younger children.

Claimant's psychiatrist made diagnosis of chronic PTSD, judge found the claimant's time at Bryn Alyn made a material contribution to those problems.

General damages	£12,500
Therapy costs	£2,000
Past vulnerability on the labour market	£2,500
Future vulnerability on the labour market	£10,000

CD: Allegations of sexual abuse including buggery by a care worker on six or seven occasions, and severe physical violence. Negligence proved in respect of only some of the allegations of buggery (not those occurring outside the school).

Agreed medical evidence that the claimant suffered PTSD and a severe mixed-personality disorder. Only limited additional damage caused by experiences at Bryn Alyn but they contributed to his inability to leave his home and to some of the costs of non-commercial care he required.

General damages	£10,000
Therapy costs	£3,000
Care costs (two-thirds of commercial rates)	£21,450
Past vulnerability on the labour market	no award
(never been employable or likely to have become so)	
Future vulnerability on the labour market	no award

JM: Allegations of indecent assault against John Allen leading to buggery proved. Indecent assaults, photographs taken and buggery by Ken Taylor while at Bryn Alyn community home also proved. Only insignificant physical abuse proved. Negligence of defendants in respect of abuse proved. PTSD, vulnerability towards episodes of depressive illness, relationship problems and irritable bowel syndrome contributed to by earlier abuse as well as abuse at Bryn Alyn community home.

General damages	£17,500
Therapy costs	no award
Past vulnerability on the labour market	no award
Future vulnerability on the labour market	no award

(These awards are due to be considered by the Court of Appeal in February 2002 – see Updates on p. 253.)

4.6   LOSS OF EARNINGS/EARNING CAPACITY

4.6.1   The legal principle underpinning assessment of claims for loss of earnings and loss of earning capacity is the compensatory principle. The claimant should be placed in the same position he would have been in if he had not suffered the wrong for which the defendant is liable. The task is to determine what the claimant would have earned absent the abuse and whether this is less than he has earned to date. Further, it is necessary to determine if the claimant still has a reduced earning capacity.

4.6.2   The basic rules associated with the calculation of these losses in personal injury claims other than child abuse claims are well known. In respect of past loss of earnings, in a conventional personal injury claim there would be an arithmetical calculation of loss of earnings based on a loss of a known amount of past loss over a known duration. In respect of future losses, there would be one or both of the following types of claim:

- an 'arithmetical' calculation involving a multiplier/multiplicand approach;

- an award for future competitive disadvantage in the open labour market, known as a *Smith* v. *Manchester* award (*Smith* v. *Manchester Corp.* (1974) 17 KIR 1, CA).

4.6.3 In child abuse cases there are typically many imponderables in terms of what the claimant would have done in the labour market but for the abuse. As a result, courts have to date tended not to adopt an arithmetical approach to the whole period of loss from the claimant leaving school until the trial. Instead, the courts have applied a broad-brush approach to the calculation of both past and future loss of earnings. In respect of past loss of earnings there may however be a past claim to be calculated on a multiplier/multiplicand basis where a claimant has been unable to work since a police enquiry forced him to consider the events of his childhood many years later.

4.6.4 In the *Flintshire* judgment Scott Baker J. set out his approach in principle to the computation of past loss of earnings as follows:

> In none of the cases (before me) has a detailed loss of earnings claim been advanced. I have approached the claims in this way. For any loss up until the date of trial, the claimant has had to persuade me that it is more likely than not that over the years since the abuse, he has earned less money than would have been the case had he not been abused. Where that question has been answered in the affirmative, I have gone on to assess the loss in monetary terms. It has not been possible to conduct the exercise on a conventional basis. Other factors, which are not the fault of the defendants, have affected the claimant's earning ability. For example, some have spent periods in prison and there have been other causes of or contributions to personality problems. Accordingly, where I am satisfied that, but for the abuse, an individual claimant would have earned more over the pre-trial period as a whole either by having a better paid job or spending more time in work, I have done my best to reflect this by making an award of a round sum.
>
> (*Various claimants* v. *Flintshire CC*, 26 July 2000, transcript p. 22)

4.6.5 Scott Baker J. observed that absent the abuse, these claimants would, in any event, have 'been very much at the lower end of the labour market'. In the event, the sums awarded for past loss of earnings in the three cases to which this approach applied were: £20,000, £20,000 and £10,000.

4.6.6 In assessing the awards for future loss of earnings Scott Baker J. found that in none of these cases was a multiplier/multiplicand approach appropriate. As Scott Baker J. explained:

> As to loss of future earning capacity here, I have followed the approach based on *Smith* v. *Manchester Corporation* (1974) 17 KIR 1. The loss does not have to be established on the balance of probabilities but as Lawton LJ pointed out in *Herod* v. *Birds Eye Foods Limited*, Kemp and Kemp 6/606 what the degree of incapacity is must depend upon the evidence before the court. It may well be that when trying to fix some figure, the court has to use its imagination and its knowledge of the world; there has to be a certain amount of speculation, but there must be some basic facts upon which the court can make its forecast.
>
> (*Various claimants* v. *Flintshire CC* (26 July 2000) transcript p. 23)

4.6.7 The sums assessed by Scott Baker J. using these criteria were £17,500 and £5,000.

4.6.8 The courts have also tended to reject an arithmetical approach for future loss of earnings claims in child abuse cases although there is no reason in principle why such a claim should not succeed. The approach which may be favoured in many child abuse claims is the approach adopted in the decision (at first instance and then upheld by the Court of Appeal) in *Blamire v. South Cumbria Health Authority*. This was not an abuse case. It involved a nurse who injured her back in a lifting accident making it permanently vulnerable. As a consequence, she was off work for various periods in the succeeding years. Eventually she became unable to continue working as a nurse and obtained part-time work in a residential home. The judge found that but for the accident the claimant would probably have pursued a longer career in nursing, and that she would now have to work as a secretary; that it would be significantly more difficult to obtain such work; and that some recurrence of back trouble could be expected during her working life. However in assessing loss of earnings he did not accept the multiplier/multiplicand approach, but awarded a broad-brush lump sum of £25,000 for future loss of wages, pension and earning capacity. The claimant appealed on the basis that the judge should have applied a conventional multiplier/multiplicand formula, which would have resulted in a six-figure loss-of-earnings award. The Court of Appeal held that:

> The judge was entitled to reject the conventional multiplier/multiplicand approach as inappropriate given the number of imponderables. There were uncertainties as to the amount the claimant would have earned if uninjured, including whether she would have had more children or only taken part-time work. There was also uncertainty as to the likely future pattern of her earnings. There could be no criticism of the judge's approach of weighing loss of pension benefits against the possibility of such benefits associated with secretarial working and taking that into account and assessing loss of earnings. Given that there was no perfect arithmetical way of calculating compensation the judge was bound to look at the matter globally and assess the present value of the risk of future financial loss.

4.6.9 Steyn LJ said that the judge at first instance,

> Had in mind that there was no perfect arithmetical way of calculating compensation in such a case. Inevitably one is driven to the broad-brush approach. The law is concerned with practical affairs and, as Lord Reid said in *British Transport Commission v. Gourley* [1956] AC 185 at p. 212, very often one is driven to making a very rough estimate of the damages.

4.6.10 Balcombe LJ said:

> There were far too many imponderables here for the judge to have been bound to take the conventional approach.

4.6.11 In view the number of 'imponderables' in many child abuse cases, the difficulties in assessing the causes and true extent of the losses suffered, the *Blamire* approach may find favour.

4.6.12 What evidence should lawyers of the claimant and defendant be looking to obtain in relation to loss of earnings? The starting point will be a medical assessment as to the way in which the claimant's psychiatric problems have impacted and will impact upon his or her ability to work. A claimant who, by reason of experiences of abuse, finds it difficult to tolerate stressful situations or authority figures may encounter difficulties in obtaining and holding down jobs. Evidence as to jobs held and reasons for leaving may be relevant. There must be 'some basic facts' (see para. 4.6.6 above) upon which the court can assess loss of earnings; evidence of the claimant's potential, whether in the form of qualifications obtained or jobs held, will be important. Another area to be explored is the sibling and parental comparisons. The question of evidence is explored in Chapter 7.

4.7 COST OF MEDICAL TREATMENT

4.7.1 Because child abuse compensation claims usually involve psychiatric injuries, the issue frequently arises as to whether the claimant may benefit from therapy. The further issue is whether the defendant should be liable for any associated costs. Claims for the private cost of therapy have now become commonplace in these cases.

4.7.2 The recoverability in principle of the private costs of medical treatment is established by s.2(4) of the Law Reform (Personal Injuries) Act 1948 (as amended) which provides that:

> In an action for damages for personal injuries . . . there shall be disregarded, in determining the reasonableness of any expenses, the possibility of avoiding those expenses or part of them by taking advantage of facilities available under the National Health Service Act 1977.

4.7.3 As a result of this provision, a defendant cannot argue that a claimant is being unreasonable in employing private medical treatment, including psychotherapy, even if such treatment is, at least in theory, available in any event on the NHS. It does not follow that a claimant will necessarily recover the private costs of medical treatment, including therapy. The issues to be considered in assessing the claim for cost of therapy were set out by Scott Baker J. in the *Flintshire* judgment:

> Here I have had to consider a number of factors before making an award. Is therapy necessary and appropriate to the extent that the claimant is likely to

benefit from it? Will he or she take it up and pay for it privately if therapy is available on the National Health Service? Is it wholly or partly attributable to the abuse? For how long is it likely to be required, how frequently and at what cost?'

4.7.4 In respect of therapy, the awards made by Scott Baker J. ranged between £5,000 and £10,000.

4.7.5 The claimant's lawyer should not overlook the fact that a claimant undergoing therapy will generally incur travelling expenses in getting to the therapist. In some cases, the claimant may incur a loss of earnings if treatment is time-consuming and/or so stressful that the claimant cannot work while undertaking the treatment.

4.8   COST OF CARE

4.8.1 In some cases where the claimant is so seriously injured by the alleged abuse that he needs a carer it will be necessary to cost this care. In *Various claimants* v. *Bryn Alyn Community Homes Ltd* Connell J. awarded a total of £3,800 for past costs of care and £17,650 for future cost of care. The claimant in this case was unable to leave home on his own to perform such tasks as signing on for benefits, attending the doctor and obtaining essential shopping such as clothes. The judge found this inability to leave home was a manifestation of the disorders from which he suffered as a result of the abuse to which he was subjected as a child. The cost of care was reduced to take into account that the claimant was abused by others for whom the defendant was not responsible. Further non-commercial costs of care were assessed at two-thirds of commercial rates.

4.9   DAMAGES UNDER THE HUMAN RIGHTS ACT 1998

4.9.1 In the case of *Z* v. *United Kingdom* [2001] 2 FLR 612 the European Court found that the four applicants, who were all children, had suffered a violation of Article 3 of the European Convention on Human Rights in that they had been subjected to inhuman and degrading treatment (see Chapter 3 para. 3.7.18–3.7.22). The court further found that the children did not have a remedy in domestic law as their claim had been struck out by the House of Lords in *X* v. *Bedfordshire County Council* [1995] 2 AC 633 (see paras 1.5.58–1.5.60). The children had been neglected by their parents but had not been removed from home despite the fact that the social workers documented that they were suffering severe abuse. The court therefore considered the appropriate awards of damages for these children. See Chapter 3 in respect of claims under the Human Rights Act.

4.9.2 The court described the injuries to the claimants as follows at paras. 113–14:

> The applicants submitted that they should be compensated for loss of future earnings and the costs of future medical expenses. Their experiences have, in different ways and to differing extents, blighted their lives. A substantial award should be made to enable them to enter life with a modicum of financial security, the potential to build an independent existence and the means to pay for therapeutic treatment and support. The applicants provided updated medical reports dated 16 May 2000 by Dr Jean Harris-Hendricks concerning their progress and prognosis for the future.
>
> (i) Z was described as having made a recovery from the serious depressive illness suffered at the time of her removal into care. While she was no longer suffering from any psychiatric illness, she had emotional, social and practical difficulties far beyond those normally carried by a girl of her age and was statistically vulnerable to anxiety and perhaps depressive illness in adult life. Her problems were classified as being of moderate severity. It was estimated that she would need psychotherapeutic treatment, outside the National Health Service, estimated at 60 to 100 sessions costing 70 to 90 pounds sterling (GBP) per session, to cope with her vulnerability particularly at periods of transition. She was likely to remain vulnerable on the labour market, though it was anticipated that she would be able to take on further education, sustain her own mental health and enter the work market. On her behalf, it was claimed: GBP 9,000 for the cost of future psychiatric treatment and GBP 40,000 for handicap on the labour market, a total of GBP 49,000.
>
> (ii) A had failed to appear, as agreed, for an interview. Dr Hendriks-Harris also commented on the lack of detailed information available concerning periods spent by him in care. She had however interviewed him on behalf of the local authority in May 1993 and had some records concerning his past treatment and problems. On that basis, she concluded that he was suffering from long-term psychiatric illness and had a poor prognosis for recovery. His ability to participate in education remained very poor. He was prone to aggression and had difficulty with normal life tasks. He was currently suffering from a reactive attachment disorder, directly resulting from severe parental neglect and abuse. The prognosis for the future was extremely bleak and he was likely to require intermittent hospitalisation. He was seriously handicapped on the labour market and was unlikely ever to hold down a job. Assuming that he might otherwise have been able to obtain low-paid manual employment earning GBP 15,000 per year and a normal working life to age 65, and taking into account uncertainties and accelerated receipt, he claimed GBP 150,000 in loss of future earnings. As he had a substantial and continuing need for psychiatric treatment outside the National Health Service (NHS), he claimed GBP 50,000 as a minimum estimate for future treatment. This made a total of GBP 200,000.
>
> (iii) B was still suffering from untreated post traumatic stress disorder and a chronic generalised anxiety disorder. He had horrific nightmares and untreated was likely to continue in the same disturbed emotional state. He

required open-ended psychiatric treatment into adult life, outside the limited provision of the NHS. This was estimated at a cost of GBP 50,000 minimum. He was vulnerable educationally and on the labour market due to chronic psychiatric disorder and limited social skills. His prospects of future employment were not as bleak as those of A, but he was likely to have substantial interruption in his employment. On the assumption of six gaps of one year, on an average manual wage of GBP 15,000 per year, he claimed GBP 90,000. This made a total of GBP 140,000.

(iv) C was described as happy in her adoptive home, though carrying a substantial burden about her origins and reminders of them. She was recurrently angry and anxious about her birth mother. She had some remaining behavioural problems which were likely to be containable with good substitute parenting. She was however more liable than other children to anxiety and there was a statistical risk of depression in adult life. She did not currently require psychiatric treatment although provision should be made for treatment in adolescence and adulthood. At a recommended 30 to 50 sessions at GBP 70 to 90, a claim was made for GBP 4,500 for future psychiatric treatment. GBP 10,000 was claimed for loss of future earnings making a total of GBP 14,500.

The reports commented that all the children would have benefited from compensation for their claims in 1994 as this would have allowed additional psychotherapeutic help, improving their prognosis. In A's case, his difficulties had been exacerbated by this lack of help while appropriate psychiatric, educational and environmental help might have substantially improved his prognosis. In B's case, more assistance in psychotherapeutic help could have reduced his current vulnerability and given a less severely gloomy prognosis. The reports also deplored that the psychotherapeutic referrals recommended for A and B in 1993 (for both) and 1998 (for B) had not been pursued by the local authority on their behalf and noted that one of the social workers had been told that there was no time or money for this work to be done.

4.9.3 The damages awarded by the European Court in Strasbourg in the case were as follows:

Z: £8,000 medical costs (£9,000 sought)
nil loss of earnings /vulnerability (£40,000 sought)
£32,000 general damages (£35,000 sought)

A: £50,000 medical costs (£50,000 sought)
£50,000 vulnerability on the labour market (£150,000 sought)
£32,000 general damages (£45,000 sought)

B: £50,000 medical costs (£50,000 sought)
£30,000 vulnerability on the labour market (£90,000 sought)
£32,000 general damages (£40,000 sought)

C: £4,000 medical costs (£4,500 sought)
nil vulnerability (£10,000 sought)
£32,000 general damages (£25,000 sought)

4.9.4 Under s.8 Human Rights Act 1998 the court has a discretion to award damages for breach of a Convention right. Section 8(4) of the 1998 Act specifies that in determining whether to make an award the court must take into account the principles applied by the European Court of Human Rights sitting in Strasbourg. However, in respect of damages the court has calculated damages on a case-by-case basis to meet the fairness of any particular situation. Awards of damages in Strasbourg have also reflected the differing levels of damages in the many member states. The Strasbourg court has not awarded exemplary or aggravated damages. A comprehensive review of the awards of damages by the European Court has now been published by the Law Commission (LC No. 266, Cm 4853).

CHAPTER 5

Limitation

5.1 Introduction and summary of the main limitation provisions
5.2 Claims in trespass to the person
5.3 Negligence claims under the 1980 Act
5.4 Negligence claims not covered by the 1980 Act
5.5 Disability
5.6 Concealment
5.7 Limitation decisions in abuse cases
5.8 Tactics
5.9 The future

5.1 INTRODUCTION AND SUMMARY OF THE MAIN LIMITATION PROVISIONS

5.1.1 A high proportion of the child abuse compensation cases now being litigated involve limitation issues. Some relate to events which took place 20 to 30 years ago or even longer. There are a number of reasons for this, including:

- one of the features of child abuse is that it is accompanied by secrecy and directions to the victim to remain silent;

- until recently, children who reported abuse were frequently not believed and having reported abuse once to a social worker or teacher did not do so again;

- reporting abuse is particularly difficult as the victim is often ashamed and embarrassed by the circumstances of the abuse and fearful of being treated as a potential risk to other children if he has been abused;

- the scope of responsibility of a public authority for a child in care and for the institutions where children are placed has only recently been recognised.

5.1.2 In the case of *Ablett and others* v. *Devon CC and others* (Sedley LJ, December 2000, unreported) when the defendants sought permission to appeal from the decision of Toulson J. refusing to order limitation to be heard as a preliminary issue, Sedley LJ described the specific difficulties in respect of abuse claims and stated:

> Inevitably there is a problem of limitation in these proceedings. I say 'inevitably' because it is in the nature of abuse of children by adults that it creates shame, fear and confusion, and these in turn produce silence. Silence is known to be one of the most pernicious fruits of abuse. It means that allegations commonly surface, if they do, only many years after the abuse has ceased.

5.1.3   Limitation is a complicated and challenging area for the practitioner. The number of reported decisions in this area illustrates the range of difficulties concerning limitation periods in personal injury and clinical negligence actions. There are to date few reported cases dealing with limitation and relating specifically to child abuse claims.

Summary of the main limitation provisions

5.1.4   The starting point for dealing with limitation is to identify the cause of action. Is the claim in trespass to the person/false imprisonment or in negligence/breach of duty? Following the House of Lords' decision in *Stubbings* v. *Webb* [1993] AC 498 the limitation period applicable to a claim in trespass to the person is *six* years from the date of the trespass or the date of the claimant's majority, whichever is the later (s.2 Limitation Act 1980). The court has no discretion to disapply this time limit. Therefore, in a child abuse claim based on trespass to the person, the claimant effectively has until the age of 24 (i.e. age 18 plus six years) in which to bring the claim. Thereafter the claim will be statute barred and the court has no discretion to permit a late claim. Date of knowledge of injury is irrelevant.

5.1.5   By contrast, in an action based on negligence the primary limitation period is three years from the claimant's date of knowledge or date of the claimant's majority, whichever is the later. Therefore, in a child abuse claim based on negligence, the claimant effectively has until the age of 21 before the claim is primarily statute barred. The provisions relating to date of knowledge set out in ss.11 and 14 Limitation Act 1980 may apply to these claims.

5.1.6   In a negligence claim, the court also has discretion to disapply the primary limitation period and permit a late claim. The rules applicable to the exercise of this discretion are set out in s.33 Limitation Act 1980.

5.1.7   Whatever the cause of action, the running of time may, in certain circumstances, be delayed or suspended by reason of disability (infancy/unsoundness of mind) or concealment: ss.28, 32 and 38 Limitation Act 1980.

5.1.8   The Limitation Act 1980 applies to the vast majority of cases but there remains a small number of very old cases, essentially those in which the cause of action accrued before 4 June 1954, which will fall to be dealt with under the older Limitation Acts.

5.2   CLAIMS IN TRESPASS TO THE PERSON

5.2.1   Before *Stubbings* v. *Webb*, trespass claims and negligence claims were dealt with according to the same rules. For example, in *Halford* v. *Brookes and another* [1991] 1 WLR 428 the Court of Appeal considered the position of the claimant who sued the defendants for murdering her daughter. It was alleged that the daughter had been murdered by the two defendants on 3 April 1978. The claimant issued a writ against the two defendants, alleging deliberate assault of her daughter, on 1 April 1987. The question of limitation was initially dealt with as a preliminary issue and the judge at first instance ruled that the claim was statute barred on the basis that it was brought after expiration of the three-year limitation period under s.11 Limitation Act 1980. The claimant appealed to the Court of Appeal, arguing that the court should exercise its discretion to allow her action to proceed pursuant to s.33 Limitation Act 1980. Her appeal was allowed. Both the judge at first instance and the Court of Appeal assumed, and it was not argued otherwise by the defendants, that the claim should be treated in the same way as a claim based on negligence, i.e. that the primary limitation period would be three years (s.11 Limitation Act 1980) and that the court had a discretion to disapply this limitation period (s.33 Limitation Act 1980). This remained the position until *Stubbings* v. *Webb*.

5.2.2   The claimant in *Stubbings* v. *Webb* had been sexually abused by her stepfather and stepbrother during her childhood. When she was over 30 years old, she issued proceedings against the abusers for deliberate assault. The assaults had begun some 24 years prior to the issue of proceedings and had ceased 15 years before the issue of proceedings. She claimed damages for psychiatric injury. Despite the fact that the events had occurred many years previously she claimed that she had not appreciated until much more recently that she had suffered psychiatric injury as a result of the sexual assaults. The claimant alleged that she did not have knowledge of significant injury until less than three years prior to the date of issue of proceedings. She sought to rely upon s.11(1) of the Limitation Act 1980, which provides:

> This section applies to any action for damages for negligence, nuisance or breach of duty (whether the duty exists by virtue of a contract or of provision made by or under a statute or independently of any contract of any sub provision) where the damages claimed by the Plaintiff for negligence, nuisance or breach of duty consists of or include damages in respect of personal injuries to the Plaintiff or any other person.

And s.11(4) which provides that:

> Except where subsection (5) below applies the period applicable is 3 years from –
>
> (a) The date on which the cause of action accrued; or
> (b) The date of knowledge (if later) of the injured person.

5.2.3 The claimant argued that her action was one for personal injuries within s.11(1) for which the primary limitation period was three years; further, that pursuant to s.11(4)(b) this three-year limitation period did not start to run until her 'date of knowledge' which was less than three years before she issued proceedings. The defendants argued that the claimant's claim, based as it was on intentional trespass to the person, did not fall within s.11; and that the claim was therefore subject to the six-year time limit prescribed by s.2 Limitation Act 1980, which states:

> An action founded on tort shall not be brought after the expiration of 6 years from the date on which the cause of action accrued.

The defendants argued that although this limitation period did not run during her minority, it had nevertheless expired many years prior to the issue of proceedings, and hence her action was time barred.

5.2.4 When the case came before the Court of Appeal, Bingham LJ (as he then was), giving the lead judgment, dealt with this issue shortly by stating that previous authorities had already construed the language of s.11 Limitation Act 1980 as embracing a claim based on unintentional and intentional trespass to the person. The defendants appealed to the House of Lords. The House of Lords, reversing the Court of Appeal, held that actions for intentional trespass to the person cannot be said to arise from 'negligence, nuisance or breach of duty' within s.11, but were actions of deliberate assault falling within s.2.

5.2.5 Since s.11 Limitation Act 1980 did not apply to a claim for trespass to the person, it followed that the claimant could not rely upon s.11(4)(b) Limitation Act 1980, i.e. the provision whereby time runs from the date of knowledge (if later than the date of accrual of the cause of action). Furthermore, she could not take advantage of the provisions of s.33 Limitation Act 1980 ('discretionary exclusion of time limit for actions in respect of personal injuries'), since plainly s.33 only applies to those claims falling within s.11.

5.2.6 The decision of the House of Lords in *Stubbings* v. *Webb* was considered by the European Court of Human Rights in *Stubbings* v. *United Kingdom* [1997] 1 FLR 105. The applicant alleged breaches of Articles 6, 8, and 14 of the European Convention on Human Rights. The European Court of

Human Rights found in favour of the UK on the basis that the existing limitation rules provided by ss.2, 11, 14 and 33 Limitation Act 1980 were within the government's margin of appreciation. The court found the provisions proportionate to the aims of securing finality and legal certainty. The rules were said to be entitled to protect defendants from stale claims and to prevent the injustice which might arise if the court were required to make decisions about long past events on the basis of unreliable evidence.

5.2.7   The European Court of Human Rights did, however, comment that:

> There has been a developing awareness in recent years of the range of problems caused by child abuse and its psychological effects on victims, and it is possible that the rules on limitation of actions applying in Member States of the Council of Europe may have to be amended to make special provision for this group of claimants in the near future.

5.2.8   The European Court set down a marker that the position of sexual abuse victims would need to be kept under review. For the present, *Stubbings* v. *Webb* is settled law subject to any reinterpretation following the decision of the House of Lords in *Lister* v. *Hesley Hall Limited* [2001] 2 WLR 1311. The decision in *Stubbings* v. *Webb* gives rise to the anomalous result that the perpetrator of abuse would be immune from proceedings after the expiry of the six-year limitation period whereas a person who *negligently* allows the abuse to take place, and is thus arguably less culpable than the abuser himself, remains open to a claim by reason of the discretion available to the court under s.33 Limitation Act 1980. This anomaly was confirmed in *S* v. *W and another (Child abuse: Damages)* [1995] 1 FLR 862 where the victim was out of time for bringing a claim against her father who abused her, but was able to bring a claim against her mother who negligently allowed the abuse to occur.

5.2.9   In *Lister* v. *Hesley Hall Ltd* the House of Lords found the defendants who ran a school vicariously liable for the torts committed by a warden who was its servant or agent. The claimants in this case had been sexually assaulted by the warden during their childhood in the early 1970s and had not issued proceedings until their late twenties. The House of Lords found the school vicariously liable for sexual assaults committed by the warden. Four of the speeches of the Lords analyse the position of the employer in terms of vicarious liability for breach of duty. Lord Millett makes clear that the liability of the employer is vicarious liability for the deliberate assault of the warden. There is no specific discussion of the limitation position. If the limitation period was an unextendable six-year period, then it appears the claims in the *Lister* case would have been statute barred by virtue of s.2 Limitation Act 1980 notwithstanding the finding of vicarious liability.

5.3   NEGLIGENCE CLAIMS UNDER THE 1980 ACT

5.3.1   The main provisions applicable to negligence are set out in s.11, 14 and 33 Limitation Act 1980. Section 11(4) provides that, except where subsec.5 (fatal claims) applies the period of limitation is three years from:

(a)   The date on which the cause of action accrued; or

(b)   The date of knowledge (if later) of the injured person.

Date of accrual of cause of action

5.3.2   A cause of action requires the existence of every fact which it would be necessary to prove to found a right to a judgment. In a negligence case this requires the existence of a duty of care; a breach of that duty; and damage arising from the breach. In a child abuse case, it is important not to overlook the fact that the cause of action will not accrue until damage has been caused. This can be a complex issue since there may be cases of indecent assault where no immediate physical pain or injury is caused to the victim at the time of the assault. Psychiatric damage may arise later. Practically, however, the issue is unlikely to be relevant since by s.11(4)(b) the limitation period does not start to run until the claimant first knows that he has suffered damage. The practitioner will therefore be mainly concerned to identify the claimant's date of knowledge, rather than the date of accrual of the cause of action.

Date of knowledge

5.3.3   The meaning of 'date of knowledge' is set out in s.14(1):

Subject to Section 1 (a) . . . references to a person's date of knowledge are references to the date on which he first had knowledge of the following facts:

(a) That the injury in question was significant; and

(b) That the injury was attributable in whole or in part to the act or omission which is alleged to constitute negligence, nuisance or breach of duty; and

(c) The identity of the Defendant; and

(d) If it is alleged that the act or omission was that of a person other than the Defendant, the identity of that person and the additional facts supporting the bringing of an action against that Defendant.

and knowledge that any acts or omissions did or did not as a matter of law involve negligence, nuisance or breach of duty is irrelevant.

5.3.4   Section 14(1) is conjunctive, i.e. knowledge of all four matters is required. It is necessary to consider each of the four matters in turn.

Section 14(1)(a): That the injury in question was significant

This is defined by s.14(2):

> An injury is significant if the person whose date of knowledge is in question would have reasonably have considered it sufficiently serious to justify him instituting proceedings for damages against a defendant who did not dispute liability and was able to satisfy a judgment.

In *Dobbie* v. *Medway Health Authority* [1994] 1 WLR 1234 (a clinical negligence case) Sir Thomas Bingham MR held that:

> The requirement that the injury of which a Plaintiff has knowledge should be 'significant' is . . . directed solely to the quantum of the injury and not to the Plaintiff's evaluation of its cause, nature or unusualness. Time does not run against a Plaintiff, even if he is aware of the injury, if he would reasonably have accepted it as a fact of life or not worth bothering about. It is otherwise if the injury is reasonably to be considered a sufficient serious injury within the statutory definition: time then runs (subject to the requirements of attributability) even if the Plaintiff believes the injury to be normal or properly caused.

The Law Commission summarised the effect of this and other decisions interpreting this section:

> There are likely to be few injuries where a Plaintiff can reasonably consider that it is not worth suing on the basis that the hypothetical Defendant posited by Section 14 (2) both admits liability and has the means to satisfy the judgment. The threshold set by the subsection is, therefore, *extremely* low. Provided that the gravity of the injury exceeds this low threshold, time will run against the Plaintiff even though it is subsequently discovered that the injury is far more serious than first thought.

5.3.5   The first reported application of s.14(1)(a) to a child abuse claim was the case of *Stubbings* v. *Webb*. In this case, ultimately the House of Lords was to conclude that s.14 Limitation Act 1980 was irrelevant to the claim since, as discussed above, a claim for intentional trespass to the person did not fall within those provisions. In the Court of Appeal interpretation of the subparagraph of s.14(1) was considered in some detail and the judgment remains relevant in considering how the courts are likely to interpret s.14(1) in abuse cases.

5.3.6   The claimant was born in January 1957 and reached 18 in January 1975. She alleged that between the ages of 2 and 14 she had been sexually and physically assaulted by the defendants. The assaults by the first defendant (adoptive father) were indecent assaults, the assaults by the second defendant (the son) included rape. In the late 1970s and early 1980s she suffered from mental illness and saw a number of doctors who made a variety of diagnoses. One doctor noted that the claimant had suffered 'sexual interference during childhood' but did not diagnose that this may have been causative of her psychiatric problems. It was only in September 1984 that the claimant met Dr Baker, a psychiatrist specialising in sexual abuse, who told her that her psychological problems might be linked with abuse she suffered during childhood. She issued proceedings in August 1987, i.e. within three years of receiving that diagnosis.

5.3.7   In the Court of Appeal Bingham LJ (as he then was) first considered the application of s.14(1)(a) in relation to the assaults allegedly committed by Mr Webb senior and formulated the issue as follows:

> Did the plaintiff within three years of her majority or at any time before 18 August 1984 (i.e. three years before the issue of the Writ) know that she suffered an impairment of her physical or mental condition such that she would reasonably have considered it sufficiently serious to justify her instituting proceedings for damages against the Defendant who did not dispute liability and who was able to satisfy a judgment? So far as impairment of the Plaintiff's physical condition is concerned, the answer must in my opinion be negative. In giving that answer I do not underestimate, dismiss or in any way minimise the distress, humiliation and degradation which conduct of the kind alleged against Mr Webb involved for a sensitive child. There is nothing in the indecent assaults and conduct alleged against him which caused her *physical* injury. There is nothing which could ground an indictment for causing actual bodily harm, nothing which could be particularised under the heading 'particulars of personal injury'. There were, of course, the assaults which the Plaintiff said she suffered from Mr Webb when she was 15, which caused her nosebleeds, but in the state of society as it existed in the late 1970s and early 1980s the Plaintiff would not reasonably have considered these assaults sufficiently serious to justify proceedings even against an acquiescent and credit ready Defendant. The rarity of such claims, if indeed there were any at all, is proof enough of that, given that domestic violence is not a recent phenomenon . . . When one turns to impairment of the Plaintiff's mental condition the position is somewhat different. The Plaintiff *could* have sued for the immediate distress caused to her by these incidents, but if this distress was regarded as a superficial emotional response without any long-term consequence I do not think the Plaintiff would reasonably have regarded it as sufficiently serious to justify proceedings. The Plaintiff did know, probably within three years of her majority and certainly well before 18 August 1984, that her mental condition was impaired sufficiently seriously to justify proceedings against an acquiescent and creditworthy Defendant.

5.3.8   Bingham LJ then considered the same test in relation to the claimant's claim against the son:

> So with reference only to her claim against Stephen I ask: did the Plaintiff within three years of her majority or at any time before 18 August 1984 know that she suffered an impairment of her physical or mental condition such that she would reasonably have considered it sufficiently serious to justify her instituting proceedings against an acquiescent and creditworthy Defendant? Again I consider physical impairment first, this time in the context of two completed acts of rape. Even in the absence of gratuitous violence, rape involves a violent violation of the victim's person, made worse in this case by the fact that the Plaintiff was aged 12 and a virgin. But in purely physical terms the impairment of the Plaintiff's condition was minor. As in Mr Webb's case there would have been very little to support an indictment of causing actual bodily harm or to plead as particulars of personal injury. There is no doubt but that the Plaintiff *could* have sued Stephen on reaching her majority, successfully if her allegations were established, but given the passage of over five years between these acts and her eighteenth birthday, by which time she had left home, I do not think she would reasonably have considered this purely physical impairment sufficiently serious to justify the institution of proceedings against an acquiescent and creditworthy Defendant. So far as mental impairment is concerned, I find no reason to differentiate between Stephen and Mr Webb; the same conclusion must in my view follow in each case.

5.3.9   Nolan LJ (as he then was) concurred:

> The question posed by the 1980 Act . . . is . . . whether . . . she should reasonably have considered her injuries sufficiently serious to justify proceedings. It may well be argued that, even if her physical injuries were relatively minor, the feelings of outrage, humiliation and despair which she must have experienced if her account is true could hardly have failed to result in mental injury. But in my judgment the available evidence does not show that she should reasonably have regarded her physical or mental injuries at that stage as sufficiently serious to justify the institution of proceedings for damages, even against hypothetically solvent and unresisting Defendants. It has to be borne in mind that until the last few years proceedings of the present kind were unheard of. The first reported civil action for rape appears to have been *W* v. *Meah* (1986) . . . I think it is also reasonable to assume that when the framers of the Limitation Act 1980 defined injuries in terms of impairment of a person's physical or mental condition they are unlikely to have had in mind the psychological traumata directly caused by domestic sexual abuse . . . different considerations have arisen since then, as a result of television programmes . . . and subsequent developments such as the Cleveland Inquiry and Child Line and increased awareness of the mental scars which sexual abuse inflicts.

5.3.10   Sir Nicholas Browne Wilkinson VC (as he then was) stated:

> In ordinary terms, I have no doubt that quite apart from any long-term psychiatric harm the alleged sexual abuse and rape caused significant injuries.

The gross interference with the physical privacy and integrity of the Plaintiff would justify a substantial award of damages in itself, even if no long-term psychiatric damage was caused.

But the word significant in Section 14 does not bear its ordinary meaning. For the purposes of that Section, an injury is only significant if the Plaintiff would 'reasonably have considered it sufficiently serious to justify her instituting proceedings for damages' against her adoptive father and brother assuming that they would admit liability and be good for the damages. In deciding what she would 'reasonably have considered' one has to have regard to the circumstances attaining in 1975, when she attained full age. The question is whether, in 1979, the Plaintiff acted reasonably in not then suing Mr Webb and Stephen Webb for the serious wrongs alleged to have been done to her. In my judgment it is important not to consider the question by reference to the social habits and conventions of 1991. Over recent years, for the first time civil actions have been brought by victims of adult rape against their assailant. As to actions against child abusers, this is apparently the first case in which the alleged victim has sought to sue her abusers. *In the present climate and state of knowledge it would in my judgment be very difficult, if not impossible, for a Plaintiff coming of age in the late 1980s to establish that she acted 'reasonably' in not starting proceedings alleging child abuse within three years of attaining her majority.* But we are concerned with the reasonableness of the Plaintiff's behaviour in the period 1975–78. At that time civil actions based on sexual assaults were unknown in this country. In my judgment it was accordingly reasonable for the Plaintiff not to have considered the injuries done to her sufficiently serious to justify starting proceedings against her adoptive father and brother. In 1975 such proceedings were unthought of and it was therefore reasonable for her not to have started such proceedings. (emphasis added)

5.3.11 One issue that arises in child abuse claims is whether there may be a date of knowledge later than the date of the abuse in circumstances where the sexual assaults do not result in any immediate injury or physical pain. Rather than consciously suffering immediate injury the victim may be persuaded by the abuser that the abuse is affection. Where this is the case and there is no physical injury, psychiatric injury may not occur until a later date when the victim realises the nature of the abuse and the falseness of the abuser's claim that the treatment was affectionate. In such cases it may be reasonable for the claimant to argue that he did not know at the time of the abuse that damage would result. This argument would be much more difficult to sustain in a case involving a penetrative sexual assault, i.e. sexual intercourse or buggery, as it is unlikely there will be no physical injury/pain at the time of the assault.

5.3.12 In some cases a claimant alleges that he complained about abuse at the time that it was committed, or wished to complain but felt that complaints were pointless. In these circumstances a court could be expected to conclude that the claimant was aware at that time of having suffered an injury. Theoretically, it could be argued that a claimant might recognise indecency by an adult as being wrong, without necessarily recognising that he or she had been damaged by it. In practice, a court is likely to conclude that a complaint, or the desire to make a complaint, is proof of knowledge of injury.

5.3.13 An important pointer to knowledge of significant injury might be the claimant discussing the abuse with his general practitioner. The claimant's GP and hospital notes should be scrutinised and any reference to the abuse would normally be taken as indicating the claimant had knowledge of having suffered a significant injury at the date of the record. In *Stubbings* v. *Webb* Bingham LJ noted that in 1976 the claimant's GP had recorded 'sexual interference during childhood' in her medical notes. Bingham LJ did not regard this as amounting to evidence of knowledge of significant injury. However, as the Court of Appeal stressed, this was at a time (1976) when knowledge and understanding of the extent and effects of sexual abuse had barely begun to develop; the position might be different now given the much greater awareness of child abuse.

5.3.14 In *Various claimants* v. *Bryn Alyn Community Homes Ltd* (Connell J., 26 June 2001, unreported) the judge in considering the date of knowledge arguments raised by claimants who had been sexually and physically abused in a care home, stated in paras. 29–30:

> Here each Claimant must have known at the time that he or she was the victim of such an assault which caused at the least some distress and more often profound disquiet, pain and resentment. They knew in ordinary language that they had been injured in a manner which could not properly be described as trivial, but which was significant. They also knew, as I conclude, that the distress suffered was attributable to the actions upon which they now rely to found their claims. Their situations were similar to that of the victim, Lesley Stubbings in *Stubbings* v. *Webb* who had been raped and persistently sexually abused, but who claimed that she did not realise that she had suffered sufficiently serious injury to justify starting proceedings for damages until she realised there might be a causal link between psychiatric problems suffered in adult life and her sexual abuse as a child. Lord Griffiths said at page 126D

> 'I have the greatest difficulty in accepting that a woman who knows she has been raped does not know she has suffered a significant injury'.

> In my view the same applies to a young person who knows that he or she has been assaulted on a regular basis; or who has been buggered, masturbated or fondled in an inappropriate way. Of course the realisation of the extent of the injury may grow with time, as may the injury itself; but in every case I conclude that these unhappy victims had the relevant knowledge before they left the community.

5.3.15 This case (which is due to heard in the Court of Appeal in February 2002) supports the view that it will be exceptional for claimants who suffered obvious physical abuse as well as sexual abuse in childhood to be able to establish a date of knowledge later than the act of abuse itself. In that case the judge allowed the claims to proceed by exercising his discretion pursuant to s.33 Limitation Act 1980.

Section 14(1)(b): That the injury was attributable in whole or in part to the act or omission which is alleged to constitute nuisance, negligence or breach of duty

5.3.16 The question that arises under this subsection is what is meant by 'attributable' and whether it entails the claimant's knowledge of fault. The authorities on this point are not easy to reconcile. In *Broadley* v. *Guy Clapham & Co* [1994] 4 All ER 439 the Court of Appeal held that the reference to 'negligence, nuisance or breach of duty' merely identified the act or omission to which the paragraph referred without adding any connotation of fault. This approach was reaffirmed by the Court of Appeal in *Dobbie* v. *Medway Health Authority* [1994] 1 WLR 1234. In that case Bingham LJ emphasised that to import an element of fault into s.14(1) would 'obviate the purpose of the subsection'.

5.3.17 The test set out by Hoffman LJ (as he then was) in *Hallam-Eames* v. *Merrett Syndicates Limited* [1996] 7 Med LR 122 at 125 has a different emphasis. He stated:

> If all that was necessary was that the Plaintiff should have known that the damage was attributable to an act or omission of the Defendant, the statute would have said so. Instead it speaks of the damage being attributable to 'the act or omission which is alleged to constitute negligence'. In other words the act or omission of which the Plaintiff must have knowledge must be that which is causally relevant for the purposes of an allegation of negligence . . . It is this idea of causal relevance which various judges of this court have tried to express by saying the Plaintiff must know 'the essence of the act or omission to which the injury is attributable' . . . Or 'the essential thrust of the case' . . . or that one should 'look at the way the Plaintiff puts his case, distil what he is complaining about and ask whether he had in broad terms knowledge of the fact on which that complaint is based.

5.3.18 In a case involving the abuse of a child in a residential home, the claim will be based on a breach of duty by the abuser for which the employer is vicariously liable (following *Lister*) and/or negligence by the employer in failing to prevent the abuse. However, it might not be sufficient for the claimant simply to know that he has been abused by staff in the home. It will be necessary for him to know or be able to ascertain something about the failings in the system which allowed such incidents to happen and enables him to allege negligence. In many cases a claimant is likely to know that the institution in which he was sexually assaulted was run in such a way as to allow staff to abuse children. If the assaults took place against the background of a harsh regime where children were fearful of physical assaults and no one protected him against the assaults he may have the necessary knowledge to allege negligence from the date of the assaults. Ignorance on the part of the claimant that, as a matter of law, these facts would give rise to a cause of action is irrelevant.

5.3.19 However, it is possible that there are factors relating to the allegations that can ultimately be made in respect of the defendant's negligence that might not be known or ascertainable earlier. For example it might not be known to the claimant (nor ascertainable) that checks by the defendant on a warden employed at a children's home revealed convictions of the warden for sexual offences prior to his employment by the defendant. If the defendant negligently employed the warden and he then sexually abused the claimant, it might be argued that the claimant did not (and could not ascertain) that the defendant had been negligent in disregarding these convictions. This failure might be the only basis on which negligence could be alleged. In these circumstances it is arguable that the claimant's relevant date of knowledge was the date the claimant discovered (or could discover) that the defendant knew of and ignored the warden's convictions.

Section 14(1)(c) The identity of the defendant

5.3.20 In relation to (c), it would be unusual for a claimant to be unaware of the identity of his abuser. In many cases the claimant will also, at the moment of the abuse, be aware of the identity of the abuser's employer.

Section 14(1)(d) If it is alleged that the act or omission was that of a person other than the defendant, the identity of that person and the additional facts supporting the bringing of an action against the defendant

5.3.21 In relation to (d) a claimant might argue that he had no idea that those responsible for operating the home, e.g. the local authority, had any responsibility. It is arguable therefore that a claimant might not necessarily possess actual knowledge of the identity of the defendant who is vicariously liable for the actions of whoever abused him. The question then would be whether the claimant had constructive knowledge pursuant to s.14(3) Limitation Act 1980, as discussed below.

Actual/constructive knowledge

5.3.22 Section 14(3) Limitation Act 1980 provides that the claimant's date of knowledge includes:

> Knowledge which he might reasonably have expected to acquire:
> (a) From facts observable to or ascertainable by him; or
> (b) From facts ascertainable by him with the help of medical or other appropriate expert advice which it is reasonable for him to seek;

> But a person shall not be fixed under this subsection with knowledge of a fact ascertainable only with the help of expert advice so long as he has taken all reasonable steps to obtain (and, where appropriate, to act on) that advice.

5.3.23 Constructive knowledge may be imputed to the claimant in respect of each of (a), (b) and (c) and (d) in s.14 (1). The claimant's knowledge will include knowledge of facts which he or she could have been expected to acquire directly or with the help of medical, legal or other expect advice which it was reasonable to seek. As a result of the decision of the Court of Appeal in *Smith* v. *Leicestershire Health Authority* [1998] Lloyd's Rep Med 77 the test is an objective rather than a subjective one, i.e. the question is whether a reasonable person in the claimant's position would have observed or ascertained the relevant facts or sought the relevant advice in order to ascertain these facts. The claimant's personal characteristics which might distinguish him from the reasonable person should be disregarded.

Section 33 Limitation Act 1980

5.3.24 Section 33 Limitation Act 1980 gives the court an unfettered discretion to disapply the three-year time limit in negligence cases. The claimant may be permitted, where it is equitable, to proceed with an action notwithstanding the expiry of the primary limitation period.

5.3.25 Section 33(1) provides:

> If it appears to the Court that it would be equitable to allow an action to proceed having regard to the degree to which:
>> (a) The provisions of Section 11 or 12 of this Act prejudice the Plaintiff or any person whom he represents; and
>> (b) Any decision of the Court under this subsection would prejudice the Defendant or any person whom he represents;
>
> The Court may direct that those provisions shall not apply to this action, or shall not apply to any specified cause of action to which the action relates.

5.3.26 The court has to examine the respective prejudices that will occur to the claimant if the claim remains statute barred and to the defendant if it is allowed to proceed. In determining the type and amount of prejudice the court is required by s.33(3) to look at 'all the circumstances of the case', without restriction and in particular with reference to six specified factors.

5.3.27 Subsection (3) sets out these six factors:

> (a) The length of, and the reasons for, delay on the part of the Claimant
>
> (b) The extent to which, having regard to the delay, the evidence adduced or likely to be adduced by the Claimant or the Defendant is or is likely to be less cogent than if the action had been brought within the time limit allowed by Section 11.

    (c)   The conduct of the Defendant after the cause of action arose, including the extent (if any) to which the Defendant responded to reasonable requests for information made by the Claimant for information or inspection for the purpose of ascertaining facts which were or might be relevant to the Claimant's cause of action against the Defendant.

    (d)   The duration of any disability of the Claimant arising after the date of the accrual of the cause of action.

    (e)   The extent to which the Claimant acted promptly and reasonably once he knew whether or not the act or omission of the Defendant, to which the injury was attributable, might be capable at that time of giving rise to an action for damages.

    (f)   The steps, if any, taken by the Claimant to obtain medical, legal or other expert advice and the nature of any such advice he may have received.

5.3.28   The burden of establishing that the court should exercise its discretion in favour of the claimant rests upon the claimant. It is necessary in each case first, to consider in general terms the question of prejudice to claimant and prejudice to defendant and then to consider the six matters identified under s.33(3) with reference to the facts of each individual case.

Prejudice to the parties

5.3.29   If the claim remains statute barred, the claimant is prejudiced in being unable to sue for compensation. The court must therefore consider, in general terms, the strength of the claimant's case on liability. If the claimant has a weak case, then little prejudice is likely to be caused to him by refusing to allow the claim to proceed. Similarly, in cases where the defendant has no defence other than limitation, the claimant will be greatly prejudiced by the case being statute barred. The value of the claimant's claim is also relevant to this test; if the claim is of nuisance value only then the prejudice to the defendant is all the greater, particularly if the claimant is publicly funded.

5.3.30   The question of prejudice to the defendants was considered by Bingham LJ in the Court of Appeal in *Stubbings* v. *Webb*:

> The most potent point relied on by the Webbs in opposing exercise of the Court's discretion in the Plaintiff's favour is the lapse of time since these events occurred. Over 30 years have elapsed since the earliest, and 20 years since the latest, of the acts complained of. Twelve years elapsed between the latest of the acts complained of and the first notification of complaint to either Mr Webb or Steven. Steven, now 38, faces claims arising out of his conduct aged 17. It is urged with great force that the Webbs should not now be required to answer these very stale accusations. There may well be compelling social arguments against raking over such ancient embers.
>
> The Plaintiff urges that her case has the appearance of truth. She voiced complaints long before she had any litigious axes to grind. She can rely, she

says on an admission made by Mr Webb to her medical advisor. If she is right, as she may be, the Webbs' inexcusable behaviour has blighted years of her life. Even now, they should be held responsible and may recompense for the wrong they did to her.

5.3.31 In this case the Court of Appeal found that the claimant's case should be allowed to proceed.

5.3.32 One consequence of 'prejudice to the claimant' test, is that it means that the prospects of a successful s.33 application are inextricably tied up with questions of liability and quantum in the case as a whole. This means that there are few benefits in determining liability as a preliminary issue. As a s.33 decision cannot be reached by the court without full investigation of the issues of liability and quantum, there may be no or very little saving in costs by having the matters heard separately. Further, a preliminary hearing in respect of limitation requires the claimant to give evidence twice in respect of the details of the abuse and this may be unnecessarily onerous for the claimant.

Section 33(3)(a) The length and reasons for delay on the part of the claimant

5.3.33 In *Coad* v. *Cornwall and Isles of Scilly Health Authority* [1997] 1 WLR 189 the Court of Appeal pointed out that the test in s.33(3)(a) was a subjective one and was not a test based on 'reasonableness'. As Rose LJ pointed out at p. 198:

> The concept of reasonableness was clearly well known to the draftsman of this legislation. It appears with mantra-like frequency in section 14(2) and (3) and section 14A(7) and (10) as well as in section 33(3)(e). The omission of that concept from section 33(3)(a) is therefore striking.

5.3.34 Ward LJ described how the test in section 33(3)(a) Limitation Act 1980 requires the court to conduct an inquiry into two factual situations. The first is the length of the delay; the second is the reason for the delay on the part of the claimant. To add 'on the part of the claimant' indicates that it is a subjective inquiry in which the court is there engaged. Having found what the reason is, the court must decide whether it is a good or bad reason or, in the language of Russell LJ in *Halford* v. *Brookes* [1991] 1 WLR 428, whether the claimant is culpable or not. There is no requirement that the claimant's reasons for delay are objectively reasonable; the words 'on the part of the claimant' indicate that it is a subjective inquiry. The issue is whether the claimant's belief in certain circumstances giving rise to the delay is a genuine belief.

5.3.35 In many cases concerned with abuse of children in residential homes the length of delay on the part of the claimant may have been substantial and the claimant will need to persuade the court to exercise its discretion.

5.3.36 Among the reasons for substantial delay which could be advanced by a claimant are the following:

- Abuse is taboo, it creates shame and fear and silences the victim who feels unable to speak about it. It may be helpful for the psychiatrist to establish the circumstances in which the claimant ultimately came to disclose the abuse to demonstrate that these circumstances had not prevailed previously. For example, many claimants first disclose abuse when placed in positions where the police require them to give the information as part of a wider inquiry. The defendant's solicitor should be alert to earlier references to abuse in medical records since, if the claimant has been able to disclose to a medical practitioner, then it is more difficult for him to argue that he felt unable to speak about the abuse at all.

- The claimant complained at the time of the abuse but the complaint was not investigated and/or believed or the claimant was punished for reporting the abuse. In these circumstances it may be reasonable for the claimant to argue he did not report the abuse again as he assumed nobody would believe him.

- If the claimant was in the care of the defendant, then a further reason for delay may be the failure of the defendant to provide counselling to the claimant to help him address and discuss the abuse he had suffered.

- The claimant was not aware that a civil remedy was open to him. Ignorance of the law will not prevent the claimant acquiring the requisite knowledge of injury under s.14 Limitation Act 1980. However, ignorance of the existence of a civil remedy was recognised in *Halford* v. *Brookes* as a justifiable reason for the claimant's delay in bringing proceedings. Many claimants who allege abuse in institutions are only aware of a civil remedy once there has been publicity, e.g. by registration requirements for a multi-party action or a police inquiry in which the claimant has been advised by the police to consult solicitors about the possibility of a claim.

Section 33(3)(b) The effect of delay on the cogency of the evidence

5.3.37 The essential question is whether it is possible to have a fair trial of the issues. In many cases the criminal trial of the abuser is the precipitating factor for the claimant to discuss the abuse and investigate a civil claim. The fact that a criminal trial of the abuser is still possible gives a strong indication that the evidence is still sufficiently cogent for a civil trial.

Other points include:

- Whether records pertaining to the claimant's time in care still exist or have been destroyed. However, if they have been destroyed by the defendant then this may be relevant to the conduct of the defendant (see s.33(2)(c)).

- Whether relevant witnesses are still alive and/or contactable, and if they are, whether their memories are so impaired by the passage of time that a fair trial of the issues is impossible.

- Where the abuser has died without being prosecuted or convicted, the defendant is prejudiced by being unable to set any evidence against the allegations being made.

- The defendant may be able to argue prejudice in respect of the investigation of causation of damage in circumstances where the claimant might have been abused elsewhere (e.g. in the family or in another home for which the defendant is not responsible).

Section 33(3)(c) Conduct of the defendant after the cause of action arose, including the defendant's response to requests for information

5.3.38 If the claimant has requested social services notes and there has been a long delay in the defendant responding to this request the claimant may be able to rely on this delay. Other examples of delay by the defendant may be refusal to provide the correct identity of the defendant.

Section 33(3)(d) The duration of any disability of the claimant

5.3.39 A person suffering from unsoundness of mind at the time of issue of proceedings may still have to take advantage of s.33(3)(d) because by virtue of the wording of s.28 Limitation Act 1980, the running of the limitation period is only suspended if the claimant was under a disability on the date when the cause of action accrued. If the claimant was not under a disability on the date of accrual of the cause of action, subsequent periods of disability become an issue for the court to consider in the exercise of its discretion. In *Yates* v. *Thakeham Tiles Ltd* ([1995] PIQR P135) the Court of Appeal held that to come within the specific provisions of s.33(3)(d) the claimant's disability had to come within the definition of s.38 Limitation Act 1980. However, subsequent authorities have indicated that where the claimant is not under a disability for the purposes s.38 Limitation Act 1980 'disabilities' (in the broader sense) from which he may none the less suffer may be taken into account as part of the general 'circumstances of the case'. In *Davies* v. *Jacobs and others* ([1999] Lloyd's Rep Med 72) Brooke LJ stated:

148

Mr Davies was never under a disability (see s.38(2) and (3) of the 1980 Act for the meaning of this word in this context). On the other hand, I accept Mr Henderson's submission that for much of the relevant period he was suffering from drug-induced hypomania to a mild degree, which cannot have assisted clarity of thought, and this is a matter which can be taken into account as one of 'the circumstances of the case'. He also underwent brain surgery in October 1995 and five weeks of radiotherapy in early 1996 which cannot have been conducive to the conduct of difficult litigation.

There is no reason why the same logic should not apply to psychiatric injuries suffered by a victim of child abuse in circumstances where the claimant is seriously affected by psychiatric symptoms but these symptoms are of a severity such that they do not place him under a disability for the purposes of the Mental Health Act 1983. Such psychiatric problems including periods of self-harm may none the less affect his ability to instruct a solicitor and to conduct litigation.

Section 33(3)(e) The extent to which the claimant acted promptly and reasonably once he knew whether or not the act or omission of the defendant to which the injury was attributable might be capable at that time of giving rise to a cause of action

5.3.40 Section 33(3)(e) is concerned exclusively with the situation where the claimant has found out that he has a cause of action in law. If he acts promptly thereafter, he will place himself in a stronger position in respect of this element of s.33.

Section 33(3)(f) The steps, if any, taken by the claimant to obtain medical, legal or other expert advice and the nature of any such advice he may have received

5.3.41 The point which may arise in child abuse claims under this subparagraph is the position of a claimant who has taken earlier legal advice but been advised he cannot bring proceedings because there is no cause of action against a public authority and/or because his action is limitation barred. A similar situation arose in *Halford* v. *Brookes*. In that case the claimant, although she was interested in pursuing a claim against those she believed to be responsible for the death of her daughter, was told by her first solicitors that the only remedy she had was an application to the Criminal Injuries Compensation Board. In the light of that advice Lord Donaldson MR concluded that:

> She cannot be blamed for accepting this advice or failing to ask other solicitors or Counsel for a second opinion, when for some reason she consulted new solicitors in July 1985 and they advised her that there was another civil remedy, she immediately applied for Legal Aid and upon this being granted at once issued her Writ.

5.3.42   In the subsequent case of *Das* v. *Ganju* [1999] 8 PIQR P260, Sir Christopher Staughton considered subsections (3)(e) and (f) of Section 33 as follows:

> I turn to items (e) and (f). In my view this case turns on the factor of wrongful advice. In no respect whatever do I think that there is ground for criticism of Mr and Mrs Das personally; and I say that despite the fact that the letter to their solicitors from the Medical Defence Union was not answered. They have, as it seems to me, struggled against misfortune, both legal and medical, for 20 years, without any fault of their own.
>
> But are they to be criticised for the fault of their lawyers? On this topic we were referred to *Whitfield* v. *North Durham Health Authority* [1995] 6 Med LR 32. There Waite LJ said at p. 35:
>
>> 'In a discretionary jurisdiction where the court is required to have regard to "all the circumstances of the case" it would clearly be inappropriate to look for hard and fast rules, but counsel were agreed in this court that the section must be read as incorporating one underlying principle. In the process of assessing equity and balancing prejudice which the section enjoins, a party's action or inaction cannot be divorced from the acts or omissions of his legal representative. The principle in that respect is analogous to that applying in cases of striking out for want of prosecution.'
>
> If that passage means that as a matter of law anything done by the lawyers must be visited on the client, it cannot in my view be reconciled with other authority. It appears to have been a concession which the court accepted. The other authority is *Thompson* v. *Brown* [1981] 1 WLR 744 and the speech of Lord Diplock at pp. 750 and 752, which I do not set out for fear of lengthening this judgment even further. I would also return to *Halford* v. *Brooks*, where again it is said that it is no reproach to the plaintiff that he has received the wrong legal advice.
>
> In this case I have no doubt that there will be prejudice to Mrs Das if her present action is struck out and she is left with a claim that must be somewhat speculative against solicitors and counsel. She will then have two hurdles to overcome – proof of the merits of her action against Dr Ganju, and proof that her counsel and solicitors were negligent.
>
> She will also, as the judge said, have to start again. He added that she will have to demonstrate that this action would have succeeded. That is not an absolute requirement. But it is a necessity if she is to recover the full amount of any damages that she would have been entitled to in this action.

5.3.43   This case confirms that the claimant may not be penalised where the claimant has sought to bring an action earlier but failed in fact to do so because of the advice of his solicitors.

5.4 NEGLIGENCE CLAIMS NOT COVERED BY THE 1980 ACT

5.4.1 The Limitation Act 1980 did not come into force until 1 May 1981. Under para. 9 Sched. 2 Limitation Act 1980 it is provided that:

> Nothing in any provision of this act shall –
>> (a) enable any action to be brought which was barred by this act or (as the case may) be the Limitation Act 1939 before the relevant date (being 1 August 1980).

It is therefore necessary to consider whether the client's claim was barred by the Limitation Act 1939 on 1 August 1980.

5.4.2 Section 2 Limitation Act 1939 provided that the limitation period for bringing an action in contract or tort was six years. However, the Law Reform (Limitation of Actions) Act 1954 amended s.2 Limitation Act 1939 so as to provide that in the case of an action for negligence nuisance or breach of duty including a claim for personal injuries the time limit was three years not six years.

5.4.3 Pursuant to s.22 Limitation Act 1939 any time limit was suspended while a client was under a disability by reason of age until he reached 21. When the 1963 Act came into force, it specifically provided that the defence provided by s.2(1) Limitation Act 1939 as amended (that is as amended to provide a three year limitation period rather than six years) could be excluded.

5.4.4 The position of claims arising prior to 1954 was considered in the speech of Lord Bridge in the House of Lords in *Arnold* v. *Central Electricity Generating Board* [1988] AC 228, [1987] 3 All ER 694 at 701:

> The only time bar of which defendants are in terms deprived of by this sub-section is the three-year time bar which accrued under section 2(1) of the 1939 Act as amended in 1954. This is made clear both by the words in parenthesis and by section 15 of the Act. There is certainly no context in section 1 which would permit the reference to s 2(1) of the 1939 Act to be construed as a reference to that subsection as originally enacted. The words in parenthesis emphasise the contrary. This is perhaps sufficient to lead to the conclusion that there is nothing in s.1 of the 1963 Act which in any way affects the availability after 1963, as before, of a defence which had accrued on the expiry of the six year period applicable to any cause of action in respect of personal injuries accruing before 4 June 1954 . . . I would hold that the 1963 Act did not operate to deprive any defendant of the time bar which had accrued on the expiry of the six-year limitation period prescribed by s 2(1) of the 1939 Act in its original form, which by virtue of s.7 of the 1954 Act continued to govern any cause of action in a personal injury case accruing before 4 June 1954.

5.4.5   The position the House of Lords dealt with in *Arnold* v. *Central Electricity Generating Board* was therefore those actions which became time barred before the 1954 Act introduced a three-year time bar rather than a six-year time bar, i.e. those accruing before 4 June 1954. Claimants with an action accruing after 1954 will be able to rely on the retrospective provisions of the 1963, 1975 and 1980 Limitation Acts.

5.4.6   In the case of *McDonnell* v. *Congregation of Christian Brothers Trustees* ([2001] PIQR P28) Mackay J. found that, where a claimant was injured by abuse that occurred in a children's home prior to 1954, but the claimant did not reach 21 until after 1957, the defendant had an accrued limitation defence under the Limitation Act 1939 and the action was time barred. The Court of Appeal upheld this decision in October 2001.

5.5   **DISABILITY**

5.5.1   Section 28(1) Limitation Act 1980 provides that:

> If on the date when any cause of action accrued for which a period of limitation is prescribed by this Act, the person to whom it accrued was under a disability, the action may be brought at any time before the expiration of 6 years from the date when he ceased to be under a disability or died (whichever first occurred) notwithstanding that the period of limitation has expired.

5.5.2   It will be apparent from the wording of this paragraph that it applies both to negligence claims (s.11 Limitation Act 1980) and trespass claims (s.2 Limitation Act 1980). However,

Section 28(1) is subject to s.28(6):

> If the action is one to which Section 11 or 12 (2) of this Act applies, subsection (1) above shall have the effect as if for the words '6 years' there were substituted the words '3 years'.

5.5.3   The effect of these sections is that if a claimant is under a disability when a cause of action accrues he will have three years from when he ceases to be under a disability to bring a claim in negligence whereas in trespass he will have six years from the date of cessation of disability.

5.5.4   Section 38(2) Limitation Act 1980 provides that:

> For the purpose of this Act a person shall be treated as under a disability while he is an infant or of unsound mind.

It is apparent therefore that there are two sorts of disability: infancy and 'unsoundness of mind'.

Infancy

5.5.5   Time will not run while the Claimant is a child but the practitioner should be alert to the consequences of the Family Law Reform Act 1969 which reduced the age of majority from 21 to 18. Under Sched. 3, para. 8 of the 1969 Act the consequential change in limitation periods only applies to causes of action which arose after the commencement date of the Act. The Act came into force on 1 January 1970.

5.5.6   Therefore for a claimant reaching the age of majority after 1970, that age of majority will be 18. For a claimant who reaches the age of majority before 1970, that age of majority will be 21.

Unsoundness of mind

5.5.7   Section 38(3) Limitation Act 1980 provides that:

> For the purpose of Section (2) above a person is of unsound mind if he is a person who, by reason of mental disorder within the meaning of the Mental Health Act 1983 is incapable of managing and administering his property and affairs.

5.5.8   Section 38(4) Limitation Act 1980 provides that:

> Without prejudice to Section 38 (3), if a person is detained under the Mental Health Act 1983 and is receiving treatment as an in-patient they will be 'conclusively presumed to be of unsound mind.

5.5.9   Section 38(3) Limitation Act 1980 defines 'unsoundness of mind' as:

- Mental disorder within the meaning of MHA 1983 (namely 'Mental illness, arrested or incomplete development of the mind, psychopathic disorder, and any other disorder or disability of mind') and
- Incapacity for administering property and affairs.

For there to be a finding of 'unsoundness of mind', both of these features must be present and the first must cause the second.

5.5.10   Where there is a possibility that the claimant is a patient, clearly a psychiatric report must be obtained and if the claimant is currently a patient, it will be necessary to identify and appoint a suitable litigation friend.

5.5.11   If the claimant is now a patient and *has been a patient for the entire period since he reached majority*, time will not have been running against him and there is no limitation issue to contend with. However, where the claimant is now a patient but has not been a patient for the entire period since the date of majority, the limitation clock will have been ticking against him since, by virtue of the wording of s.28(1) Limitation Act 1980, the running of the limitation period is only suspended if the claimant was under a disability *on the date when the cause of action accrued*. Therefore, if the claimant was not under a disability on the date when the cause of action accrued, but is now under a disability, the period or periods of disability will be a matter for the court to consider in the exercise of its discretion under s.33 Limitation Act, and this is specifically provided for under s.33(3)(d).

5.5.12   Section 33 Limitation Act 1980 only applies to negligence claims. As discussed above there is no similar provision in relation to trespass claims and it follows that in trespass claims where the claimant was not under a disability on the date when the cause of action accrued, or ceases to be under a disability for any period (however short) thereafter the six-year period will start to run even if the claimant subsequently becomes subject to a disability during that six-year period.

5.6   CONCEALMENT

5.6.1   Section 32 of the 1980 Act so far as relevant, provides:

> (1) . . . where in the case of any action for which a period of limitation is prescribed by this Act, either – (a) the action is based upon the fraud of the defendant; or (b) any fact relevant to the claimant's right of action has been deliberately concealed from him by the defendant; or (c) the action is for relief from the consequences of the mistake; the period of limitation shall not begin to run until the plaintiff has discovered the fraud, concealment, or mistake (as the case may be) or could with reasonable diligence have discovered it. . . .

> (2) For the purposes of subsection (1) above, deliberate commission of a breach of duty in circumstances in which it is unlikely to be discovered for some time amounts to deliberate concealment of the facts involved in that breach of duty.

5.6.2   Section 32 Limitation Act 1980 can be used in respect of actions in tort or trespass. In cases where the six-year limitation period is unextendable it may be particularly relevant to consider whether there has been a concealment of any fact relevant to the claimant's right of action.

5.6.3   In the case of *Cave* v. *Robinson Jarvis and Rolf* [2001] EWCA Civ 245, the Court of Appeal confirmed the earlier decision of a two-judge court in

Brocklesby v. *Armitage & Guest* [2001] 1 All ER 172 in respect of the interpretation of section 32 Limitation Act 1980. Potter LJ summarised the facts in *Brocklesby* as follows:

> In that case, the claimant purchased a property from a company with the aid of a building society loan in 1989. Three months later, he agreed to transfer the money back to the company in consideration for the company obtaining his release from his obligations to the building society. The defendant solicitors were instructed to act for both parties. The claimant executed the transfer, but thereafter the solicitors omitted to complete the transaction by procuring his release from the building society. The claimant did not become aware of this until mid-1992 when so informed by the building society, which later sued him for the balance of the loan. In 1997 the claimant sued the solicitors for negligence, relying on s.32(1)(b) of the 1980 Act and alleging that the solicitors had been guilty of 'deliberate commission of a breach of duty' within the meaning of s.32(2). The claimant did not allege, however, that the solicitors were aware that they were in breach of duty. The solicitors contended (as the defendants before us contend) that s.32(2), when relied on in amplification of s.32(1)(b), requires not only that the act or omission in question should be deliberate, but also that the person committing it should be aware that it amounted to a breach of duty.

5.6.4   Potter J. set out essential reasoning in the judgment of Morritt LJ in *Brocklesby* as appears at [2001] 1 All ER 180g–181b:

> When one turns to the terms of s.32 of the 1980 Act itself, under sub-s.(1) there is a clear contrast between the action based on fraud and para (b), the concealment of any fact relevant to the plaintiff's right of action being deliberate. The requirement is that the fact relevant to the cause of action has been deliberately concealed from him by the defendant. But sub-s.(2) amplifies what is meant by deliberate concealment and requires that for the purposes of sub-s.(1) deliberate commission of a breach of duty, etc., amounts to deliberate concealment of the facts involved in the breach of duty. Generally speaking, and I do not say that there may not be exceptions, the civil law and, so far as I know, the criminal law, does not require that a person should know the legal consequences of the act which he commits. Generally speaking, if he knows of the act and he intends the act, but is unaware of the legal consequences, his unawareness is immaterial for it is trite law that ignorance of the law is no defence. It appears to me that had Parliament intended in the case of a deliberate concealment under s.32(1)(b) of the 1980 Act, as amplified by sub-s.(2), that there should be both deliberate commission of an act in the sense of knowingly and intentionally committing the act and also knowledge that such commission gave rise to a particular legal consequence, then it required clearer words to spell that out than are to be found in sub-ss.(2) or (1).
>
> Accordingly, *the conclusion I reach is that it is not necessary for the purpose of extending the limitation period pursuant to s.32(1)(b) of the 1980 Act to demonstrate that the fact relevant to the claimant's right of action has been deliberately concealed in any sense greater than that the commission of the act was deliberate in the sense of being intentional and that that act or omission, as the case may be, did involve a breach of duty whether or not the actor appreciated the legal consequence.* [emphasis added]

5.6.5   The Court of Appeal held that that the reasoning in *Brocklesby* as set out by Morritt LJ was binding upon them and should be applied in the *Cave* Case.

5.6.6   Following the decisions in *Brocklesby* and *Cave* the position is that if any element relevant to the claimant's right of action has been concealed (and it is sufficient for concealment that in the circumstances the breach of duty is unlikely to be discovered for some time) then the limitation period does not begin to run until the claimant has discovered the concealment. There may be circumstances in which facts relevant to the claimant's right of action against an abuser or the employer of an abuser are concealed and the claimant can seek to rely on s.32.

5.7   LIMITATION DECISIONS IN ABUSE CASES

5.7.1   There are very few limitation decisions relating directly to child abuse claims. The following are relevant.

Stubbings v. Webb (CA)

5.7.2   The Court of Appeal decision in *Stubbings* v. *Webb* treated the claim as if it fell within the provisions of ss.11, 14 and 33 Limitation Act 1980. The analysis remains relevant in assessing how the courts apply these sections in abuse cases. The relevant sections are set out above.

Various claimants v. Flintshire CC

5.7.3   In the North Wales children's homes litigation judgment of Scott Baker J. in only one case was there a specific limitation issue. In the case of DW, the defendants contended that the claim was statute barred. In this case DW's cause of action had accrued at the latest by January 1985 when he left the home in which he was abused, but because he did not attain 18 until 3 May 1989 the period was extended for three years thereafter, i.e. to 2 May 1992. Proceedings in this case were not commenced until 16 July 1999. It followed that the claim was out of time unless DW only acquired the requisite knowledge of injury less than three years before 16 July 1999. Defendants' counsel argued that it was up to the claimant to prove that he only acquired the requisite knowledge within three years before 16 July 1999 and in the absence of medical evidence to this effect he was unable to establish a date of knowledge later than his majority.

5.7.4   Mr Justice Scott Baker noted that the events complained of by DW began when he was at or near his fourteenth birthday. Whether or not he can be said to have appreciated that he had suffered a significant injury, it was clear that for more than three years before he began proceedings he was telling people he had been abused in the home. The existence of publicity about the widespread abuse in the North Wales Homes began well before 1996 and therefore the claimant either knew that the defendants were responsible for his assaults or could have so ascertained with reasonable enquiry.

5.7.5   In evidence, DW said that it was only when he was seen by a prison doctor, two years before trial that he found that he could speak honestly and in detail to somebody about what had happened to him in care. Mr Justice Scott Baker concluded that DW's claim was out of time. However, he then went on to consider his discretion under s.33 Limitation Act. Bearing in mind the provisions of s.33 he concluded that it would be equitable to allow the action to proceed. He stated as follows:

> There is, it seems to me, minimal prejudice to the Defendants who have largely admitted the aspects of the claim that I have found proved. The position would have been otherwise with regard to the allegations of sexual abuse that I have found unproved. Furthermore, I am well aware that it is very painful for many, if not all, of these claimants to bring to the forefront of their minds and relive events that occurred long ago. The Waterhouse Inquiry has brought matters into the public domain and recently helped this painful exercise. I do not think the evidence on the matters I have found established is any less cogent than it would have been had the action been brought in the time allowed and I think it would be wrong to prevent (DW) from recovering relatively modest damages for abhorrent behaviour on the part of the Defendants.

Ablett and others v. Devon CC/The Home Office

5.7.6   Ablett and others were former inmates of Forde Park Approved School and were claiming against the Home Office/Devon County Council for physical and sexual abuse in the school. A group of 15 lead cases was selected for trial. The allegations related to events between 1957 and 1985. In an interlocutory decision at first instance Toulson J., the judge managing the case, was called upon to determine whether the issue of limitation ought to be hived off and tried as a preliminary issue. He decided that it should not. The defendants appealed to the Court of Appeal where Lord Justice Sedley considered the limitation issue generally and the question of whether it should be determined as a preliminary issue:

> Inevitably there is a problem of limitation in these proceedings. I say 'inevitably' because it is in the nature of abuse of children by adults that it creates shame, fear and confusion, and these in turn produce silence. Silence is known

157

to be one of the most pernicious fruits of abuse. It means that allegations commonly surface, if they do, only many years after the abuse has ceased.

In the present case Miss Thirlwall QC for Devon County Council has impressed upon me that this has the effect that a very large number, the great majority, of those individuals implicated by name in the abuse are dead or in some cases unable to be traced. Others survive but are unwell. None of that immunises the two defendant authorities from liability if it is otherwise established, but it does create a serious problem for the Court of Trial in deciding what allegations have been made out in the absence of the individuals implicated in them. What is not inevitable is that a defendant, especially when that defendant is a public authority, will plead limitation rather than accept responsibility for as much or as little as can reliably be established at such a distance of time. These defendants, however, have exercised their undoubted right to plead the Limitation Act in bar of the actions. In consequence two main groups of issues will form part of the litigation. First, what was the date of each claimant's knowledge for the purposes of section 14 of the Limitation Act 1980? Second, if that date of knowledge fell beyond the limitation period, ought the time bar to be lifted by virtue of Section 33 of the Act?

The question Toulson J. was called upon to decide as part of his case management function was whether the issues which were thus raised ought to be hived off and tried as preliminary issues. He decided that they should not. In a carefully reasoned judgment, he weighed the pros and cons and gave his reasons for coming down on the side of a single trial. Essentially they were these. As to date of knowledge, there was expert evidence before the judge suggesting that these claimants were confused and damaged individuals whose own understanding and mental processes were likely to be inextricably bound up with the evidence and issues which also went to liability. As to the power to disapply the bar, if that came in question, the judge said:

'It does not seem to me that one could justly refuse to exercise the Court's discretion under Section 33 to allow the claim to continue, if the question of primary limitation had been determined against the claimant, without being sure that one had really fully and sufficiently understood what had allegedly happened to the person and its affect on him.'

Toulson J. recognised in his judgment that if limitation were to be hived off and went the defendants' way, there would be a real saving of time and costs. He also recognised that if it was hived off but went the claimants' way, it would not only add to the total expenditure of time and money, but it would mean the claimants having to go twice through the ordeal of giving evidence, together with the expert witnesses. Balancing these against each other, the judge concluded that a preliminary trial could not be shown to be likely to produce better or cheaper justice. I stress that one element of his reasoning was the fact that the issues in a preliminary trial would have to go deep into the very issues which would also form the subject-matter of any trial on liability because of the need to probe into the history and present mental state of each claimant.

In my judgement Toulson J. was not only entitled to reach this conclusion, which is enough for present purposes; if I had to consider the question I would say that he had reached an undoubtedly correct conclusion. Latham LJ, considering these applications on paper, took the same view.

For these reasons, I would refuse permission to appeal against the order of Toulson J.

Various claimants v. (1) *Bryn Alyn Community Homes Ltd* and (2) *The Royal and Sun Alliance plc* (Connell, J., unreported, 26 June 2001)

5.7.7   Connell J. considered the position of a claimant who in 1979 had been placed in the first defendants' care home and was there subjected to physical abuse. The claimant suffered psychiatric injuries as a result of the abuse. At trial, Connell J. held that the claimant's claim was outside the limitation period but that the court should exercise its discretion under s.33 Limitation Act to allow the claim to proceed. At para. 33 he stated that:

> In my view it would be manifestly unjust now to prevent those who prove their claims to the relevant standard from benefiting from those claims because they have lacked the confidence and ability to talk to others at an earlier stage about their very unhappy and embarrassing experiences. I conclude this injustice far outweighs the prejudice which the second defendants have suffered through the late presentation of these claims and I shall exercise my discretion by disapplying the provisions of section 11 in every case.

5.8   TACTICS

5.8.1   Two tactical questions arise in relation to limitation. First, what steps should the claimant's solicitor take in order to protect the position of a claimant whose claim is already likely to be statute barred and who will need to rely on the court's discretion pursuant to s.33 Limitation Act 1980? Second, should either side be seeking an order for limitation to be tried as a preliminary issue?

5.8.2   To deal with the first point, the claimant's solicitor should take steps to notify the claim to the intended defendant at the earliest possible opportunity. The claimant's solicitor should invite the defendant to confirm that receipt of the letter before action will precipitate limitation in the sense that time will then cease to run against the claimant for a specified period (e.g. of a few months in order that a claimant can then obtain medical evidence and issue proceedings). The claimant's solicitor should advise the defendant that a refusal to afford the claimant a limitation 'holiday' in these terms will force the claimant to issue proceedings immediately with a consequent increase in costs.

5.8.3   In respect of limitation as a preliminary issue, there will in fact seldom be significant cost saving in respect of child abuse claims by the trial of limitation as a preliminary issue. A court cannot properly exercise its discretion under s.33 Limitation Act 1980 in such cases without determining the full circumstances in which the abuse is alleged to have occurred, the strength of the case on liability and causation and the extent of the damage caused. These points are addressed by Lord Justice Sedley in the *Forde Park* litigation, quoted above.

5.8.4 The question of limitation as a preliminary issue also highlights the importance for the claimant of identifying the correct defendants, and the correct causes of action at the beginning of the litigation. The claimant needs to avoid the situation where he has to apply to amend his statement of case at a later date in the litigation, to add additional defendants or plead additional causes of action. If the original claim was issued after the expiry of the primary limitation period then any application to amend will likewise have to be made after the expiry of the primary limitation period and in considering whether to grant the amendment the court would have to consider the exercise of its discretion under s.33 – thus in effect provoking the court to a preliminary hearing of the s.33 issue.

5.9 THE FUTURE

5.9.1 Looking to the future, several developments may be expected:

- The number of reported limitation decisions in child abuse cases will rise significantly as much of the multi-party litigation initiated in recent years comes to trial.

- The six-year limitation period in respect of trespass to the person claims following the House of Lords decision in *Stubbings* v. *Webb* may need to be reconsidered. The Law Commission in its recent report *Limitation of Actions* (see below) has recommended the outright abolition of the six-year rule and the integration of trespass claims into a new 'core regime' applicable to all personal injury claims. Even if the Law Commission's proposals are not enacted by Parliament, the *Stubbings* decision may none the less be challenged on the basis of ECHR/Human Rights Act and/or the decision in *Lister* v. *Hesley Hall Ltd.*

- The Law Commission in its recent report *Limitation of Actions* has proposed a wholesale reform of limitation law, detailed analysis of which is outside the scope of this Chapter. The Law Commission considered whether limitation periods should be applied at all in child sexual abuse cases, but concluded that they should. The Law Commission has proposed a new limitation regime relating to personal injuries action based on time running from the date of 'discoverability' and has suggested that child abuse claims should be treated like other personal injury cases within this regime. In its original proposals in 1998 the Law Commission suggested the introduction of a 'long stop' limitation period in all personal injury claims but after consultation has rejected this in its most recent report, recognising that this would be particularly unfair to child abuse claimants as a group given the particular difficulties that they face.

CHAPTER 6

Criminal injuries compensation

6.1   INTRODUCTION

6.1.1   The Criminal Injuries Compensation Authority (CICA) and its predecessor the Criminal Injuries Compensation Board (CICB) are state-funded compensation schemes for victims of crimes of violence within Great Britain. Many victims of child abuse have received awards under the various schemes operated by the CICA and CICB. Consequently, it is incumbent on the claimant's lawyer to consider the possibility of an application for criminal injuries compensation.

6.1.2   This chapter deals primarily with the two schemes presently operated by the CICA. The first of these governs applications made on or after 1 April 1996 (the 1996 scheme). The second governs applications made on or after 1 April 2001 (the 2001 scheme). Copies of these schemes can be obtained from the CICA.

6.1.3   The forerunner to the CICA was the CICB. The CICB was created by the government in 1964 and underwent several revisions over the ensuing three decades. In 1994, the Home Office (by way of parliamentary answer) introduced a new scheme based on a tariff system for injuries. This was successfully challenged by way of judicial review in *R* v. *Secretary of State for the Home Department, ex parte Fire Brigades Union* [1995] 2 AC 513. This decision of the House of Lords meant that all applications submitted during 1994–5 had to be reconsidered and the government was obliged to enact legislation, the Criminal Injuries Compensation Act 1995 (the 1995 Act) to bring the 1996 scheme into force. This Act came into force on 1 April 1996. The CICB continued to deal with applications made before that date.

6.1.4   The 2001 scheme makes certain changes to the operation of the 1996 scheme (paras. 83–6 of the 2001 scheme).

6.1.5   In the case of CICB applications received after the date of commencement of each of the CICB schemes but relating to injuries suffered before it, the applicable scheme was the scheme in existence at the time of the injury.

6.1.6   The underlying policy of the 1996 and 2001 schemes can be found in the 1995 Act. The courts have always tried to give effect to the underlying policy of the CICA and CICB by adopting the interpretation of a reasonable and literate man (*R* v. *Criminal Injuries Compensation Board, ex parte Webb* [1986] 3 WLR 251). In addition, the 1995 Act is a framework statute. When the government introduced the bill, it was unable to detail its actual workings so a number of assurances were given about how the scheme would operate in force. After *Pepper* v. *Hart* [1993] AC 593 those assurances influence the interpretation of the various schemes.

6.1.7   The 1996 and 2001 schemes should be read with their accompanying guides. With regard to the 1996 scheme, the CICA has published *A Guide to the Criminal Injuries Compensation Scheme* (Issue Number One (4/96) and Issue Number Two (4/99)). With regard to the 2001 scheme, the CICA has published *A Guide to the Criminal Injuries Compensation Scheme (2001)* Issue Number Two (7/01). There are two further CICA guides: the *Guide to Applicants for Loss of Earnings and Special Expenses*; and the *Guide to Applicants for Compensation in Fatal Cases.* In addition, the CICA publishes a short guide entitled *Child Abuse and the Criminal Injuries Compensation Scheme.* The CICA also publishes a set of annual reports and accounts (which contains useful information as to the CICA's policy in certain claims); has a website at www.cica.gov.uk and has published a further brief guide *Compensation for Victims of Violent Crime.*

6.2   THE STRUCTURE OF THE CICA

6.2.1   The CICA is a non-departmental public body, but not a statutory body. It has no distinct legal personality. The decisions of the CICA's administrative officers come under the jurisdiction of the Parliamentary Commissioner for Administration by virtue of s.10 of the 1995 Act. Both the CICB and the CICA have a complaints procedure. The guides to the 1996 and 2001 schemes specify time limits for acknowledging and dealing with applications, reviews and appeals and making payments. A senior member of staff will investigate complaints about the way in which an application has been dealt with, but not the merits of the decision.

6.2.2 The CICA employs claims officers who will determine applications for compensation. Appeals against those determinations are heard by the Criminal Injuries Compensation Appeal Panel (CICAP) which is independent of the CICA.

6.2.3 Certain foreign countries provide compensation schemes for their own citizens. Those countries which are signatories to the *Council of Europe's Convention on the Compensation of Victims of Violent Crime* (HMSO 1988), have or propose to have reciprocal arrangements whereby one state will compensate the citizens of another country if they sustain criminal injury within its jurisdiction. The United Kingdom ratified this treaty on 1 February 1990. From 1 June 1990, British citizens are eligible for compensation under the arrangements established in any other state which is a party to the Convention and within whose jurisdiction a criminal injury was sustained.

6.3   JUDICIAL REVIEW OF THE CICB/CICA'S DECISIONS

6.3.1 Although the CICB was not created by statute, and essentially its payments are *ex gratia*, its administration is subject to judicial review *(R* v. *Criminal Injuries Compensation Board, ex parte Lain* [1967] 2 QB 864). The CICA derives its authority from statute and as a public body it is subject to judicial review. Consequently, the 1996 and 2001 schemes explicitly provide for written reasons to be given for their decisions.

6.3.2 *R* v. *Criminal Injuries Compensation Board, ex parte Cook* [1996] 1 WLR 1037 CA concerned the degree of detail which the CICB should give when advising applicants of its decision to refuse or reduce an award having exercised its discretion. The Court of Appeal stated that while the CICB's reasons for refusing compensation should contain sufficient detail to enable the reader to know what conclusion had been reached on the principal important issue, it was not a requirement that they should deal with every material consideration to which they had regard. The court went on to say that what was required was an assessment of the propriety of the CICB's decision not an evaluation of its merits. In other words, a court will not substitute its own reasoning for that of the CICB or the CICA.

6.4   MAKING THE APPLICATION

Initial enquiries by CICA

6.4.1   On receipt of the application, the CICA will write to the police, medical authorities and any other relevant authority to verify the allegations. The police will be asked to confirm that the injury was reported to them, and whether in their view it was attributable to a crime of violence or resulted to any extent from the applicant's own conduct. They will also be asked whether the applicant is known to them and the outcome of criminal proceedings. Where these are pending, it has been the CICA's practice to defer determination of the application but only where it considers that the proceedings are likely to have a bearing on the outcome of the application.

6.4.2   In cases involving the abuse of children, the police are likely to have a major influence on the determination of an application. In cases where a number of applicants have brought allegations against the same abuser, the CICA has shown itself willing to deal with the applicants in a group. In these circumstances there may be corroborative evidence on the police file which may assist the CICA in reaching decisions. Where allegations are made by a stand-alone applicant (i.e. an applicant who is alone in making allegations against a particular alleged abuser), and relate to events which are alleged to have occurred many years previously, it is vital to consider what corroborative evidence might be made available to the CICA. For instance, the applicant may have attended a particular hospital after the abuse, or may have reported the matter to social services or school authorities. However, the CICA has no powers to compel a person or authority to give up its records. It is unlikely that the police will allow an applicant to inspect the criminal file.

6.4.3   The CICA makes its decision on the civil standard, i.e. the balance of probabilities. Section 3(2) of the 1995 Act provides: 'Where, in accordance with any provision of the Scheme, it falls to one person to satisfy another as to any matter, the standard of proof required shall be that applicable in civil proceedings.' See paras. 64 of the 1996 and 2001 schemes.

6.4.4   The 1996 and 2001 schemes provide that an application must be made within two years of the date of the incident. This time limit may be waived in certain circumstances (see below). In view of the time limit, an application should be lodged as soon as practicable. Thus, while vital corroborative evidence may ultimately emerge from the criminal and civil cases, the application should not be delayed pending their outcome. However, the CICA may delay a final determination until these processes are complete.

CICA powers of investigation

6.4.5   The CICA has wide powers on the receipt of an application to make investigations. If discrepancies or issues arise from the CICA's initial search for information, then it can make further enquiries of the applicant. The CICA can also make 'directions and arrangements' under the schemes for the conduct of the application including imposing conditions. If, for example, the applicant's medical prognosis is unclear, the CICA can delay the consideration of the application. The CICA can also require the applicant to submit to a medical examination (for which reasonable expenses can be paid).

The initial decision

6.4.6   The claims officers of the CICA make the initial determination of what award (if any) should be made (para. 3 of the 1996 and 2001 schemes). There are effectively two steps in this decision making process. First, whether the applicant is eligible for an award. The claims officer has to consider here whether the injury complained was a crime of violence, whether the applicant complied with the rules relating to the reporting of the injury, and whether the applicant's conduct or character make an award inappropriate. The second step concerns the amount of the award under the relevant scheme.

Making the award

6.4.7   Normally an award of compensation is paid to the applicant by cheque as a single lump sum. However, the CICB or the CICA may make other arrangements for the payment of the award, including its administration on the applicant's behalf: para. 9 of the old scheme and s.3(1)(b) of the 1995 Act. Section 3(1)(d) of the 1995 Act allows the CICA to make structured settlements. Payments from such settlements are tax exempt: s.8 of the 1995 Act.

6.4.8   The terms of the 1996 and 2001 schemes allow a claims officer to make arrangements for the management of an award not only where the applicant does not have mental capacity, but also if the officer considers it to be in the applicant's best interests, for instance where their past history suggests that they might dissipate the award.

6.5 REVIEWS AND APPEALS

Review

6.5.1 Under the 1996 and 2001 schemes, the applicant may, if dissatisfied with the initial decision taken by the claims officer, make an application for a review of that decision: paras. 58–60 of the 1996 and 2001 schemes. The applicant has 90 days from the date of the letter notifying him of the initial decision to seek a review by a more senior claims officer although he can apply to extend this period if his request is based on good reasons and it is in the interests of justice: para. 59 of the 1996 and 2001 schemes.

6.5.2 The grounds for applying for a review are set out in para. 58 of the 1996 and 2001 schemes. Note that the review application should be signed by the applicant, not the lawyer. The CICA can refuse to accept an application for review on these grounds.

6.5.3 The review is heard by another more senior claims officer who considers the application afresh together with any further evidence submitted by the applicant. It should be noted that the review process may reduce further or entirely disallow an award which has been made at first instance in which case the applicant's only option is to appeal. The outcome of the review process will be communicated to the applicant and, once again, its reasons must be stated.

Appeal

6.5.4 The procedure for appeal can be found in paras. 61–71 of the 1996 and 2001 schemes.

6.5.5 An appeal can either be heard on paper or by way of hearing. Under para. 76 of the 1996 and 2001 scheme, oral appeals are held in private and they are confidential. An applicant in a child abuse case should be warned that his or her abuser may be invited by the Appeals Panel to attend and give evidence.

6.5.6 An oral hearing is a complete reconsideration of the case. The appeal panel can take into account matters which were not mentioned beforehand. Written notice of the date of the hearing will be sent to the Applicant and the CICA at least 21 days in advance. This notice may be accompanied by a copy of the documents submitted by the application and the CICA. The hearing will take place before at least two adjudicators. The CICA appoints a claims officer to present the appeal on its behalf. All parties to the hearing have the right to call, examine and cross-examine witnesses, but the panel has no power to issue a witness summons. It is for the applicant to arrange the attendance of his own witnesses. The panel can take into account hearsay and opinion evidence, and may accept evidence in writing.

6.5.7 The practice of the appeals panel is to hand over statements made by other parties in the criminal investigation to the applicant and his lawyer on the day of the hearing. The applicant's lawyer has only a very short time to read such statements and take instructions. The police file is also unavailable to the applicant. The applicant therefore may not know what evidence the CICAP has seen, or how that evidence operates to reduce or withhold his award. See *R* v. *Chief Constable of Cheshire, ex parte Berry* (1985) unreported and *R* v. *CICB, ex parte Brady* (1987) *The Times*, 11 March. In *Berry*, the CICB was not the respondent but the court had cause to review the CICB's practice of giving out witness statements on the day of the hearing. The CICB had given an undertaking to the police that they would hold onto such statement until immediately before the hearing. The Chief Constable's request for this undertaking was not held to be perverse. The court held that the release of statements immediately before the hearing did not amount to a denial of natural justice. In *Brady*, the court suggested that the applicant could request an adjournment of the hearing, which could be reasonably considered by the CICB. (See also *R* v. *CICB, ex parte Gould* (1989) unreported.)

6.5.8 The compatibility with human rights of these types of procedural rules was considered in relation to the Motor Insurers' Bureau in *Evans* v. *Secretary of State for the Environment, Transport and the Regions and the Motor Insurers Bureau* [2001] 2 CMLR 10. Mr Evans challenged the operation of the appeal process available to victims of untraced drivers under Article 6.1 of the European Convention on Human Rights (now incorporated into domestic law by the Human Rights Act 1998). Mr Evans said that the appeal process had not allowed for any exchange of expert or lay witness evidence. He had never had any proper opportunity to deal with expert and video evidence which had been produced by the MIB late in the appeal process. The matter came before Buckley J. who felt that it was not clear that the MIB agreement in question showed sufficient compliance with Article 6.1 of the Convention.

6.5.9 There is no exchange of witness evidence under the CICA schemes although applicants are invited to put forward their own evidence. Applicants do not necessarily see all the CICA's evidence until the day of their appeal, at which time it may be too late to deal with it effectively. The CICA's procedures may therefore be vulnerable to challenge under the Human Rights Act 1998, in appropriate cases.

6.6　CRIMINAL INJURY

Definition

6.6.1　Under para. 6 of the 1996 and 2001 scheme, the applicant must have sustained a criminal injury on or after 1 August 1964 to be eligible for an award. Under para. 8 of the 1996 and 2001 scheme, criminal injuries are defined as personal injuries (i.e. personal or mental injuries) sustained in Great Britain and directly attributable to a 'crime of violence'. There is no definition of 'crime of violence' in either the CICB or the CICA schemes. In *R* v. *Criminal Injuries Compensation Board, ex parte Webb* [1986] QB 184 the Court of Appeal approved the CICB's submission that a crime of violence is 'one where the definition of the crime itself involves either direct infliction of force on the victims, or at least a hostile act directed towards the victim or class of victims'. A definition was provided by s.109(1)(a)(ii) of the Criminal Justice Act 1988 but this was never brought into force. A personal injury is a criminal injury when it is directly attributable to conduct constituting an offence which requires proof of intent to cause death or personal injury or recklessness as to whether death or personal injury is caused. An attempt to commit a crime of violence is also a 'crime of violence' for the purposes of the scheme.

Omissions amounting to criminal injuries

6.6.2　Personal injuries are not criminal injuries even though they are caused by a breach of a set of rules, unless that breach can be construed as constituting the external elements of a crime of violence. This means that omissions on the part of offenders may lead to a criminal injury. It is therefore submitted that the neglect of a child which may be a crime under the Children and Young Persons Act 1933 (as amended by subsequent legislation) leading to injury may be a crime of violence for the purposes of the CICA.

Consent

6.6.3　Almost all sexual offences against persons under 16 will rank as crimes of violence. In the criminal law, a person under 16 cannot give any consent which would prevent a sexual act being an assault. The CICA schemes state that rape, incest and buggery are clear examples of crimes of violence for the purpose of applications on behalf of sexually abused children. There may be difficulties where the alleged offender has simply invited the child to commit an indecent act, in which case there is no assault: *Fairclough* v. *Whipp* [1951] 2 All ER 834.

6.6.4 However in certain circumstances, a sexual offence such as buggery may not necessarily be a crime of violence under the schemes, even where it involves a child. In *R* v. *Criminal Injuries Compensation Appeals Panel ex parte A (A Minor)* [2001] 2 WLR 1452, two applicants had been subjected to acts of buggery when under the age of 16. Both were refused compensation on the grounds that while victims of a crime, they were not victims of a crime of violence. CICAP found that the two applicants had consented to the criminal acts. The first applicant, A, had been born in 1976 and, at the age of 13, had been involved in acts of buggery with his abuser, a 53-year-old man, C. A had apparently been the agent of the act of buggery with his abuser. The CICAP held that he had consented to these acts. The second Applicant, B, claimed to have been the victim of buggery by other pupils at an approved school in the 1960s. The CICAP found B to be an unreliable witness and was not satisfied that he had not consented to the acts of buggery.

6.6.5 A and B applied for judicial review of the CICAP's decision which was granted at first instance in the High Court. Collins J. held that where a person aged 12 or 13 was buggered, it was inevitable that he would suffer trauma and injury and the act of buggery on him, regardless of his consent, was a crime of violence. The CICAP appealed against this decision.

6.6.6 The Court of Appeal held that the judge at first instance had substituted his own judgment for that of the CICAP (by saying that such acts must cause trauma), a course which could not be justified. It was impossible to say that the CICAP were irrational in concluding that acts committed consensually were not crimes of violence. The CICAP also argued that the offences for which C had been convicted were offences under ss.12 and 13 of the Sexual Offences Act 1956, which were not created to protect children but to prevent unnatural behaviour. Both participants in such behaviour were equally guilty under the 1956 Act. It followed that an act of buggery would not necessarily involve an assault. Since the consent of either party was irrelevant to guilt, the age of the participants was irrelevant. The issue of consent was central in deciding whether a 'reasonable and literate man' would consider whether this was a crime of violence: *R* v. *Criminal Injuries Compensation Board, ex parte Webb* [1987] QB 74.

The assailant's state of mind

6.6.7 In the case of children who are 16 or over, the state of mind of the assailant should not be relevant to the making of an award. For instance, if a man rapes a 17 year old, the fact that he honestly believes that his victim is consenting may excuse him from liability under the law. However, it does not preclude the making of an award. In a case described in *Legal Action* in 1987 (p. 16), the rapist was acquitted by the criminal court. The CICB single member refused the award because he was not satisfied that the applicant had not consented. The Board held that the outcome of the trial was irrelevant and made a full award on the basis of her evidence.

Absence of conviction

6.6.8 It is not necessary for there to be a conviction against the offender, or a prosecution, for an award to be made (para. 10 of the 1995 and 2001 schemes). Similarly, the CICA is not bound by the failure of a civil action. What is required is that the alleged offender's conduct can be shown, on the available evidence and on the balance of probabilities to amount to a crime of violence. In *Re G (A Ward) (Criminal Injuries: Compensation)* [1993] 1 FLR 103 CA, the fact that a father had been cleared of the sexual abuse of his child did not prevent the guardian *ad litem* from applying to the CICB. See also *Re G (A Minor) (Ward: Criminal Injuries Compensation)* [1990] 1 WLR 1120 CA).

6.7   PERSONAL INJURY

Definition

6.7.1 Paragraph 8 of the 1996 and 2001 schemes provides that *'For the purposes of this Scheme, "criminal injury" means one or more personal injuries as described in the following paragraph [8], being an injury sustained in Great Britain and directly attributable to . . .'*

6.7.2 Paragraph 9 of the 1996 scheme then defines 'personal injury':

> For the purposes of this Scheme, personal injury includes physical injury (including fatal injury), mental injury (that is, a medically recognised psychiatric or psychological illness) and disease (that is, a medically recognised illness or condition).

6.7.3 The definition of 'personal injury' in para. 9 of the 2001 scheme omits the words 'psychological illness' and introduces the words 'sexual offence' alongside 'physical injury'. The change in the wording appears to take account of the rise in claims made by victims of sexual abuse. The reason for the omission of the word 'psychological illness' is unclear, since note 8 on page 27 of the scheme refers to 'psychological symptoms'.

6.7.4 Threats of violence leading to physical or mental injury can lead to an award. The CICB has awarded compensation to a young girl who was forced into prostitution by threats of violence (CICB, 1983 para. 20; s.2 Sexual Offences Act 1956). Where a child becomes pregnant as a result of rape, compensation will include an additional sum (para. 27 1996 scheme and page 32 2001 scheme under the heading 'pregnancy').

6.7.5 Mental injury does not have to follow physical injury. However, the CICA schemes follow the common law position as stated in *Alcock* v. *Chief Constable of South Yorkshire* [1992] 1 AC 310 by distinguishing the conditions which need to be met before mental injury can become payable. Both schemes contain definitions of 'mental illness and temporary anxiety'. The 1996 scheme defines mental injury as a 'medically recognised psychiatric or psychological illness'. Note 2 of the 1996 tariff states: 'shock or nervous shock' may be taken to include conditions attributed to PTSD, depression and similar generic terms covering:

> (a) such psychological symptoms as anxiety, tension, insomnia, irritability, loss of confidence, agoraphobia and preoccupation with thoughts of guilt or self-harm; and (b) related physical symptoms such as alopecia, asthma, eczema, enuresis and psoriasis. Disability in this context will include impaired work (or school) performance, significant adverse effects on social relationships and sexual dysfunction.

Notes 8–11 on p. 27 of the 2001 scheme contain more detail and define the type of diagnosis which the CICA expects to see.

Psychiatrists/psychologists

6.7.6 The terms of the 1996 scheme indicate that the CICA prefers psychiatric evidence to that of psychologists and psychotherapists. Page 25 of the 1996 tariff stated that disabling and permanently disabling mental disorder was to be confirmed by 'psychiatric diagnosis'. However, at the same time, para. 9 referred to 'medically recognised or psychological illness'. Note 2 to the 1996 tariff referred to 'psychological symptoms'.

6.7.7 The CICA (under the 1996 scheme) will not necessarily refuse to accept the expert evidence of a psychologist or psychotherapist but a large claim which rests on the establishment of a permanently disabling disorder should be supported by a psychiatrist. The 2001 scheme makes the position clearer. Again there are references to both psychiatric and psychological injuries but Note 10 on p. 27 states: ' "Psychiatric diagnosis/ prognosis" means that the disabling mental illness has been diagnosed or the prognosis made by a psychiatrist or clinical psychologist.'

6.7.8 When instructing a psychiatrist or clinical psychologist in cases involving the CICA, the expert should be referred to the terms of the applicable scheme and should assess the case according to the relevant definitions.

6.7.9   Paragraph 9 of the 1996 scheme provides that a person who has a 'close relationship of love and affection with a victim of a crime of violence' may be able to make a claim for mental injury as long as that mental injury comes under the criteria described above. In *W* v. *Criminal Injuries Compensation Board* [1999] SCLR 921 the applicant claimed compensation for the psychological trauma she suffered on the discovery that her husband had sexually abused her daughters. The Board had rejected her claim on the basis that while such secondary claims could be made under the terms of the scheme, there was insufficient evidence in this case. The court granted the applicant's judicial review petition. Paragraph 4 of the 1990 CICB scheme stated that the injury must be 'directly attributable' to the crime of violence. The Board had failed to address the proper question as a matter of fact as to the proximity of her injury with regard to time and space to the crime of violence.

6.8   WHO MAY APPLY TO THE CICA

6.8.1   Paragraph 6(a) of the 1996 and 2001 schemes provides that either the applicant or a person on his behalf may make an application. An application may be brought on behalf of a child or a person without mental capacity. See para. 3.10 for the detailed provisions.

6.8.2   Where the applicant is a child, then the application may be brought by an adult with parental rights over the child. See para. 3.7 of the *Guide* to both the 1996 and 2001 schemes. Where the assailants are the parents, and the child has been taken into care, the application is made by the local authority. The Family Division has issued a practice direction which provides that where a child is a ward of court and has a right to make a claim for compensation, application must be made by the guardian ad litem for permission to apply and to disclose to the CICA such documents as are considered necessary to establish eligibility and quantum. The same application can be made by a director of social services or any other person having care or control of a child. Where an application for permission to apply to the CICA is made by the Official Solicitor, the court should consider only whether the claim for compensation is arguable and whether it is in the child's interests to pursue it.

6.8.3   No award will be made where it is likely that the assailant or any likely assailant will benefit (para. 15 of the 1996 and para. 16 of the 2001 schemes). The award must not be against the child's interests, e.g. where an award might exacerbate family tensions, or hinder a family reconciliation, or force the child to undergo a distressing medical examination.

6.8.4 An award of less than £1,000 will normally be paid to those having parental responsibility for the child. However, the CICA has the power to keep the child's award until the child's majority.

6.9 THE PRE-1979 ABUSE RULE

6.9.1 Paragraph 7(b) of the 1996 and 2001 schemes provides that no compensation will be paid in the following circumstances:

> where the criminal injury was sustained before 1 October 1979 and the victim and the assailant were living together at the time as members of the same family.

6.9.2 This rules originates in para. 7 of the 1969 CICB scheme which provided that compensation would not be payable in such cases. This was revised by para. 28(b) of the 1979 scheme, which came into force on 1 October 1979. The rule bars claims brought in respect of intra-familial abuse before 1979.

6.9.3 The rule has been tested in *R* v. *Criminal Injuries Compensation Board, ex parte Staten* [1972] 1 All ER 1034 where it was held that the question of whether the parties were living together as members of the same family was essentially a question of fact to be decided by the CICB. In *R* v. *Criminal Injuries Compensation Board, ex parte R* (1996) unreported, the court held that a child who was injured by his mother's cohabitee was excluded from compensation. The court observed that the correct approach was to take a broad look at what the situation or set up was in fact.

6.9.4 In historic abuse cases, a victim of pre-1979 intra-familial abuse will be an adult, and is likely to have cut off all contact with the abuser. In *R* v. *Criminal Injuries Compensation Board, ex parte P* [1994] 1 All ER 870 CA, the applicants claimed compensation for sexual abuse committed pre-1979 by their stepfathers. This was denied on the grounds that the injuries had been inflicted by a member of the family living in the same household as the applicants. The court held that while the legality of the scheme could be judicially reviewed, it could not be said that the decision to institute the bar was irrational.

6.9.5 However, it is important to define the exact meaning of 'living together at the time as members of the same family'. Sometimes abuse in an intra-familial setting will be committed by members of the same family who do not live with the applicant, such as grandfathers or uncles.

6.9.6 The position of foster children is uncertain. It is submitted that there is a distinction in childcare law between the position of children who are fostered and children who are either adopted by or natural offspring of their parents. Foster children are 'boarded out' to foster parents and hence are not 'members of the same family' as their foster parents.

6.9.7   Under para. 16 of the 1996 scheme and para. 17 of the 2001 scheme (cases not excluded by the pre-1979 rule), different considerations apply. Where the abuser and victim are living in the same household as members of the same family, the CICA can withhold an award unless the assailant has been prosecuted in connection with the offence. The exception to this is where the claims officers considers that there are practical, technical or other good reasons why a prosecution has not been brought.

6.10   THE TWO-YEAR TIME LIMIT

6.10.1   Paragraph 17 of the 1996 and para. 18 of the 2001 schemes lay down the condition that the application must be made within two years of the date of the incident, but that this time limit will be waived where 'by reason of the particular circumstances of the case, it is reasonable and in the interests of justice to do so'. The time limit under the CICB schemes was three years and was introduced in 1969 because of the difficulties in investigating late claims, in particular the absence of police and medical records. Paragraph 18 of the 1996 scheme and para. 19 of the 2001 scheme state that is for the applicant to make out his case.

6.10.2   Typically, child abuse applications are made long after the two-year time limit has expired. The CICA has shown a sympathetic approach to claims brought out of time where there is sufficient evidence to enable them to be satisfied that the allegations are true, for example, a recent criminal conviction. Paragraph 7.4 of the *Guide* to both the 1996 and 2001 schemes mentions those 'whose ability to help themselves is or was impaired', i.e. those with learning difficulties, and the CICA is sympathetic to claims brought out of time by such people. The CICA will generally waive the time limit where an application is brought within a reasonable time of a child reaching majority.

6.10.3   In *R* v. *Criminal Injuries Compensation Board, ex parte A* [1992] COD 379 the Board refused to waive the three-year time limit in a case where the applicant, A, had allegedly been sexually assaulted by her stepfather many years before making the application. The chairman of the Panel stated that he had been forced to conclude that A's failure to apply was because either she did not wish to make the application or because she had been advised that she had no prospect of success. The court held that the chairman should have considered the impact of abuse on an applicant in addition to other possible explanations. It should never be assumed that the time limit will be waived: see *R* v. *CICB, ex parte Wilson* (1991) LEXIS, 5 February 1991, DC. On a judicial review application relating to a refusal to waive the time limit, the court will not substitute its own discretion for that of the CICA.

6.10.4 The CICA should give reasons for any refusal to waive the time limit. In *X* v. *Criminal Injuries Compensation Board* ([1999] SCLR 1066, the petitioner's claim had been based on allegations of sexual abuse as a child. His claim was brought late, but he argued that there were exceptional circumstances in his case since he had suffered and continued to suffer serious psychiatric problems relating to the abuse. Lord Penrose said that the CICB scheme contained a 'substantial judicial component', and therefore their functions were quasi-judicial. It was clear from the practice of the CICB that they acknowledged a duty to give reasons for a decision as to whether to waive the time limit. Therefore, in the circumstances, a bald statement that the circumstances were not exceptional was necessarily defective.

6.11 COOPERATION WITH THE AUTHORITIES AND CRIMINAL CONVICTIONS

Cooperation with the authorities

6.11.1 The applicant must report the incident without delay to the police and thereafter cooperate with them in bringing the offender to justice. The applicant must also cooperate with the CICA. Paragraph 8.1 of the *Guide* to both the 1996 and 2001 schemes states:

> Payment of compensation for injury as a result of a crime of violence is intended to be an expression of public sympathy and support for innocent victims. The original Scheme, introduced in 1964, envisaged that it would be inappropriate for those with significant criminal records or whose own conduct led to their being injured, to receive compensation from public funds. It was also felt that people who failed to co-operate in bringing the offender to justice should not benefit from such payments. These provisions continue in this Scheme.

6.11.2 Under para. 13(a) of both the 1996 and 2001 schemes, a claims officer may withhold or reduce an award where he considers that the applicant failed to take, without delay, all reasonable steps to inform the police, or other body or person considered by the CICA to be appropriate for the purpose, of the circumstances giving rise to the injury. However, the CICA will take a sympathetic view where the delay in reporting the incident to the police is clearly attributable to youth, old age, or to some physical or mental incapacity or psychological effects of the crime.

6.11.3   By para. 13(b) of the 1996 and 2001 schemes, a claims officer may withhold or reduce an award where he considers that the applicant failed to co-operate with the police or other body in attempting to bring the assailant to justice. Paragraphs 8.3 to 8.12 of the *Guide* to both the 1996 and 2001 schemes contain further advice on the CICA's policy in this situation.

6.11.4   Therefore, where the applicant makes the first disclosure of abuse to his lawyer, he should be advised to report his allegations to the police immediately. See also para. 8.8 of the *Guide* to both the 1996 and 2001 schemes. It may be helpful to obtain a letter from the police stating that in their view the applicant did everything possible to cooperate.

Criminal convictions

6.11.5   Paragraph 13(e) of the 1996 and 2001 schemes provides that an award may be withheld or reduced by the reason of the applicant's character as shown by his criminal convictions or by evidence available to the claims officer.

6.11.6   Both the 1996 and the 2001 schemes use a penalty points system to determine whether there should be a reduction or refusal of the award. Convictions which are spent under the Rehabilitation of Offenders Act 1974 are ignored (see para. 8.16 of the *Guide* to both the 1996 and 2001 schemes).

6.11.7   The penalty point system is not absolute. Under para. 8.17 of the *Guide* to the 1996 scheme, the CICA may take into account 'the particular circumstances of the claim and other related factors . . . or there may be evidence of rehabilitation not otherwise indicated by the points system which may be taken into account'.

6.11.8   In January 1999, the CICAP considered at a special series of hearings claims from adult male applicants who claimed to have been sexually abused in care homes in the north-west of England (CICAP: The Panel's Policy on Abuse in Childhood – M.E. Lewer QC May 2000). In most of these cases, the CICAP had to consider the effect of the applicant's criminal record pursuant to para. 13(e). The CICAP was provided with psychological reports for each applicant and evidence of a general nature from a consultant clinical psychologist. The psychological evidence considered the extent to which abuse had caused or contributed to subsequent psychological dysfunction in the applicant's life, especially conduct which led to convictions. The Chairman of the CICAP, M.E. Lewer QC, noted that:

> The psychologist accepted that any psychological dysfunction exhibited by applicants in later life was multifactorial, and that PTSD following abuse was one of many factors that might contribute to the development of a personality disorder. It could not be said to have caused it. Except in relation to some primary events e.g. criminal behaviour while absconding, it would

not be right to regard it as directly causative of crime; and for later sequelae it had to be considered with other factors. The ability of trauma associated with abuse to influence behaviour diminished with the passage of time. In particular with crimes, he could not say that someone's responsibility for committing a crime was impaired as a result of the abuse.

6.11.9   The chairman summarised the CICAP's approach as follows:

> In considering an applicant's convictions, the Panel's view is that each case clearly depends on its own particular facts. It notes that convictions in the early years after the abuse, when the effect of abuse is likely to be most severe, are often spent and do not fall to be considered. However, the Panel gives weight to the point that one object of placing applicants in care has been to protect them from crime, and that children had been abused when they were at a vulnerable age in the very institution where they had been sent for care and protection. The Panel also gives significant weight to the fact, when it occurs, that an applicant subsequently decides to cooperate with the police and to face the ordeal of giving, or being prepared to give, evidence against the abuser so that he may be brought to justice. Those general considerations and the fact that on the evidence the abuse was one of the factors that had contributed to subsequent offending places abused offenders, in the Panel's view, in a special category. This leads the Panel to take a more sympathetic approach to convictions which are not spent than would be the case if these factors were not present. In some instances, and in recognition of the abuse suffered, a reduced award is likely to be appropriate. But the Panel takes the view that serious criminality, particularly recent serious offences involving violence or substantial prison sentences, cannot be ignored and, in some cases, it concludes that a combination of the nature and seriousness of the offence and the distance in time between that offending and the abuse produces a situation in which it is inappropriate that there should be any award.

6.12   ASSESSMENT OF COMPENSATION

The 1996 scheme

6.12.1   Under the 1996 scheme, there are three main categories for sexual and physical abuse of children: (i) Physical abuse of children (where individual injuries do not otherwise qualify; (ii) Sexual abuse of children (not otherwise covered by sexual assault); and (iii) Sexual assault (single incident – victim any age). A single serious injury or the establishment of an injury coming under the heading of shock (see above) may result in a higher award. The tariff for the abuse of children is based on the length of time over which the child is abused, and the severity of that abuse. No account is taken of the actual effect of the abuse on the child in question (unless the award can be brought under the heading of shock).

6.12.2 There are four levels of award for nervous shock. The lowest, an award of £1,000, is payable in respect of a disabling but temporary mental anxiety which has been medically verified. The higher three categories of disabling but temporary mental anxiety must be confirmed by a psychiatric prognosis. The top award for mental injury is a 'permanently disabling disorder confirmed by psychiatric prognosis' which attracts an award of £20,000.

6.12.3 Paragraph 30 allows for a claim for loss of earnings where the applicant has lost earnings or earning capacity for longer than 28 weeks as a direct consequence of the injury.

The 2001 scheme

6.12.4 The position regarding awards for child abuse and mental injury has been substantially amended under the 2001 scheme.

6.12.5 The number of subcategories of sexual assault/abuse have been increased and a new subcategory, an assault 'resulting in serious internal bodily injuries' has been introduced. Non-consensual vaginal and/or anal intercourse includes a new subcategory defined as 'resulting in permanently disabling mental illness confirmed by psychiatric prognosis'. The highest award is now £33,000 for intercourse 'resulting in serious internal bodily injury with permanent disabling mental illness confirmed by psychiatric prognosis'.

6.12.6 Mental injury awards are set out on p. 27 of the 2001 scheme. A 'Permanent mental illness, confirmed by psychiatric prognosis' which is 'seriously disabling' now attracts an award of £27,000.

The period and type of abuse

6.12.7 Whether the application comes under the 1996 or the 2001 schemes, care must be taken to ascertain exactly how long the abuse lasted, and the precise type of abuse which occurred. An award based only on those matters for which the abuser was convicted may be inadequate if the indictment is limited to specimen offences.

Multiple incidences of abuse

6.12.8 Under the 2001 scheme, note 13 of the *Guide* deals specifically with multiple incidences of abuse, and provides that: 'Where the applicant is entitled to compensation for the series of assaults, she/he will qualify for an award as the victim of a pattern of abuse rather than for a separate award for each incident.'

6.12.9 Applicants may wish for each and every crime of violence which they have suffered to be included in their application. Note 13 of the *Guide* to the 2001 scheme suggests that the CICA will only compensate for the 'single most recent incident, if in relation to the earlier incidents she/he failed to report them to the police without delay and/or failed to cooperate with the police in bringing the assailant to justice'. In practice, incidents of minor violence are unlikely to be compensated (under either the 1996 or the 2001 schemes) if they have never been reported to the police, and where they have occurred many years back. A comprehensive application which provides detailed allegations, supporting evidence, sources of enquiry for the CICA to pursue, and reasoned argument on the issues of time limits and reporting to the authorities, etc. is far more likely to succeed than a bare application.

Causation

6.12.10 Paragraph 7.8 of the *Guide* to the 1996 scheme states:

> You will only be compensated for injuries directly resulting from a crime of violence or threat of violence [or either of the two victimising events]. This means that we must satisfy ourselves, on the basis of all the available facts, that not only was the incident in which you were injured a crime of violence [or either of the other two victimising events] but also that the incident was the substantial cause of your injury.

Paragraph 7.8 of the *Guide* to the 2001 scheme contains similar wording.

Contraction of a disease

6.12.11 Paragraph 9 of the 1996 scheme provides that, if a child contracts a disease as a result of a sexual offence, this will qualify for an award. The tariff requires a 'medically recognised illness/condition'. The 2001 scheme goes further and creates a new tariff for disease contracted as a result of sexual assault. Page 32 the 2001 scheme distinguishes between a 'sexually transmitted disease other than HIV/AIDS' and 'infection with HIV/AIDS'.

Effects on award of other payments

6.12.12 Any award made under the schemes will be reduced by the full value of any award which the applicant obtains in civil litigation, or which is ordered by a criminal court (paras. 48 and 49 of the 1996 and 2001 schemes).

6.13 COSTS

6.13.1 Paragraph 74 of the 1996 and 2001 schemes permits the reimbursement of reasonable expenses incurred by the applicant and any other person, i.e. a witness who attends a hearing. However, no further costs are allowable, but the cost of photographs showing the extent of any injuries is usually reimbursed.

6.13.2 It should be noted that legal help may be available for part of the costs and disbursements of a solicitor instructed in a CICA claim. Under the terms of the Legal Aid Act 1988, Green Form advice and assistance was available for CICB/CICA claims. In 1998, Green Form became legal advice and assistance and in 2000, legal help. Under the terms of the Legal Aid Act 1988, CICA claims are not subject to any deduction in respect of legal help costs. This is because such awards are made by reason of statute. The position under the new public funding rules is not expressly stated. However, enquiries of the Legal Services Commission have indicated that legal help payments are not to be deducted from any compensation which the applicant receives.

6.13.3 Interim payments will be not made by the Commission to subsidise disbursements. Furthermore, legal help does not cover the costs of representation at a hearing, though it may cover the preparation for that hearing.

6.13.4 Alternatively, a solicitor may enter into a contingency fee arrangement with the applicant, under which costs are limited to a specified proportion of damages recovered. Such arrangements do not solve the difficulty of financing disbursements, especially where the time taken to progress the application to conclusion may be in excess of two years.

6.13.5 In practice, expert and other evidence which is obtained under the terms of a public-funding certificate granted for the purposes of civil litigation may be used to assist a CICA claim. However, a public-funding certificate does not cover a CICA claim, and the Commission would disallow on assessment costs incurred solely for the purposes of advancing a CICA claim.

6.13.6 Paragraph 20 of the 1996 scheme and paragraph 21 of the 2001 scheme allow the CICA to commission its own medical evidence. It may be appropriate to suggest this to the CICA when the applicant cannot afford to obtain his own medical evidence, or cannot obtain a disbursement loan.

CHAPTER 7

Evidence and experts

7.1 THE STANDARD OF PROOF

7.1.1 Where a claim involves allegations of sexual abuse or serious physical abuse, then there may either have been a criminal prosecution, or there may be a criminal investigation in process. The claimant's case will be considerably stronger on the facts if the alleged abuser has been convicted in a criminal court in relation to the same acts against the claimant. However, there may be a number of good reasons why such a prosecution has not occurred including:

- the abuser's death;
- the abuser's disappearance;
- the abuser's extreme ill-health;
- the conviction of the abuser for other offences, so that a prosecution for further offences relating to the claimant cannot be justified;

The absence of a conviction or even an acquittal will not be fatal to such a claim being brought. The standard of proof in civil proceedings is on the balance of probabilities rather than the criminal standard of beyond reasonable doubt.

7.1.2 In considering the standard of proof, the court in civil proceedings will take into account the test confirmed by the majority in the House of Lords in *Re H and R* (Child Sexual Abuse: Standard of Proof) [1996] 1 FLR 80. This test states that the standard of proof is the balance of probabilities, but, the more serious the allegation, the more cogent the evidence required to establish that the events happened on the balance-of-probabilities standard. Lord Nicholls in a majority speech described how:

> Where the matters in issue are facts the standard of proof required in non-criminal proceedings is the preponderance of probability, usually referred to as the balance of probability. This is the established general principle . . . The balance of probability standard means that a court is satisfied an event occurred if the court considers that, on the evidence, the occurrence of the event was more likely than not. When assessing the probabilities the court will have in mind as a factor, to whatever extent is appropriate in the particular case, that the more serious the allegation the less likely it is that the event occurred and, hence, the stronger should be the evidence before the court concludes that the allegation is established on the balance of probability. Fraud is usually less likely than negligence. Deliberate physical injury is usually less likely than accidental physical injury. A stepfather is usually less likely to have repeatedly raped and had non-consensual oral sex with his under-age stepdaughter than on some occasion to have lost his temper and slapped her. Built into the preponderance of probability standard is a serious degree of flexibility in respect of the seriousness of the allegation. Although the result is much the same, this does not mean that where a serious allegation is in issue the standard of proof required is higher. It means only that the inherent probability or improbability of an event is itself a matter to be taken into account when weighing the probabilities and deciding whether, on balance, the event occurred. The more improbable the event, the stronger must be the evidence that it did occur before, on the balance of probability, its occurrence will be established. Ungoed-Thomas J. expressed this neatly in *Re Dellow's Will Trusts, Lloyds Bank* v. *Institute of Cancer Research* [1964] 1 WLR 451 at p. 455:
>
> > 'The more serious the allegation, the more cogent is the evidence required to overcome the unlikelihood of what is alleged and thus to prove it.'
>
> This test accords with the approach adopted in early authorities such as the well-known judgment of Morris LJ in *Hornal* v. *Neuberger Products Ltd* [1957] 1 QB 247 at p. 266. This test also provides a means by which the balance of probability standard can accommodate one's instinctive feeling that even in civil proceedings a court should be more sure before finding serious allegations proved than when deciding less serious or trivial matters.

7.2   THE CLAIMANT'S STATEMENT

7.2.1   The formalities required to be complied with in a witness statement are set out in the Civil Procedure Rules at CPR 32.8 and Practice Direction 32 para. 17.1 (32PD-017). The practice direction specifically provides that 'the witness statement must, if practicable, be in the intended witness's own words'. As with any other litigation, the content of the claimant's statement will depend on the individual circumstances of the case. In most cases involving child abuse, it will be necessary for the statement to deal with the claimant's pre-abuse history, the details of the abuse and the claimant's post-abuse history. The following is a non-exhaustive list of the matters which should be included in a claimant's statement:

1. The claimant's name, address and date of birth.

2. A paragraph explaining that the statement deals with abuse suffered by the claimant between certain dates.

3. Details of the claimant's immediate family including the whereabouts and occupations of any siblings. If a claimant is the only child in a family to be abused, a comparison with the development of brothers and sisters may be relevant in assessing the impact of abuse.

4. The claimant's education and development prior to the abuse, including any allegations of abuse prior to the abuse which forms the basis of the claim.

5. If there was social services involvement, the claimant should, where possible, identify the date and circumstances in which any care order was made and/or details of the circumstances of his removal from his natural family, his social workers at the material time, together with any other professionals whom he saw, e.g. a child psychiatrist.

6. The circumstances in which the abuse took place and the identity of the abuser. The claimant's relationship with the abuser prior to the abuse.

7. Details of the abuse: the type of abuse, when it began, the frequency of the abuse and the length of time over which it continued.

8. Details of any witnesses. Witnesses would include not only those who saw the abuse, but also those to whom the claimant may have disclosed at the time or who suspected that the claimant was being abused.

9. Details of any complaints made by the claimant or others at the time of the abuse or shortly afterwards.

10. The claimant's education and general development as a child after the abuse, including any allegations of abuse after the abuse which forms the basis of the claim.

11. The claimant's history as an adult and an explanation as to (a) why he did not report the abuse at the time or later; (b) how he came to report the matter to the police, social services or his solicitor.

12. Details of the various institutions (such as schools, hospitals, psychiatric institutions) which he has attended throughout his life either before or after the relevant abuse, and the approximate times of attendance. The client should describe briefly any period of offending.

13. Details of the impact of the abuse on the claimant as an adult.

14. Details of any treatment which the claimant has undergone or is about to undergo.

15. The claimant's plans for the future, i.e. education, employment, etc.

7.2.2 Certain situations such as abuse in care homes will require additional issues to be addressed. In particular it is important to deal with the way in which the home functioned, since very often this provides the answer to the means by which the abuse was allowed to continue:

1. The claimant's first impression of the home on arrival.

2. A description of the number of children and staff in the home, their names and whether the claimant is still in contact with any of those people at the present time.

3. The layout of the home. If possible, the claimant should draw a map. Sometimes the layout of the home reveals how abusers gained access to their victims.

4. The way in which the home operated on a day-to-day basis, i.e. mealtimes, activities during the day, school lessons and bedtimes.

5. The enforcement of discipline in the home. For example, care-home staff might have allowed older children to abuse younger or weaker children. Alternatively, staff may have used a 'points' or 'token' system whereby good behaviour would earn privileges for children.

6. Visits to the home by social workers or other professionals, e.g. doctors. How often these occurred and whether they were monitored by staff.

7. Whether the claimant witnessed the abuse of other children.

8. Whether the claimant can remember any rumours or gossip regarding children or staff at the home. Whether any child was a 'favourite' of a member of staff, or a member of staff or a child suddenly left the home.

9. Whether the claimant can remember seeing physical signs of abuse, such as bloodstains on sheets or psychological signs such as bedwetting, self-mutilation by children or abscondences from the home.

10. Whether there was inappropriate/sexual conversation and activity between children and/or staff, e.g. the showing of horror or pornographic videos. Sometimes sex education or body searches are used as a cover for abuse.

11. Whether there was any complaints procedure, and whether any complaints were investigated and the way in which any investigation was handled.

12. Whether the claimant can remember any books being kept in the home.

7.3 OTHER LAY WITNESS EVIDENCE

7.3.1 The lawyer should consider whether there are other witnesses whose evidence will assist the claimant's case. In group actions, there will be a number of supporting statements from other claimants. However, in certain circumstances, witnesses such as care-home staff, teachers and neighbours may be able to corroborate some part of the claimant's case.

7.3.2   The claimant should be encouraged to name any potential witnesses. Very often he will still be in contact with these people as they may well still remain in the area where the abuse took place. Regrettably, many witnesses are reluctant to give statements in these types of cases. There are also bound to be problems locating such witnesses. Nevertheless, often simple enquiries (i.e. through directory enquiries) may be sufficient without incurring the expense of an enquiry agent. It is important that the lawyer draws up a list of potential witnesses as soon as practicable and in particular the steps taken to locate those witnesses. This should also be done with regard to sources of evidence, such as hospitals or employers. Child abuse cases do require a methodical search for evidence, particularly in cases when there is very little evidence in support of the claimant's allegations. It is also important for the lawyer to consider all the potential sources of information, before making the decision as to whether a search in one particular direction is justified.

7.3.3   It is also possible (at a relatively low price) to put a discreet advertisement in the local newspaper requesting witnesses, although this should be discussed with the client first as it may draw unwanted attention to the client.

7.4   DOCUMENTARY RECORDS

Social services records

7.4.1   Social services records are one of the most valuable sources of information in a child abuse claim, since they provide a contemporaneous record of the client's experiences as a child. The form and content of social services records vary between local authorities. The placement of the child by social services may dictate the type of records which will have been compiled. The Schedule attached to the Administration of Children's Homes Regulations 1951 (SI 1951 No. 1217) provides a list of records to be kept at any care home subject to those regulations. Similarly, Regulation 10 of the Boarding-Out of Children Regulations 1955 (SI 1955 No. 1377) describes the case records to be kept by local authorities and voluntary organisations (see Chapter 2). At the same time, social services guidance documents may specify the type of records which should be kept depending on the childcare situation.

7.4.2   The following is a non-exhaustive list of the type of records which are found in these cases:

1. Social workers' files. Any child in the care of social services should have an allocated social worker, and that social worker's file will contain the most detailed information on the child's progress. Typically, the file will contain the following:

   (a) A background history on the child and his family together with a record of contact between the child and his family.

   (b) If there have been court proceedings, a court report from a guardian ad litem, a probation officer or a court welfare officer.

   (c) Reports from external professionals such as psychiatrists or teachers.

   (d) Medical records.

   (e) If the child is in care, the six-monthly statutory child care reviews.

   (f) Internal memoranda requesting a placement.

   (g) Items from the child, such as drawings and letters.

2. External professionals' records. Records compiled by teachers and educational psychologists are generally to be found with the local education authority, or, in some circumstances, the particular school which the claimant attended. Records compiled by psychiatrists and psychologists are generally kept by the local health authority, the hospital or the GP's surgery.

3. Minutes of the local authority social services committee. Such committees are ultimately responsible for any child in the care. They may decide to place a child in a private home outside their area or to approve foster parents. Their decisions are normally made on the recommendation of social workers.

4. Records of senior managers and administrators. These are the people who carry out the executive functions of social services. They are responsible for drawing up policy documents, monitoring and supervision, recruitment, allocation and resources, infrastructure, as well as the running of homes.

5. Enquiries of local multi-disciplinary committees. These committees are responsible for preventing child abuse, and are made up of various agencies, such as the police, social services and health professionals. Where a child dies within the local authority's area, they are generally responsible for carrying out an inquiry.

6. Records of foster parents. Some foster parents keep their own records which are sometimes found on the social worker's files.

Lost social services notes

7.4.3   Where the claimant's lawyer is informed that social services notes have been lost or destroyed, it is important to ascertain:

1.   The policy of social services as to storage of records both at the material time and now. The length of time that records are kept, and where they are stored, and the document-destruction policy.

2.   If any policy existing now or at the time was not followed, whether there was any explanation or investigation into why the policy was not followed.

3.   The identity of the person who authorised the destruction of the notes, and whether there was an investigation into that destruction.

Medical records

7.4.4   These will include all the records from the claimant's childhood and adult life. If the claimant has undergone lengthy periods of treatment, for example in psychiatric institutions (including in prison), the cost of obtaining copies of records may raise a CPR proportionality issue. It may be appropriate for the claimant's solicitor to ask the medico-legal experts to inspect the original records at the location where they are held, to save the costs of copying.

Public inquiries, internal inquiries and press reports

7.4.5   It is not uncommon for local authorities and other childcare institutions to hold their own internal inquiries although these are not necessarily released to the public. Press articles arising out of child abuse investigations and press reports at the time of the abuse may provide useful material.

Criminal convictions and other records

7.4.6   The claimant's criminal record can be obtained by application on his authority to the local police station. Other records which may be relevant to a child abuse claim are:

1.   Employment records.

2.   Inland Revenue records.

3.   Department of Social Security benefit records.

4.   Prison and probation records.

Evidence arising from criminal investigations

7.4.7   Any police investigation into allegations of child abuse will provide useful information for a claim. However, the police will not release any information obtained in the course of a criminal investigation (apart from the claimant's own criminal statement), before that process is complete. At the conclusion of the investigation they will generally decline to release the remaining records except under the cover of a court order.

7.5   PUBLIC INTEREST IMMUNITY

7.5.1   Social services records typically contain highly confidential information relating to children in a local authority's care as well as information obtained in confidence from or on third parties. The following should be read in the light of the provisions of the Data Protection Act 1998 (DPA 1998) and the Freedom of Information Act 2000 (FOIA 2000) which are discussed in para. 7.6 below. It is not entirely clear how the doctrine of public interest immunity, the DPA 1998 and the FOIA 2000 will work together, although, certainly, the public interest immunity argument is still relied upon by local authorities and other organisations.

7.5.2   Rule 31.19(1) of the CPR 1998 allows a party to withhold disclosure or inspection on the grounds of public interest. When presented with a request for disclosure of social services records, the local authority is obliged to consider whether those records are subject to public interest immunity. This means that (in the opinion of the local authority) the production or disclosure of the records would harm the public interest generally. However, if the local authority is satisfied that the public interest is in favour of disclosure, i.e. the immunity is outweighed by the interests of justice, then it may disclose the relevant material *R* v. *Chief Constable of the West Midlands, ex p. Wiley* [1995] 1 AC 274.

7.5.3   The court is under a duty to consider the issue of public interest immunity, even if neither party in the proceedings has raised it.

7.5.4   The public interest to be protected is the effective performance of the local authority in respect of its duties towards children in its care. The performance of those duties includes maintaining the utmost confidence in the local authority's system of record keeping in childcare cases, as well as the storing of information relating to third parties. For example, certain regulations such as the Foster Placement (Children) Regulations 1991 (SI 1991 No. 910) include regulations relating to retention and confidentiality of records.

7.5.5   Claims for public interest immunity may be either:

1. A claim that the document ought not to be disclosed because of the class of documents to which it belongs.

2. A claim that the documents ought not to be disclosed because of its contents.

7.5.6   In *Re D (Infants)* [1970] 1 WLR 599 the court considered records produced under the Boarding-Out of Children Regulations (SI 1955 No.1377) (the 1955 Regulations). The court held that it would be quite contrary to established practice if such records were disclosed. Furthermore, disclosure would be contrary to public policy because social workers keeping such records would forever be under the threat of attack for expressing adverse opinions on persons within the records.

7.5.7   In *Re S (Minors) (Wardship: Police Investigation)* [1987] 3 WLR 847 the court held that case records kept under the 1955 Regulations were confidential records and were protected from disclosure. In *Re S and W (Minors) (Confidential Reports)* (1983) 4 FLR 290 it was held that reports in respect of a child considered for fostering were immune from production. In *DPP* v. *Morrow* ([1994] Crim LR 58) public interest immunity attached to files relating to prospective adoptive parents held by the local social services.

7.5.8   In *D* v. *NSPCC* [1978] AC 171 the NSPCC was able to withhold disclosure of documents identifying an informant who had wrongly suggested that a mother was beating her child.

7.5.9   However, in *Re M (A Minor) (Disclosure of Material)* [1990] 2 FLR 36 the approach, where automatic immunity was granted in respect of social work records, was reconsidered. It was established that social work and analogous records are in a special category of immunity, justified by the particular circumstances of the welfare of the children. However, there is no absolute rule against disclosure and each case will be judged on its own merits. The court should weigh up competing interests in a balancing operation: on the one hand, the public interest in the proper administration of public justice by making all relevant material available to the litigants, and, on the other hand, the public interest in not harming society as a whole by releasing highly confidential information. (See also *Air Canada* v. *Secretary of State for Trade (No.2)* [1983] 2 AC 394.)

7.5.10   Articles 6.1 and 8 of the European Convention on Human Rights will be relevant to any public interest immunity hearing. Police files (see *Leander* v. *Sweden* [1987] 9 EHRR 433) and local authority social services files (see *Gaskin* v. *UK* [1990] 1 FLR 167) relating to an individual fall under the principle of the right to private and family life under Article 8. Article

6.1 of the Convention confers upon a person the right to a 'fair and public hearing'.

7.5.11 In the case of child abuse claimants, the following practical considerations which may be relevant to the court's decision as to whether public interest immunity should attach to records:

1. Whether the records relate to children who are now adults.

2. Whether it is open to the local authority to 'blank out' names of third parties.

3. Rule 31.6 of the CPR provides that standard disclosure includes documents which may have a positive or negative effect on either party's case.

4. Whether full disclosure would enable the defendant to prepare a proper defence, particularly in a case where the material events have occurred a long time in the past, and limitation is at issue.

7.6   THE DATA PROTECTION ACT 1998 AND THE FREEDOM OF INFORMATION ACT 2000

The Data Protection Act 1998 (DPA 1998)

7.6.1 The Data Protection Act 1998 (the Act) came into force on 1 March 2000 and was passed pursuant to the UK's obligations under the European Data Protection Directive (95/46/EC). It lays down new principles regarding rights of access to data. The Act defines data under section 1(1)(c) and that definition includes social services, health and education records brought into being both before and after the Act.

7.6.2 Section 7 of the Act provides that a data subject (i.e. a person who is the subject of data) is entitled to make a written request (upon payment of a prescribed fee) to a data controller (i.e. the person holding the data). Upon submission of that request, the data subject is entitled to obtain the information constituting any personal data of which that individual is the data subject and any information available to the data controller as to the source of those data: s.7(1)(c)(i)–(ii).

7.6.3 The rights of the data subject to receive information and access personal data are defined as the 'subject information provisions' under s.1 of the Act. However, s.30 of the Act allowed the Secretary of State to make regulations exempting certain personal data from the 'subject information provisions'. Such personal data includes 'accessible records' i.e. data which is processed for health, education and social work purposes: s.68(1)(a)–(c).

7.6.4 The exemption regulations relating to health, education and social work records have now been made and are listed below:

1. The Data Protection (Subject Access Modification) (Social Work) Order 2000 (SI 2000 No. 415).
2. The Data Protection (Subject Access Modification) (Education) Order 2000 (SI 2000 No. 414).
3. The Data Protection (Subject Access Modification) (Health) Order 2000 (SI 2000 No. 413).

7.6.5 These regulations came into force on 1 March 2000. They provide for partial exemption from the provisions of the Act which confer rights on data subjects to gain access to data held about them. For example Regulation 5(1) of SI 2000 No. 413 states that personal data to which the Regulations apply are exempt from the obligations set in s.7(1)(b)–(d) of the Act (i.e. the right to receive information relating to records). This restriction is stated to be limited to the extent to which the application of that right to information would be likely to prejudice the carrying out of social work by reason of the fact that serious harm to the physical or mental health or condition of the data subject or any other person would be likely to be caused.

The Freedom of Information Act 2000 (FOIA 2000)

7.6.6 This Act is being brought into force by stages. It establishes a general right of access to information held by public authorities, in particular the right to know whether information is held by a public authority, and the right of access to that information. However, the Act is subject to numerous exceptions and limitations. It makes limited amendments to the Data Protection Act 1998.

7.7   PRE-ACTION DISCLOSURE OF RECORDS

7.7.1 The provision of information, in particular pre-action disclosure of social services notes remains a problem in child abuse litigation. There are instances of certain insurers and public authorities simply refusing to hand over any records, despite the rights to information which presently exist under the DPA 1998. Section 7(9) DPA 1998 states that a person may make application to the court if information has been withheld in contravention of the provisions of the Act. Section 13 DPA 1998 allows for compensation. Any action would be taken out under Part 7 or Part 8 of the CPR (see p. 3841 III PAT [58.1] CPR, Vol. 2). There is also the possibility of taking out an application for pre-action disclosure under the CPR 31.16, which sets out the ground on which such an application must be based. One suggested basis for such an application would be that the claimant can only plead his case properly by reference to his own social services notes, and so avoid the need for a costly amendment to those pleadings later on.

7.8   THE ROLE OF EXPERTS

7.8.1   Child abuse claims will typically require supporting evidence from the following types of experts. It is important that the lawyer ensures that the relevant expert has detailed instructions, and that he is provided (as far as is practicable) with the claimant's medical and social services records.

Liability

7.8.2   In a claim against a social services department, the social care expert advises on the standard of care applicable at the time of the material events. Social care experts are experienced social workers who can examine the relevant records together with any witness statements, and comment on errors and substandard practice. As in any professional negligence claim, it is important to identify an expert with the relevant experience to comment on the actions complained of. In particular, the social work expert will need to demonstrate that they have experience:

- at the relevant level of qualification of the staff whose actions are being attacked;
- at the date of the actions complained of;
- in the same field of social work/care as the actions complained of.

It may be necessary to identify a director of social services as an expert if the actions complained of are the overall control exercised by a local authority in respect of a child. Alternatively, if the complaint is in respect of Home Office Inspections, a Home Office Inspector will be the relevant expert.

Quantum: psychiatric/psychological injuries

7.8.3   The most prominent feature of child abuse is the mental injury to the claimant. Lawyers in this area of the law have instructed both psychologists and psychiatrists. It is necessary to consider the distinction between the two specialisms. A consultant psychiatrist is a qualified medical practitioner and is defined as 'a medically qualified physician who specializes

193

in the study of and treatment of mental disorders' (*Oxford Concise Medical Dictionary*). A psychologist has no medical training but has completed at least a first degree in psychology. He is defined as 'a person who is engaged in the scientific study of the mind' (*Oxford Concise Medical Dictionary*). A clinical psychologist has been trained in aspects of the assessment of treatment of the ill and handicapped and usually works in a hospital as part of a multidisciplinary team.

7.8.4 In a child abuse compensation claim where it is necessary to establish a medically recognised psychiatric illness, the opinion of a qualified medical practitioner, i.e. a psychiatrist will be required. However, it should be noted that mental health institutions employ both types of specialist and that the experience of the particular expert (whether they be a psychiatrist or a psychologist) is crucial to the quality of the supporting evidence. It should be noted that the new CICA Scheme introduced in April 2001 stipulates that psychiatric injury (in certain circumstances) can be supported by either a psychiatrist or a clinical psychologist

7.8.5 The lawyer should also consider whether there is a viable claim for treatment. The psychiatrist/psychologist should advise on the type and length of treatment which is suitable for the claimant. The treatment itself is best undertaken by a psychotherapist registered by the UK Council for Psychotherapy. The British Association for Behavioural and Cognitive Psychotherapies publishes a list of suitably qualified psychotherapists for each area of the country. Alternatively, the psychiatrist/psychologist may suggest counselling. Counsellors are generally accredited by the British Association for Counselling.

7.8.6 Certain claimants are unable to travel to treatment. It may be necessary to instruct a nursing care expert (with a specialism in psychiatry), who can visit the claimant in his home and provide such support and treatment as is necessary.

7.8.7 Abuse may have damaged a claimant's educational progress, in particular where that claimant suffers from a pre-existing learning difficulty. In appropriate cases, the lawyer should consider the instruction of an educational psychologist. Such a psychologist has been trained in aspects of the cognitive and emotional development of children.

Quantum: physical Injuries

7.8.8 Abuse may cause permanent physical damage. Intercourse (anal or vaginal) may lead to permanent physical damage or the contraction of a sexually transmitted disease. The relevant experts are a gynaecologist in the case of a female claimant and a coloproctologist in the case of an anal injury. It is necessary for claimants to consider whether they are willing to undergo an invasive physical examination since this can be an extremely traumatic process.

7.8.9 Other physical injuries caused by abuse may include broken bones, head injuries, self-mutilation. Claimants have complained of being provided with badly fitting shoes while in homes, which have caused foot and spinal problems later in life. In such cases an orthopaedic surgeon who has experience of paediatric injuries and who may be able to recognise a non-accidental injury, will be suitable.

Expert evidence in general

7.8.10 In the case of *Various claimants* v. *Flintshire County Council* (26 July 2000, unreported) Scott Baker J. commented on the quality of evidence, which a court might expect in a child abuse case:

> I make three points about the expert evidence. First, there has been a great deal of unnecessary duplication and consequently cost, and secondly a disappointingly large number of the experts (there had been 14 experts in the case) have given me the impression of being rather less than completely objective and impartial. Maybe that has been because of emotive nature of the case, or maybe because the effect the abuse has had on an individual's life is very much more a matter of 'feel' than precise analysis and calculation. Bearing in mind that this is a group action I would have had more assistance if one or two experts could have set out the general principles that should be applied by psychiatrists and psychologists in assessing the causes of personality and psychological problems in cases such as this rather than have every expert set out in his report in his own words his views and then, perhaps expand them during oral evidence.
>
> It is of course helpful to have experts in individual cases flag up documents or highlight aspects of the evidence that may support a particular conclusion. What is not helpful is for an expert to pick out pieces of evidence or entries in documents that support the conclusion his side seeks to reach while not looking for or discarding material that points the other way. One of the difficulties for the expert, I readily accept, is that the cornerstone of any opinion will be the abuse or facts eventually established at the trial.
>
> I appreciate that with such a large number of cases and claimants living all over the country that it will not be physically possible to have the same expert in every case. However it should be possible to have one or two experts dealing with generic matters and some limitaton on the number of experts dealing with specific cases.

7.8.11 Scott Baker J. drew attention to the duties and responsibilities of expert witnesses in civil cases as set out in *The Ikarian Reefer* [1993] 2 Lloyd's Rep 68. He pointed out that there appeared to have been little attempt in the present cases for the experts to meet to try and identify and isolate their differences.

7.8.12 In *Various Claimants* v. *Bryn Alyn Community Homes Ltd and another* (26 June 2001, unreported), Connell J. noted with approval that the comments of Scott Baker J. on expert evidence had been observed.

Generic reports

7.8.13 In actions involving a number of claimants injured in the same institution it may be helpful for the social work expert and/or the psychiatric expert to prepare a generic report describing the common themes that occur in the individual cases. For example the nature of the regime, its failure to comply with the statutory provisions in force at the time and any regulations covering the home or institution. Further, the activities of particular abusers may be traced in such a report with reference to different victims showing the methods of operation of that particular abuser. A generic psychiatric report may be helpful in setting out the research in respect of child abuse and the type of injuries and symptoms frequently experienced by such victims. It may also help to identify the reasons why complaints can sometimes only be made many years after the events

Joint experts

7.8.14 The possibility of examination by a joint expert should be considered in all cases. In cases where a joint examination by a psychiatrist or any other medical expert is appropriate, the claimant's solicitor should at an early stage forward a list of two or three possible experts in each specialism to the defendant's solicitors and ask them to agree to a joint expert. Examination by a joint expert has the obvious advantage in these cases that claimants are saved from having to go through the details of their experiences with two experts.

CHAPTER 8

Practical guidance in running child abuse compensation claims

8.1 Case handling
8.2 The conflict between the criminal and the civil process
8.3 Public funding
8.4 Private funding, conditional fee agreements and insurance

8.1 CASE HANDLING

The impact of child abuse

8.1.1 It is essential for any practitioner dealing with cases involving child abuse to have a basic understanding of the effect of abuse on children and adults. This is important not only with regard to causation and quantum assessment, but also in the context of abusive situations and how they occur. There is a suggested reading list for lawyers in the Appendices.

8.1.2 The effect of child abuse also has implications for case handling, since the compensation process can have an adverse effect on the claimant's mental health and his ability to give instructions. Anecdotal evidence from lawyers involved in such claims suggests that some claimants experience extreme difficulties in replying to correspondence from their lawyers, providing statements and attending appointments with experts. At the same time, certain claimants can be extremely demanding of the lawyer's time and resources.

8.1.3 It should be pointed out that it is not the lawyer's responsibility to assume a therapeutic role for his client. If the client wishes to seek help and support, a comprehensive list of local advice and support centres is to be found in the *Directory and Book Services National Resource Direction* (see Appendices).

8.1.4 Indeed, in child abuse compensation claims, it is vital that the lawyer maintains a strictly professional approach to the client at all times. The following is a list of practical points which have been formed from the writers' experience. It is by no means exhaustive and may not be appropriate or possible in all cases.

- At first interview, the lawyer should refrain from asking the client to make a full disclosure of all of his experiences, but rather ascertain where the likely sources of information are. From a practical point of view, the client's statement may take many hours, or the client may already have made a statement to the police or a psychiatrist which can be incorporated into a full civil statement (see Chapter 7). The Appendices contain a Statement of Case in an application for public funding, and para. 8.3 describes the kind of information which the Legal Services Commission requires in such applications.

- The lawyer should set out a structured caseplan for the client, and explain exactly what will be required of the client for the case to progress. For instance, a client in a CICA claim should be warned that he may have to face his abuser in an appeal hearing. Similarly, a client who refuses examination by a psychiatrist may prejudice the progress of his own litigation case.

- The client should be advised as soon as possible of: (a) the likely costs of the case; (b) the expected level of damages; (c) the length of time the case will take to conclude; (d) limitation advice. These are all matters which would normally be discussed at the outset of a normal personal injury case. While it may be very difficult to give a victim of child abuse an accurate view at the outset of the case, an early and realistic assessment will dispel any false preconceptions which the client may have formed about the compensation process.

- The lawyer should agree a medium of communication with the client. Some victims of child abuse live chaotic lives, and frequently change addresses. This means that correspondence does not reach them, and the lawyer has no means of speedy communication. This can have disastrous consequences for a case, for instance where there has been non-compliance with court directions. The client should be warned at the outset of his case, that failure to give instructions and cooperate with the legal process could lead to the dismissal of the compensation claim.

- The abuse of children constitutes criminal activity. Clients should always be advised at the outset of their claim to report the matter to the police if they have not already done so. Certain police investigations in this country have begun from the allegations of one single complainant. In addition, social services and voluntary organisations will sometimes institute their own internal investigations if allegations are brought to their attention. This is obviously a matter for the client to decide. At the outset of any claim, it will be unclear whether any investigation on the part of the authorities will enhance the claim. However, it is perfectly possible that the police are already investigating a similar set of circumstances.

- The lawyer should ensure that he has the time and the resources to progress the client's case, having regard to his existing caseload. Child abuse compensation claims can be extremely time-consuming and complex. The client's statement may well take a number of hours to complete, quite apart from the time spent instructing experts, obtaining documentation, and dealing with the defendant. The documentation produced, including medical notes, social services records, statement and psychiatrist's reports can run into hundreds of pages. Consequently, a barrister advising on the case or a psychiatrist examining the claimant may need to spend a considerable amount of time on the case, before any advice or report is produced. The consequent cost should be worked out beforehand and authorised either by the client in a private case or the Legal Services Commission in a publicly funded case.

- It is important to ascertain the exact nature of the client's instructions at the outset of the case. Certain victims of abuse may state, at the outset of their case, that they are not interested in obtaining compensation, but rather that they wish to ensure that no one else has to suffer their own experiences. Certainly, there are other options open to a client, such as utilising a local authority's complaints procedures or requesting a public inquiry into that local authority's residential care (see Chapter 2). For instance, the client may require nothing less than to bring his opponent into a court of law. This may not be practical in the context of a reasonable offer of settlement and the continuing provision of public funding.

- The lawyer should take extreme care when dealing with the media. The publication of a story in a newspaper regarding the claimant's or a group of claimants' cases has been known to cause great distress to the claimants themselves. Furthermore, it is not unusual for claimants to remain in the actual area where they suffered abuse. The sudden appearance of a newspaper article can make them the object of unwanted attention. There are legal constraints on the reporting of cases involving children (see Chapter 2). Practically, the lawyer may have very little control over what is produced by a newspaper. At the very least, some warning should be given to the client if at all possible.

Mental capacity

8.1.5　Many victims of child abuse suffer serious psychiatric problems for which they may require treatment by way of psychotherapy or counselling, or in some cases as an in-patient within a mental health institution. Where there is evidence of mental disturbance in a claimant, the lawyer should consider whether he can accept instructions directly from that person as a client (see Ch. 12.01 of the *Guide to the Professional Conduct of Solicitors* (Law Society)). Section 1 of the Mental Health Act 1983 defines the various categories of mental disorder for purposes of the Act. It adds at s.1(3) that a person does not suffer from mental disorder by reason only of promiscuity, or other immoral conduct, sexual deviancy or dependence on alcohol or drugs. Where the claimant is resident in a hospital under the provisions of the Mental Health Act 1983, the issue of mental capacity can be answered by the treating psychiatrist. The position will be less clear where the claimant lives in the community, and is under the care of a community psychiatric nurse or a psychiatric social worker.

8.1.6   In addition, the British Medical Association together with the Law Society has published a handbook entitled *Assessment of Mental Capacity: Guidance for doctors and lawyers* (Law Society/BMA, December 1995) which sets out the factors which should be considered when considering whether a person has mental capacity. The book states that 'any doctor should be able to take a psychiatric history and to conduct a basic mental state examination' (*Assessment of Mental Capacity*, para. 13.2.1).

8.1.7   The handbook stresses the importance of the primary diagnostic decision being taken by a medical practitioner (by contrast with a clinical psychologist). The doctor or medical practitioner could be the claimant's own GP, but it is submitted that it would be preferable to seek the opinion of the treating psychiatrist who is familiar with the claimant's history and who can give an opinion. The handbook goes on to say that 'It is important to choose a specialist based not so much on the specialist's detailed research knowledge but upon his or her clinical acquaintance with the condition and experience of caring for patients with that condition' (Ibid.). Furthermore, the handbook states that 'in a complex medico-legal case, it may be important for a lawyer to choose a doctor with particular experience in medico-legal work' (Ibid., para. 13.2.3).

8.1.8   There is also a body of caselaw which has grown up on the issue of mental capacity in the fields of consent to medical treatment and community care. In *Re MB* (*An Adult: Medical Treatment*) [1997] 2 FCR 541 the Court of Appeal laid down the following principles:

1. Every adult is presumed to have capacity, unless shown to the contrary.

2. Capacity should be considered in relation to the particular decision, in other words the more serious the decision, the greater the capacity required.

3. If a patient does have capacity, then the issue of best interests does not arise. It does not matter if the decision is one which would not be made by a person of ordinary prudence and, indeed, may be irrational or founded on no good reason.

4. A person lacks capacity if some impairment or disturbance of mental functioning renders the person unable to make a decision. That inability to make a decision will occur when:

    (a) the person is unable to comprehend and retain the information which is material to the decision, especially about the likely consequences;

    (b) the patient is unable to use the information and weigh it in the balance as part of the process of arriving at the decision.

5. Temporary factors such as confusion, shock, fatigue or pain may erode capacity, but these factors would need to be operating to such an extent that the ability to decide is nullified.

8.1.9 It should be noted that the above case concerned the withholding of consent to medical treatment. It is less clear what the position would be where a victim of child abuse with mental health problems is required to instruct lawyers, undergo the stress of litigation and take decisions relating to substantial amounts of compensation.

8.1.10 Where the claimant does not have mental capacity, the lawyer will need to appoint a litigation friend. Under the CPR (Part 21) this is usually a member of the claimant's family. However, in cases where the claimant has been taken into care at an early age (for instance as a result of intrafamilial abuse), the option of a family member as litigation friend may not be possible. In such circumstances, it may be possible to request the Official Solicitor to act as litigation friend, although it should be stressed that such a course is only a 'last resort'.

8.1.11 It is vital to determine the issue of mental capacity at an early stage as it is crucial to a number of issues, in particular:

- whether the claimant requires a litigation friend;
- whether the Court of Protection need to be involved in the litigation;
- limitation.

8.1.12 Section 28 of the Limitation Act 1980 provides:

> if on the date when any cause of action accrued for which a period of limitation is prescribed by this Act, the person to whom it accrued was under a disability, the action may be brought at any time before the expiration of six years from the date when he ceased to be under a disability or died (whichever first occurred) notwithstanding that the period of limitation has expired.

Section 38(2) of the Limitation Act 1980 provides:

> For the purpose of this Act a person shall be treated as under a disability while he is an infant or of unsound mind.

Section 38(3) of the Limitation Act 1980 provides:

> For the purpose of section (2) above a person is of unsound mind if he is a person who, by reason of mental disorder within the meaning of the Mental Health Act 1983 is incapable of managing and administering his property and affairs.

Section 38(4) of the Limitation Act 1980 provides that without prejudice to section 38(3) if a person is detained under the Mental Health Act 1983 and is receiving treatment as an in-patient they will be 'conclusively presumed to be of unsound mind'.

Detention in a mental hospital is only one way of showing the requisite disability for the purposes of the Act.

The definition of 'unsound mind' in the Limitation Act 1980 requires two elements to be satisfied:

> (i)   the Claimant must be incapable of managing and administering his property and affairs; and
>
> (ii)   the reason for this disability must be that the claimant is suffering from 'mental disorder' as defined in section 1(2) Mental Health Act 1983 which states:
>
>> 'mental disorder means illness, arrested or incomplete development of mind, psychopathic disorder and any other disorder or disability of mind'.

Further guidance is contained in the Review of the Mental Health Act 1959 (Cmnd 7320) and White paper, Reform of Mental Health Legislation (Cmnd 8405).

There is very little authority on what constitutes mental incapacity in respect of psychiatric damage, particularly in respect of mental disorder following sexual abuse – this is a point which may well need to be explored by the courts in this context.

In Heywood and Massey, *Court of Protection Practice*, thirteenth edition, in identifying patients that are subject to the jurisdiction of the Court of Protection it is stated that:

> The question of degree of incapacity of managing and administering a patient's property and affairs must be related to all the circumstances including the state in which the patient lives, the complexity and importance of the property and affairs which he has to manage and administer, and the Court has a discretion of deciding whether in the circumstances and upon the facts it is right for a receiver to be appointed.

This suggests the test is a subjective one and is based on the unreported decision of Mr Justice Wilberforce (as he then was) in the case of *Re CAF* 1961 No. 2363 (23 March 1962).

8.2   THE CONFLICT BETWEEN THE CRIMINAL AND THE CIVIL PROCESS

8.2.1   The claimant may approach a solicitor to investigate a claim for compensation before he has made any report to the police, or after the criminal process, i.e. the trial has finished. Where the criminal process is still ongoing, the police are generally careful about what information is furnished to compensation lawyers acting for prosecution witnesses. A defence lawyer acting for a person accused of child abuse will be looking for weaknesses in the prosecution case. It may be well be put to a prosecution witness that his story has been concocted in order to obtain compensation, or that he has put his account of events together from talking to other prosecution witnesses.

8.2.2   Defence lawyers may also apply for orders from a criminal court for sight of the civil lawyer's file. There are limits to such applications, but a successful application can provide material for cross-examination including for instance a psychiatric opinion on the claimant which comments on his mental instability or the fact that he has added to his disclosures since making his police statement.

8.2.3   Lawyers who defend defendants accused of child abuse often find that because events have occurred a long time ago, their clients find it difficult to recall the detail of events or offer any positive information to discredit the prosecution evidence. Complainants may come forward after the criminal process has begun, and so be added to the list of prosecution witnesses. The Crown Prosecution may be selective in what is disclosed and so it is for the Defendant's lawyers to make application for disclosure of documentation. For an examination of this particular issue, see article by McDonald, L., 13 April 2001 'Defending child abuse cases – tips and pitfalls', *New Law Journal*.

8.2.4   Consequently, a civil lawyer may be faced with the immediate problem of whether to issue civil proceedings and/or make application to the CICA on behalf of the claimant, or wait until the criminal process is complete. On balance it is recommended that civil proceedings and/or a CICA claim be instituted as soon as practicable. There are several reasons for taking this course. First, the criminal process may take years to complete, during which time the claimant will be unable to recover compensation including the cost of therapy. Unless agreement can be reached with the defendant that limitation issues are precipitated at the date of notification of the claim, proceedings will have to be issued as soon as possible. Any delay will significantly prejudice the claimant's limitation position and give rise to the risk of further witnesses dying or disappearing. Second, the issues which are placed before a criminal court are very different to those which come before a civil court. A person may be acquitted before a criminal court, but that does not necessarily mean that a civil court or the CICA cannot make an award. Third, the publicity surrounding police investigations into child abuse and the resultant compensation claims means that many people will be well aware, whether they have consulted a lawyer or not, that they may be entitled to compensation.

8.2.5   However, the civil lawyer should warn the claimant that his compensation claim is bound to be an issue in the criminal process. In group actions it is recommended that claimants should be advised by their civil lawyers not to speak to one another regarding the civil and criminal cases. Furthermore, the solicitors involved in the group action should not discuss the details of their client's case. This limits the scope of any defence argument based on collusion between witnesses. Finally, it is open to the lawyer acting for the defendant in a civil case to apply for a stay of proceedings, while the criminal case is heard.

8.3   PUBLIC FUNDING

8.3.1   Child abuse compensation claims are one of the few types of personal injury claims which still attract public funding. The present rules relating to public funding were introduced under the Access to Justice Act 1999 (the 1999 Act). Section 6(6) of the 1999 Act provides that only certain categories of case will be eligible for public funding. It provides for a Funding Code to be drawn up to state which categories of cases are eligible for public funding. Schedule 2 para. 1(a) to the 1999 Act excludes from the scope of public funding negligently inflicted personal injury. However, s.8.1 of the present Funding Code includes within the categories of cases eligible for public funding, claims against 'public authorities concerning serious wrongdoing, abuse of position or power or significant breach of human rights'. Furthermore para. 1(a) is not intended to exclude cases about personal injury arising from an alleged assault of deliberate abuse.

8.3.2   Originally, only those with a Legal Services Commission (LSC) personal injury franchise could be granted public-funding certificates in abuse cases. The LSC has now proposed that the franchise for actions against the police should be extended to include 'an allegation of deliberate abuse of any person whilst in the care of a public authority or institution, whether or not falling within any other franchise category other than clinical negligence'. This proposal is expected to be brought into force in December 2001.

8.3.3 The LSC has also proposed that a new franchise be set up to include child abuse and the abuse of vulnerable persons entitled 'Mistreatment by those responsible for care'.

8.3.4 There are several levels of public funding. Legal help is available for the preparation of claims to the CICA (see Chapter 6) and for the preparation of applications for legal representation. Public-funding certificates are still available for certain types of personal injury claims against public authorities and claims which involve an issue of human rights. All public-funding applications which relate to allegations of child abuse should be submitted to the Manchester Area Office of the LSC, which has been designated as the central office for child abuse claims, irrespective of which area of the country they relate to.

8.3.5 An example of a letter in support of a public funding application in an abuse claim is given at Appendix 2. The LSC has not announced any formal guidelines for the assessment of applications. However, in the experience of the writers, the following are the main criteria upon which the LSC will base its decision:

1. Whether the claimant is likely to be able to prove the occurrence of the abuse. This will be satisfied by the criminal conviction of the abuser. If the alleged abuser has not been convicted, a decision by the police to investigate may be sufficient. In a multi-party action, the LSC will be aware that corroborative evidence is likely to be available from other claimants.

2. Whether the likely quantum of the claim will satisfy the costs–benefits ratio. A brief description of the nature and extent of the abuse together with details of the long term effect on the claimant will be required.

3. Whether the proposed defendant is solvent or insured.

4. If the claim appears to be statute barred, whether the applicant can give a satisfactory explanation for failing to bring proceedings earlier.

8.4 PRIVATE FUNDING, CONDITIONAL FEE AGREEMENTS AND INSURANCE

8.4.1 Where the applicant is ineligible to apply for a public-funding certificate on financial grounds, securing alternative case funding may be difficult. The possible availability of legal expenses insurance in a household insurance policy should not be overlooked. In abuse cases there are two common problems: securing 'after the event' insurance and the position of a privately funded claimant in a group action in which most litigants are publicly funded.

8.4.2   A privately paying/CFA claimant in a multi-party action is potentially liable not only for those generic costs (including generic disbursements and
counsel's fees) which are not covered by any CFA, but also for a share of
the defendant's costs if the action is lost. Costs are at the discretion of the
court, and consequently it is possible for the court to award the entire
generic costs of the defendant against a single private claimant in an un-
successful group action.

8.4.3   Therefore, one approach which might be adopted in a group action is to invite the defendants to agree that private claimants' claims will be dealt
with at the conclusion of the action without the need for them to be added
onto the Claim Form and so incur a costs risk.

The insolvent defendant

8.4.4   Most claims are against institutions rather than individuals. One reason for
this is that individuals who have been convicted of abuse are often insol-
vent or of limited means and cannot pay a claim. However, the claimant
should check his own household insurance policy. Some such policies
contain a provision whereby the insurer will discharge an unsatisfied judgment debt. This may enable the claimant to bring a claim against an insol-
vent defendant which is ultimately paid by the claimant's own insurer.

The case of John Doe

MR JOHN DOE
STATEMENT OF CASE IN SUPPORT OF PUBLIC-FUNDING APPLICATION

Introduction

John Doe was taken into care during the 1980s by Wessex County Council. He was placed at a controlled community home where he was sexually and physically abused by a member of staff. At the age of 16 he left care.

In 2000, John Doe was contacted by police in connection with an investigation into the care home where he had been abused. After his abuser has been convicted of abuse, he proceeds to instruct solicitors, who apply for public funding on his behalf. On receipt of a public funding certificate, a Letter of Claim is sent to Wessex County Council and a psychiatrist is instructed. Proceedings are then issued (including a Schedule of Loss and Damage), and a Defence is filed. There then follow Case Management Directions.

The facts

The Applicant, Mr John Doe was born on 20 July 1971 and is now 30 years of age. He is currently unemployed and is living at 15 Acacia Avenue, Christminster, Wessex.

He wishes to bring a claim against Wessex County Council in respect of sexual and emotional abuse which he suffered at The Elms Children's Home in Casterbridge from 1983 to 1987.

We enclose the following statements and reports by way of background:

1. Statement of Mr John Doe.

2. Exhibit JD1 Schedule of Mr Doe's convictions.

3. Newspaper report from the Casterbridge Clarion dated 6 July 2001.

4. Caselaw (short report on the case of *Various Claimants* v. *Bryn Alyn Community Homes Ltd and Others*) (QBD (Connell J.) 26 June 2001)

Mr Doe was placed in care at The Elms Children's Home at the age of 12 following the death of his father. His mother had mental health problems and was physically abusive towards her children. He was taken into care by Wessex County Council. Mr Doe suffered abuse here from 1983 to 1987 by which time he was 16 years old and left the home voluntarily. His statement gives some details as to his experiences both before being placed in care, at para. 5, and during his time in care, at paras. 12–16. So far we have not had time to take a detailed statement from him on his experiences.

While at The Elms Children's Home, Mr Doe was sexually abused by the manager of the home, Mr Reginald Smith. Mr Smith took Mr Doe away with him on numerous occasions to his own home and this is where the instances of sexual abuse occurred. The abuse that he suffered involved buggery and oral sex.

Mr Doe left The Elms in 1987 when he reached the age of 16. He developed a heroin addiction and began offending. These offences continued for roughly six years up until 1993 when he met his partner, Jane. At this stage he found employment as a security guard and continued in this employment until June 2000 when the police contacted him in connection with the criminal investigation that is the subject-matter of this action. Following the police investigation and the re-emergence of the incidents of sexual abuse in his past, Mr Doe suffered serious mental health problems and he has been unable to work since January 2001. He has been treated as an outpatient of Christminster General Hospital since June 2001.

The police investigation

In early 2000 another victim of Reginald Smith informed the Police Child Protection Team at Casterbridge police station that she had been abused by him while at The Elms. In June 2000 Mr Doe was approached by the police regarding their criminal investigations because the other victim had mentioned him in her statement. Mr Smith was arrested and charged but pleaded not guilty. Mr Doe gave evidence against him and in June 2001 he was convicted of six out of eight indictments. He was sentenced to seven years' imprisonment.

Duty of care

We understand that The Elms was owned and managed by the local authority, Wessex County Council. Wessex County Council would have owed Mr Doe a duty of care to take reasonable steps to ensure his safety and well-being while he was a child in their care, to monitor any deterioration in his behaviour, and to seek to address any such deterioration in behaviour. This duty of care arose when Mr Doe was placed in care and continued up until the time that he left care at the age of 16.

Breach of duty

We allege that this duty of care was breached.

Mr Doe's claim is centred around the abuse that he suffered while at The Elms Children's Home, since this is when the incidents of sexual abuse occurred.

1. In 1983 Mr Doe made a complaint to the headmaster of Casterbridge Secondary School, Mr Healey, that Mr Smith was being violent towards him. Social services were contacted and said that they would investigate, but regrettably nothing was done. On

the contrary, Mr Randall, a Social Worker, persuaded Mr Doe that it would not be in his interests to make such allegations of physical abuse. There is apparently a complete record of this incident in Mr Doe's social services records.

2. In 1984 Mr Doe told Miss Hamilton, a residential social worker, that he was being abused by Mr Smith and said that Mr Smith would not leave him alone. She confronted Mr Smith about the allegations but soon left the Elms, allegedly having been intimidated by Mr Smith.

3. Mr Doe attended Dr Black, a GP in Casterbridge, in 1984 because he had problems with anal bleeding. Dr Black reported the matter to social services. There is, again, apparently a complete record of this incident in Mr Doe's social services records.

In spite of all of these warning signs, Wessex County Council Social Services appear to have taken no positive action. Indeed, we would argue that nobody from social services came to inspect The Elms following these allegations.

Vicarious liability

It was recently determined in *Lister and others* v. *Hesley Hall Ltd* [2001] UKHL 22 that, where an employer is responsible for the care and welfare of children and he entrusts this responsibility to a warden in a home, the employer is vicariously liable for the acts of his employees that occur within the home.

For these reasons, we have assessed Mr Doe's chances of success at 60 per cent to 80 per cent, and probably at the higher end of the scale towards 80 per cent.

Causation and damage

As a result of the abuse that he endured, we allege that Mr Doe has suffered:

1. Physical damage

2. Severe emotional and psychological damage

3. Loss of earnings in the region of £15,000 through inability to work due to mental illness since the time of the police investigation and the criminal trial

4. Loss of advantage in the labour market when seeking further employment in the future based again on his current loss of earnings of £30,000, with the potential for increase if he is unable to find work in the future.

We would venture a tentative assessment of general damages for pain, suffering and loss of amenity at £50,000. We attach a copy of a reported case from Butterworth's Personal Injury Service dated 27 March 2001, which bears certain similarities to Mr Doe's case. In addition to the claim for loss of earnings (which we have assessed at £15,000), we would add a claim for psychotherapy, assessed at £10,000. This would need to be substantiated by psychiatric evidence. This amounts to a total claim for roughly £75,000.

The issue of causation is clearly demonstrated by the fact that Mr Doe was engaged in a period of continuous employment between 1993 and 2001, but his work began to deteriorate following his visit from the police and the re-emergence of the incidents of sexual abuse in his past, which finally forced him to stop working in January 2001.

Limitation

Under the Limitation Act 1980, Mr Doe's claim against the local authority in negligence would have become statute barred on 19 July 1992 when he reached his twenty-first birthday, unless he had a later date of knowledge.

The court may conclude that Mr Doe had knowledge of significant injury by 1983 (if not earlier). However, we consider that he would have strong grounds for persuading a court to disapply the limitation period under s.33 of the Limitation Act 1980. We attach the judgment for *Various claimants* v. *Bryn Alyn Community Homes Ltd*, in which the court used its discretion under the Limitation Act 1980 and allowed a claim, with facts analogous to those of the present claim, to proceed.

Finally, we believe that there are at least six other parties bringing similar claims against Wessex County Council, however, this has not yet been confirmed. We are attempting to make contact with those firms acting for those claimants.

13 July 2001

[LETTER OF CLAIM]

13 August 2001

Legal Department
Wessex County Council
The Town Hall
Market Square
Wessex

Dear Sirs

Re: John Doe

We act for Mr John Doe of 15 Acacia Road, Christminster, Wessex. Mr Doe was born on 20 July 1971 and his National Insurance number is NRS04856. Mr Doe is currently unemployed and is in receipt of income support and disability living allowance.

Please note that Mr Doe holds a certificate of public funding for the purposes of taking action against Wessex County Council issued on 1 August 2001 out of the Manchester Area Office under certificate number OEDNIR156784/1/A/2.

We are instructed by Mr Doe that he was taken into care by Wessex County Council in 1983. He was placed at The Elms Children's Home in Casterbridge up until 1987 when he left care. During his time at The Elms, Mr Doe was repeatedly sexually abused by the manager of the home, Mr Reginald Smith. Mr Smith took Mr Doe away with him most weekends to his own home and this is where the numerous instances of sexual abuse occurred. The sexual abuse included acts of buggery and oral sex.

Mr Doe left the Elms in 1987 when he reached the age of 16. After leaving care, Mr Doe developed a drug addiction and he began offending.

This way of life continued for approximately six years until 1993 when he met his present partner. At this stage, he found employment as a security guard. He continued in regular employment from 1993 until July 2000 when he was contacted by Wessex police in connection with a criminal investigation into events which occurred at The Elm's Children's Home.

As you are no doubt aware the conduct of Mr Smith was the subject-matter of a criminal investigation conducted by police in Christminster.

The police investigation originated from allegations in relation to Mr Smith's conduct made to the police by another of his victims. During the course of making these allegations, Mr Doe was referred to by this victim.

In June 2000, Mr Doe was approached by the police with regard to their criminal investigations. He was interviewed and gave details of all the incidents which had occurred while he was at The Elms.

In June 2001, Mr Smith was convicted of abusing Mr Doe and other children in his care in the Wessex Crown Court.

Following the police investigation and, as a result of having to recount the incidents of sexual abuse in his past, Mr Doe developed mental health problems. In June 2001 he was admitted to Christminster Hospital. He has not worked since that time.

We allege that Wessex Social Services owed Mr Doe a duty of care at the time he was in The Elms Children's Home to take reasonable steps to ensure his safety and well-being, to monitor any deterioration in his behaviour and to seek to address that deterioration in behaviour. In particular, we allege that Mr Doe made complaints about the abuse he was suffering which should have been acted upon by Wessex Social Services:

1. In 1983 Mr Doe made a complaint to the headmaster of Casterbridge Secondary School, Mr Healey, to the effect that Mr Smith had been violent towards him. Social services were contacted and said that they would investigate, but nothing was done. On the contrary, Mr Doe's social worker at the time, Mr Randall, persuaded Mr Doe that it would not be in his interests to make allegations of physical abuse. We believe that there is a complete record of this incident in Mr Doe's social services records.

2. In 1983 Mr Doe told Miss Hamilton, a residential social worker, that he was being abused by Mr Smith and that Mr Smith would not leave him alone. Apparently, Miss Hamilton confronted Mr Smith about the allegations but soon left The Elms Children's Home, allegedly having been intimidated by Mr Smith.

3. In 1984 Mr Doe attended Dr Black, a GP in Casterbridge, because he was suffering with anal bleeding. Dr Black reported the matter to social services but no action was taken. There is, again, apparently a complete record of this incident in Mr Doe's social services records.

In spite of these warning signs, nobody from Wessex Social Services came to inspect The Elms or took any action at all.

We understand that The Elms Children's Home was a controlled community home subject to the provisions of the Community Homes Regulations 1972 (SI 1972 No. 319). We would also point out that Wessex Social Services would have owed Mr Doe a general duty of care under the provisions of the Child Care Act 1980. The existence of such statutory duties is relevant to the establishment of a common law duty as between Wessex County Council and Mr Doe. We reserve the right to make further detailed allegations of negligence when we have been allowed access to Mr Doe's social services records (see below).

In addition, Mr Smith was an employee of Wessex County Council and consequently you are vicariously liable for assaults committed by Mr Smith in the course of his employment with the local authority (*Lister and others* v. *Hesley Hall Limited* [2001] UK HL 22).

As a result of the abuse that Mr Doe endured we are instructed that he has suffered:

1. Physical damage (in particular anal bleeding).

2. Severe psychiatric and emotional damage.

3. Loss of earnings and/or disadvantage in the job market.

With regard to limitation, Mr Doe reached his majority on 20 July 1992. It is not conceded that Mr Doe acquired requisite knowledge for the purposes of the Limitation Act 1980 more than three years prior to the date of this letter. Without prejudice to that contention, if necessary, our client will ask the court to exercise its discretion pursuant to s.33 Limitation Act 1980 and will rely in particular on the following facts and matters:

1. The difficulties Mr Doe has had in discussing the events set out above, contributed to by the lack of assistance he received from social services, which would have helped him to discuss the abuse earlier.

2. The fact that the evidence has remained sufficiently cogent for the police to investigate the events and to secure a conviction against Mr Smith.

3. Mr Doe acted promptly and reasonably once he understood that his complaints of abuse were part of a wider police investigation and that it was appropriate to consult solicitors.

This list is not exhaustive. In order to save costs, we invite you to confirm that from the date of receipt of this letter time will not run against Mr Doe for a period of six months in order that he may prepare his claim for issue and service. If such confirmation is not forthcoming from you within 28 days, Mr Doe will be compelled to issue proceedings to protect his position with a consequent increase in costs. We reserve the right to draw this letter to the attention of the court in appropriate circumstances.

We believe that there are a number of other parties from The Elms Children's Home bringing similar claims against Wessex County Council. We would be grateful if you could confirm whether you have received letters from their solicitors.

This is a case where your records relating to our client's care and the management and inspection of The Elms held by social services should be disclosed without it being necessary for us to make application to the court. We believe that you are likely to have or have had in your possession, some or all of the following documents relevant to issues arising, or likely to arise in relation to the claimants' cases, although this is not intended to be an exhaustive list, full disclosure of all notes and records is required:

1. (a) Social workers' file on Mr Doe
   (b) External professionals' records on Mr Doe including educational records
   (c) Care order in respect of Mr Doe

2. Records from The Elms Children's Home from 1983 to 1987
   (a) Day book
   (b) Visitors' book
   (c) Punishment book
   (d) Accident book
   (e) Medicine and health care
   (f) Admission and discharge register
   (g) Menu record/diet sheet
   (h) Staff files relating to Reginald Smith and Miss Hamilton
   (i) Staff-meeting minutes relating to Mr Doe, Reginald Smith and Miss Hamilton
   (j) Mr Doe's individual care-home file

We propose to obtain a psychiatric report concerning our client's injuries. In order to save costs, we invite you to agree to the instruction of a psychiatric expert on a joint basis. We nominate the following three experts.

Dr Judith Stonemason, Consultant Psychiatrist – Christminster Hospital, Christminster, Wessex

Dr Gabriel Oak, Consultant Psychiatrist – Sandbourne Hospital, Sandbourne, Wessex

Dr Thomas Hardy, Consultant Psychiatrist – Swinburne Mental Health Unit, Swinburne, Wessex

Please confirm the name and address of your insurers. A copy of this letter is attached for you to send to your insurers.

Finally, we expect an acknowledgment of this letter within 21 days by yourselves or your insurers.

Yours faithfully,

[LETTER OF INSTRUCTION TO PSYCHIATRIST]

28 September 2001

Dr Thomas Hardy
Swinburne Mental Health Unit
Swinburne
Wessex

Dear Dr Hardy

Our Client: Mr John Doe
Address: 15 Acacia Avenue, Christminster, Wessex
Date of birth: 20 July 1971
Telephone Number: (00123) 2223303

We act for Mr John Doe who is bringing a claim against Wessex County Council in respect of sexual and emotional abuse in The Elms Children's Home in Casterbridge between 1983 and 1987.

We enclose:

1. Mr Doe's statement made for the purposes of his civil claim. You will note that the abuser, Smith, was convicted at Casterbridge Crown Court in June 2001 of sexual offences against Mr Doe.

2. Mr Doe's GP's notes from 1972 to date (we were not able to obtain any notes from Mr Doe's first year).

3. Mr Doe's psychiatric notes from Christminster Hospital from June 2001 to date.

4. Mr Doe's social services notes from 1983 to 1985. (We have requested a full set of notes from the defendant, but the enclosed copies are those which Mr Doe has himself supplied to us, and they are incomplete.)

Your report should address the following points:

1. Is Mr Doe suffering and/or has he in the past suffered from an identifiable psychiatric illness, and, if so, please identify the illness or illnesses?

2. If he is suffering and/or has suffered from an identifiable psychiatric illness, to what extent is this attributable to the sexual and emotional abuse that he suffered at The Elms Children's Home between 1983 and 1987?

3. Having regard to Question 2, please describe in detail how you consider Mr Doe's experiences at Elms Children's Home have affected his:
   (a) Family life
   (b) Ability to have relationships
   (c) Ability to work

4. Considering the issue of causation in more detail, please comment on the causative significance of abuse suffered by Mr Doe at The Elms Children's Home in relation to the following matters:

(a) Mr Doe's persistent criminal offending and drug abuse between 1987 and 1993

(b) Mr Doe's breakdown and loss of employment in early 2001

5. What is the prognosis? Particularly with reference to:
    (a) Mr Doe's future employment status
    (b) Mr Doe's future therapy requirements. If you consider that Mr Doe would benefit from psychiatric treatment and/or counselling, please set out your recommendation for treatment and the cost of such treatment on a private basis.
    (c) What is your prognosis once Mr Doe has undergone such treatment, if you feel this is possible to predict at this stage?

6. Is Mr Doe now or has he ever been a patient within the meaning of the Mental Health Act 1983? If yes, please identify the period or periods during which he was a patient.

7. You will note that Mr Doe's allegations relate to events which occurred between 1983 and 1987. Mr Doe first instructed us in connection with this claim on 2 July 2001. Are there any aspects of his psychiatric condition which have a bearing on the length and reasons for the time taken to instruct us?

We would be grateful if you could make an appointment to see our client for the purposes of preparing your report. You may telephone him at his home, for the purposes of making such appointment.

We confirm that our client has the benefit of public funding for his claim and we undertake to be responsible for your reasonable fee subject to assessment.

Yours faithfully,

[CLAIMANT'S STATEMENT OF CASE]

<u>Claim No. . . .</u>

IN THE HIGH COURT OF JUSTICE

QUEEN'S BENCH DIVISION

IN THE [. . .] DISTRICT REGISTRY

BETWEEN:

<table>
<tr><td></td><td>**JOHN DOE**</td><td><u>Claimant</u></td></tr>
<tr><td></td><td>– and –</td><td></td></tr>
<tr><td></td><td>**WESSEX COUNTY COUNCIL**</td><td><u>Defendant</u></td></tr>
</table>

<u>PARTICULARS OF CLAIM</u>

Introduction

1. The defendant was at all relevant times a statutory body whose duties included the duty to provide proper social services functions pursuant to s.2 of and sched. 1 to the Local Authority Social Services Act 1970.

2. The defendant has not disclosed social services records in respect of the claimant and these particulars are drafted without the benefit of these records. The events referred to relate to the claimant's childhood. Once the records are disclosed it may become necessary to amend or add to the particulars.

Statutory backdrop

3. In the course of providing social services functions, the defendant received into care children living in the area of Wessex. The duties of the defendant in respect of a child in its care were at the relevant time set out in the Child Care Act 1980.

4. Further pursuant to the Local Authority Social Services Act 1970 and the Child Care Act 1980, the defendant was responsible for the provision, management, supervision and maintenance of community homes including children's homes.

5. At all relevant times the defendant was responsible for the management control supervision and maintenance of The Elms Children's Home (Elms), Casterbridge, Wessex. Elms Children's Home was a controlled community home subject to the provisions of the Community Homes Regulations 1972.

6. Pursuant to s.18 of the Child Care Act 1980, the defendant in reaching any decision in relation to the claimant, had a duty to give first consideration to the need to safeguard and promote the welfare of the claimant throughout his childhood; so far as was practicable

217

to ascertain the wishes and feelings of the claimant regarding such decisions; and to give due consideration to them, having regard to his age and understanding.

Direct duty of care owed by the defendant

7. At all relevant times the defendant owed to those children taken into its care and those children placed at community homes under its supervision and management a common law duty of care.

8. The claimant was born on 20 July 1971. In 1983, the claimant was taken into the care of the defendant. Thereafter the defendant assumed responsibility for the welfare of the claimant and owed a duty of care to the claimant as set out below.

9. The common law duty of care owed by the defendant to the claimant pursuant to para. 7 above included the following duties:

   (a) A duty to act in the place of the child's parents and to provide the claimant with the standard of care which could be expected of a reasonable parent.
   (b) A duty to take reasonable steps to protect the claimant from physical, emotional, psychiatric or psychological injury while he remained in the care of the defendant.
   (c) A duty to provide a home and education for the claimant for such period as he remained in the care of the defendant.
   (d) A duty to place the claimant at all times in a home where his safety would be secured and/or monitored by the defendant.
   (e) A duty to safeguard and promote the claimant's development in a manner appropriate to the claimant's stage of development at any given time.
   (f) A duty to provide any medical treatment which the claimant required by arranging referral to a suitable medical specialist or otherwise.
   (g) A duty to secure the claimant's right to family life.
   (h) A duty at all times to provide a competent and suitably qualified and/or experienced social worker or workers whose responsibility it was to monitor the physical, psychiatric and psychological welfare of the claimant.

Vicarious duty of care owed by the defendant

10. Further, at all relevant times each of the social workers employed by the defendant who was allocated as the social worker for the claimant owed the claimant a duty of care. The duty of care of each social worker for the period for which they were allocated to the claimant included:

    (a) A duty to not to injure the claimant and to protect the claimant from physical, emotional, psychiatric and psychological damage.
    (b) A duty to monitor the claimant's physical, emotional, psychiatric and psychological welfare.
    (c) A duty to make arrangements to provide such medical (including psychiatric and therapeutic) treatment as was reasonably necessary for the claimant's welfare and to arrange for his referral to such medical specialists as he required.
    (d) A duty to visit the claimant and ascertain his views, wishes, anxieties and complaints in as far as was appropriate to his age and understanding.

(e) A duty to have regard to long-term planning for the claimant and for his long-term welfare in addition to his immediate needs.

11. Further, each of the members of staff employed by the defendant at The Elms Children's Home who was responsible for the care of the claimant owed to the claimant a duty of care which included:

(a) A duty not to injure the claimant and to protect the claimant from physical, emotional, psychiatric and psychological damage.

(b) A duty to monitor the claimant's physical, emotional, psychiatric and psychological welfare.

(c) A duty to make arrangements to provide such medical (including psychiatric and therapeutic) treatment as was reasonably necessary for the claimant's welfare and to arrange for his referral to such medical specialists as he required.

(d) A duty to ascertain the claimant's views, wishes, anxieties and complaints in as far as was appropriate to his age and understanding.

12. At all relevant times the defendant was vicariously liable for the acts of its servants or agents employed for the purpose of caring for children taken into care by the defendant including the claimant. The defendant is vicariously liable in respect of any injury caused to the claimant by such servant or agent in whose care the claimant was placed however caused.

13. Further, the defendant is vicariously liable in respect of any breach of duty of care on the part of any of its servants or agents including those employed at The Elms Children's Home.

Placements

14. When taken into the care of the defendant in about January 1983 the claimant was a vulnerable child. He had been neglected by his parents and was a small, undernourished child. His father was an alcoholic and seldom at the family home; his mother worked as a cleaner at night and the claimant was frequently locked out of his home

15. The claimant was placed at The Elms Children's Home in 1983. Elms was under the supervision of Mr Reginald Smith, who was employed by the defendant to run Elms and to supervise the home.

16. The claimant remained at The Elms Children's Home until he was discharged from care in 1987 aged 16 years.

Complaints of abuse

17. While living at The Elm's Children's Home, the claimant was sexually abused by Reginald Smith. Before abusing the claimant, Reginald Smith groomed the claimant for abuse. This grooming involved Reginald Smith spending substantial periods of time with the claimant. At weekends Reginald Smith took the claimant to his own home which was in the grounds of The Elms Children's Home. At Reginald Smith's home, the claimant was allowed to watch television and to smoke cigarettes. Further, Reginald Smith on numerous occasions took the claimant out to tea and bought the claimant presents.

18. The claimant who had been removed from his family as a result of their neglect of him had no other experience of a loving relationship. He was very vulnerable to such grooming treatment. Further, having been locked out of his own home he found Reginald Smith's home a welcoming and attractive place to go at weekends.

19. After approximately two months of treating the claimant in a privileged way, Reginald Smith began to abuse the claimant sexually. While the claimant was in Reginald Smith's home, Reginald Smith kissed and cuddled the claimant and touched his penis. At the time the claimant understood this to be an affectionate way for Reginald Smith to treat him as he had known no other affection from an adult; and Reginald Smith led him to believe it was a proper way for an adult to show affection to a child.

20. Thereafter when Reginald Smith took the claimant to his home, Reginald Smith touched the claimant's penis while he was masturbating. Further, he then asked the claimant to touch his penis until Reginald Smith ejaculated.

21. On the claimant's thirteenth birthday, Reginald Smith took the claimant out and bought the claimant a large number of presents. That night Reginald Smith took the claimant to his bed, removed his night clothes, turned him onto his tummy, rubbed jelly on his anus and buggered him. Reginald Smith withdrew his penis before ejaculating and ejaculated over the claimant's bare back. The claimant suffered extreme fear and pain as a result of this incident. He also suffered anal bleeding.

22. Thereafter Reginald Smith buggered the claimant on at least a further six occasions over the next 12 months.

23. Further, Reginald Smith forced the claimant to perform oral sex on him by forcing his penis into the claimant's mouth. He then ejaculated into the claimant's mouth. The claimant found this extremely frightening. He cried and tried to run away from Reginald Smith's home. When he tried to do so, Reginald Smith grabbed him and hit him.

Reports of abuse

24. In 1983 the claimant made a complaint to the headmaster of Casterbridge Secondary School, Mr Healey, that Mr Reginald Smith had been violent towards him. Subsequently, the claimant was told by the headmaster that the defendant's social services had been contacted and had indicated that they would investigate. As far as the claimant is aware no action was taken by the defendant. However, the claimant's social worker, Mr Randall, told the claimant that if he persisted with allegations against Reginald Smith he would be removed to a tougher children's home.

25. In 1983 the claimant told Miss Hamilton, a residential social worker, that he was being sexually abused by Mr Reginald Smith and that Mr Reginald Smith would not leave him alone. Soon after the claimant made this complaint Miss Hamilton left The Elms Children's Home. The claimant believes Miss Hamilton had confronted Mr Reginald Smith about the allegations but was intimidated by Mr Reginald Smith.

26. In 1984 the claimant attended Dr Black, a GP in Casterbridge because he was suffering with anal bleeding. Dr Black reported this to the defendant's social services but no action was taken.

Causation

27. The abuse of the claimant committed while he was at the defendant's Children's Home is set out in paragraphs 19–23 above. Such abuse caused serious damage to the claimant. This damage was caused by an employee of the defendant acting in breach of his duty to take care of the claimant. The defendant is vicariously liable for the said abuse and breach of duty and is thereby itself in breach of duty to the claimant.

28. Further, the abuse was caused or materially contributed to by the negligence of the defendant and/or its servants or agents for whom the defendant is vicariously liable in that it:

Particulars of negligence

(a) Employed Mr Reginald Smith as a manager at Elm's Children's Home when he was totally unsuitable as an employee in a children's home.

(b) Allowed Mr Reginald Smith to work unsupervised with children before ascertaining whether he was a suitable employee to do so and failing to ascertain that he was not.

(c) Employed other staff at Elms who were not sufficiently vigilant to prevent the claimant being abused by Mr Reginald Smith.

(d) Failed to take reasonable steps to implement a proper system of care and supervision at Elms which would keep the children there reasonably safe from injury and abuse.

(e) Failed to carry out regular and adequate medical examinations to ensure that any injury to the claimant at Elms was identified, diagnosed and suitably and adequately treated. When anal bleeding was reported by the claimant's GP, the defendant failed to follow up this report or take steps to investigate why the claimant suffered anal bleeding.

(f) Failed to provide a social worker or suitable responsible adult who was prepared to listen to the complaints of the claimant in respect of the abuse he was suffering, and to take these complaints seriously.

(g) Failed to investigate properly or at all the complaints made by the claimant to his headmaster.

(h) Failed to deal with the claimant's welfare in a suitable or appropriate manner when it was known or ought to have been known that he was a vulnerable child with no adult figure he could trust or look to for help and support.

29. As a result of the abuse by Reginald Smith for which the defendant is vicariously liable and/or as a result of the negligence of the defendant, its servants or agents for whom the defendant is vicariously liable the claimant has suffered severe personal injury, loss and damage as follows:

Particulars of injury

(a) Pain and suffering at the time of the abuse set out above, including anal bleeding.

(b) Psychiatric damage including post-traumatic stress disorder and personality as set out in the appended report of Doctor [. . .], Consultant Psychiatrist, dated 22 December 2001.

221

Particulars of loss and damage

(c) The claimant's expenses and losses are contained in the appended schedule and include the cost of treatment as assessed by Doctor [. . .], loss of earnings and vulnerability on the labour market. In particular, following the police investigation and the fact that the claimant has been forced to consider the above incidents of sexual abuse in his past, he developed serious mental health problems, and in June 2001 was admitted to Christminster Hospital. He has not worked since that time.

Disclosure of abuse

30. In July 2000, the claimant was contacted by Wessex police in connection with the criminal investigation into the activities of Reginald Smith. This was the first time that the claimant had been asked about these events and he had been unable to disclose them to any other person since leaving Elms. It was very distressing for him to recount the events to the police.

31. Following the police investigation, Reginald Smith was charged with a number of counts of sexual offences committed at The Elms Children's Home. In June 2001, Mr Reginald Smith was convicted of buggery in respect of the claimant. Mr Reginald Smith was also convicted of a number of other offences and sentenced to a total period of 12 years' imprisonment at Wessex Crown Court. The claimant relies, pursuant to the provisions of the Civil Evidence Act 1968, upon the conviction of Mr Smith as evidence that he was sexualy abused by Mr Smith.

Limitation

32. The claimant asks the court to exercise its discretion pursuant to s.33 Limitation Act 1980 to allow this action to proceed in all the circumstances of the case and having regard to the fact that:

(a) The lapse of time has been caused by the difficulty that the claimant has in discussing the events set out above. This has been contributed to by the lack of assistance he had from the defendant by way of counselling or social work support which would have helped him to discuss the abuse earlier. Further, when he did try to report the activities of Mr Reginald Smith they were not properly investigated and he was threatened by an employee of the defendant with a move to a tougher home. No steps were taken at any time to provide counselling for him or to prevent Reginald Smith from having contact with him.

(b) The evidence remains sufficiently cogent for the police to investigate the events; and to charge Mr Reginald Smith with criminal offences; and for a jury to convict him.

(c) The defendant has failed to respond to requests for the claimant's social services records to be disclosed.

(d) The claimant remained under a disability by reason of his minority until 20 July 1991. Thereafter he has been suffering psychiatric injury as a result of the events set out above whether or not he has for any of this period been under a disability by reason of mental disorder. The claimant reserves the right to argue in respect of any or all of the period that his psychiatric disorder has been such as to render him under a disability.

(e) The claimant will further rely on the fact that pursuant to Article 3 of the European Convention for the Protection of Human Rights and Fundamental Freedoms the defendant, as a public authority, was and remained under an obligation to investigate the abuse Mr Smith perpetrated on the claimant and thereby subjecting him to inhuman and degrading treatment.

(f) The claimant acted promptly and reasonably once he understood that his complaints of abuse were part of a wider police investigation.

(g) The claimant acted promptly in seeking legal and expert advice after the police enquiry proceeded.

33. Further, the claimant contends that, where it is alleged that the defendant is vicariously liable for physical and/or sexual abuse, the existence of a duty of care between the defendant and the claimant prior to the abuse taking place results in a special relationship and/or assumption of responsibility for the claimant so that any injury caused to the claimant in such circumstances whether by a deliberate act or otherwise constitutes a breach of duty, and the claim is properly categorised as one of breach of duty coming within ss.11, 14 and 33 of the Limitation Act 1980.

34. Further, the claimant claims interest on the damages awarded pursuant to s.35A of the Supreme Court Act 1981 as follows:

(a) on general damages at 2 per cent from the date of service of these proceedings; and

(b) on special damages at the full special account rate from the date on which any head of loss has crystallised (being 8 per cent to 1 August 1999; 7 per cent thereafter); and on continuing losses at half the special account rate.

And the claimant claims:

1. damages exceeding £50,000 including an award in excess of £1,000 for the claimant's pain, suffering and loss of amenity.

2. interest.

STATEMENT OF TRUTH

I believe the facts stated in these particulars of claim are true.

Full Name: ....

Solicitor: ....

Signature: ....

[CLAIMANT'S SCHEDULE OF LOSS AND DAMAGE]

IN THE HIGH COURT OF JUSTICE   CASE NO.

CHRISTMINSTER DISTRICT REGISTRY

QUEEN'S BENCH DIVISION

JOHN DOE   Claimant

– and –

WESSEX COUNTY COUNCIL   Defendant

SCHEDULE OF LOSS AND DAMAGE
(as at 15 January 2002)

Claimant born on 20 July 1971

Received into the defendant's care 13 May 1983

At The Elms Children's Home

May 1983 to July 1987

Discharged from care 20 July 1987

1. General damages for pain, suffering and loss of amenity

The claimant has set out in his Particulars of Claim details of the events including sexual abuse which caused him physical and emotional pain and suffering while he was at The Elms Children's Home.

In respect of the psychiatric damage suffered by the claimant he relies on the report of Thomas Hardy, consultant psychiatrist served with the particulars. Dr Hardy describes how the abuse that the claimant suffered was so traumatic as to precipitate a serious psychiatric illness. As a result of these traumas, the claimant suffers post traumatic stress disorder and depression, he is at increased risk of suicidal behaviour, alcohol and drug addiction and has required in-patient and out-patient treatment at Christminster Hospital since 10 June 2001.

Damages to be assessed

2. Interest on general damages

The claimant claims interest at 2 per cent from the date of service of proceedings.

Damages to be assessed

3. Loss of earnings, vulnerability in the labour market and cost of treatment

The claimant left care on 20 July 1987 and was unemployed until 5 July 1993. During this period, the claimant developed a drug problem and began offending. He spent a total of one year in prison between the years 1987 to 1993.

In 1993 the claimant settled down in a relationship with his current partner and from 1 July 1993 found regular employment as a security guard working for various firms in the Christminster area, for a period of six and a half years until 15 January 2001 when he had to abandon his employment as a result of suffering severe psychiatric illness (as per the report of Dr Thomas Hardy).

The claimant claims loss of earnings on the basis of his proven ability to work as a security guard as demonstrated by his employment between 1993 and 2001 for the periods and net rates as follows (calculated as in the report of Geoffrey Pleasance, Occupational Psychologist and adjusted to give approximate net rates).

A. PAST LOSS OF EARNINGS

First period

All figures are net of income tax and national insurance.

From 20 July 1987 to 5 July 1993:

1987	£7,141
1988	£7,843
1989	£8,500
1990	£9,100
1991	£9,034
1992	£9,760
1993	£9,310
Total	£60,688

Less one year's average earnings throughout the period 1987 to 1993 to take account of one year in prison: £8,688

Net claim: £52,000

Second period

From 15 January 2001 to date of schedule (15 January 2002)

At the time of losing his job in January 2001, the claimant was earning £12,000 net.

15 January 2001 to 31 March 2001: £2,500

From 1 April 2001, the claimant's net earnings would have increased to £13,200

1 April 2001 to 15 January 2001: £10,450

Net claim: £12,950

TOTAL PAST LOSS OF EARNINGS: £64,950

B. FUTURE LOSS OF EARNINGS

The report of Dr Hardy states that the claimant is 'severely disadvantaged on the open labour market by reason of his condition. He will require at least five years of psychotherapy before he can realistically be expected to return to the open labour market'.

Mr Pleasance states that the claimant will need at least one year to find employment after completing any course of therapy and thereafter will be disadvantaged on the open labour market by reason of his medical history. The claimant therefore claims six years' loss of earnings.

Multiplicand: £13,200
Multiplier: 4.5

TOTAL NET FUTURE LOSS OF EARNINGS: £57,400

C. VULNERABILITY ON THE LABOUR MARKET

In addition, the claimant claims a global sum to compensate him for his vulnerability on the labour market and his inability to work due to psychiatric illness and to compensate him for the loss of opportunity to find employment. The claimant has in the region of 30 years' working life ahead of him.

TOTAL: TO BE ASSESSED

D. COSTS OF TREATMENT

Dr Hardy has recommended that the claimant undergo a course of psychotherapy. The claimant will require one session per week at £50 per session for five years at the clinic of Julie Care, Psychotherapist, which is located in Sandbourne, Wessex, a distance of ten miles from the claimant.

Cost of therapy: £13,000

Estimated travel fares: £1,000

TOTAL CLAIM FOR TREATMENT: £14,000

E. INTEREST ON PAST LOSSES

The claimant claims interest on past losses assessed at half the special account rate from the date that he would have obtained employment in 1987 to date.

First period of loss of earnings: 20 July 1987 to 5 July 1993 = £52,000. Interest taken from mid-point 1 June 1990 giving a total of 47.05 per cent on £24,466.

Second period of loss of earnings: 15 January 2001 to 15 January 2002 = £12,950 @ 3.5 per cent (half the special account rate) on £12,950 = £453.25.

1. **GENERAL DAMAGES: TO BE ASSESSED**

2. **INTEREST ON GENERAL DAMAGES: TO BE ASSESSED**

3. **LOSS OF EARNINGS, VULNERABILITY ON THE LABOUR MARKET AND COST OF TREATMENT**

A. **PAST LOSS OF EARNINGS: £64,950**

B. **FUTURE LOSS OF EARNINGS: £57,400**

C. **VULNERABILITY ON THE LABOUR MARKET: TO BE ASSESSED**

D. **COST OF TREATMENT: £14,000**

E. **INTEREST ON PAST LOSSES: £24,919.25**

TOTAL SPECIAL DAMAGES: £161,269.25

Served on 15 January 2001

[DEFENCE]

<u>Claim No. . . .</u>

IN THE HIGH COURT OF JUSTICE

QUEEN'S BENCH DIVISION

IN THE [. . .] DISTRICT REGISTRY

BETWEEN:

JOHN DOE   <u>**Claimant**</u>

– and –

WESSEX COUNTY COUNCIL   <u>**Defendant**</u>

<u>DEFENCE</u>

1. Paragraph 1 of the particulars of claim is admitted.

2. The defendant has been unable to identify whether the claimant was placed in its care or to produce any records relating to the claimant because all of the defendant's records relating to the period of 1981 to 1988 were destroyed in an arson attack on the defendant's premises on 1 October 1996.

3. The defendant admits that the statutory provisions referred to in paras. 3–6 of the particulars of claim were in force at the relevant time. No admission is made as to the relevance of any of these provisions to the claimant's case and the claimant will be required to prove such relevance.

4. In respect of para. 7 of the Particulars of Claim it is admitted that the defendant has a general duty of care in respect of children removed from their homes into its care. No admission is made as to the extent of any duty of care owed to children taken into its care or as to the extent of any duty owed to the claimant, if any.

5. In respect of para. 8 of the Particulars of Claim, the claimant is required to prove his date of birth and the date he is alleged to have been taken into care as the defendant cannot identify any records relating to the claimant.

6. In respect of para. 9 of the Particulars of Claim, the claimant is required to prove the relevance of each duty pleaded to the facts of the claimant's case.

7. In respect of paras. 10–13 of the particulars of claim, the defendant admits that it is vicariously liable for the actions of its servants or agents while they were acting within the course of their employment but not otherwise. The defendant admits that, in so far as staff employed by the defendant were allocated to care for particular children, they owed duties to those children.

8. The claimant is required to prove:

    (a) The circumstances in which any servant or agent of the defendant was placed in a position in which he or she owed a duty of care to the claimant.

    (b) The scope and extent of any such duty owed by a servant or agent of the defendant to the claimant.

    (c) The circumstances in which any factual allegations that he may prove occurred.

    (d) That such allegations as the claimant may prove constituted a breach of duty by a servant or agent of the defendant.

    (e) That the relevant servant or agent of the defendant was acting in the course of his employment at the relevant time and in connection with the relevant circumstances of any such alleged breach of duty.

9. In respect of paras. 14–16 of the Particulars of Claim, the Defendant, having no record of the claimant, does not admit that the claimant was taken into its care on the date alleged or at all and makes no admissions as to the home circumstances of the claimant prior to any such date of receipt into care as the claimant may prove.

10. The defendant admits in respect of the single count of buggery against the claimant for which Mr Reginald Smith was convicted that this offence took place. The claimant makes no further admissions as to the facts of any of the complaints of abuse set out in paras. 17–23 of the Particulars of Claim. The claimant is required to prove the circumstances in which the act of buggery against the claimant for which Mr Reginald Smith was convicted occurred and that Mr Reginald Smith was acting in the course of his employment with the defendant at the time of this offence. The claimant has failed to identify which of the acts of buggery alleged was the count on which Mr Reginald Smith was convicted.

11. The defendant makes no admissions as to the alleged reports made by the claimant to Mr Healey, Miss Hamilton and Doctor Black as set out in paras. 24–26 of the Particulars of Claim: the defendant has no record of these reports. The defendant has attempted to trace Miss Hamilton but unfortunately she was killed in a road traffic accident while travelling in Spain in 1998. It is specifically denied that the claimant made any such report to Mr Randall.

12. The claimant has not to date provided copies of any medical records and is required to prove the attendance at the surgery of Doctor Black, the findings alleged and the relevance of such findings to the allegations against the defendant.

13. In respect of paras. 27–28, the claimant is required to prove each allegation abuse other than the single count for which Mr Reginald Smith was convicted. Further, the claimant is required to prove in respect of each allegation, including that for which Mr Reginald Smith was convicted that Mr Reginald Smith was acting in the course of his employment.

14. The defendant denies the allegations of negligence set out in para. 28 of the Particulars of Claim. In so far as the claimant is able to establish any of the allegations of abuse it is alleged that such events took place in private outside the area of the school to which pupils had access; and the defendant did not and could not have known of or have prevented such abuse occurring in as far as the allegations made are proved.

15. The claimant has not pleaded any facts or matters which should or could have placed

the defendant on notice that Mr Reginald Smith was not a suitable employee to work in a children's home. The defendant will rely on the impeccable references they obtained in respect of Mr Reginald Smith prior to his employment and on the fact that detailed appraisals of Mr Reginald Smith's performance while he was working at The Elms Children's Home showed him to be an entirely satisfactory employee. Further, the defendant will apply to strike out this part of the claim.

16. The abuse alleged, if and in as far as it is proved to have taken place, took place in Mr Reginald Smith's private home or car and it would not have been reasonable, practical or permissible for the defendant to monitor its employee's activities in his own home or car.

17. It is denied that the claimant made the allegations alleged to Mr Randall. It is alleged that Mr Randall was a suitable and competent social worker to whom the claimant could have made complaints and in whom the claimant could have confided.

18. It is denied that any such loss or damage as the claimant proves he has suffered was caused by any negligence on the part of the defendant or by any actions of any employees for whom the defendant was vicariously liable in respect of such actions.

19. The defendant does not accept the claimant's medical evidence and will seek to rely on its own independent expert.

20. The action was commenced in August 2001, more than 12 years after the claimant reached the age of 18 years.

21. In so far as the claimant relies on deliberate acts of abuse by Mr Reginald Smith the action was commenced more than six years outside the limitation period prescribed by s.2 Limitation Act 1980 and is statute barred. The court has no discretion to extend the limitation period in respect of these allegations and the defendant will apply to strike out this part of the claim.

22. In so far as the claimant relies on allegations of negligence, the action was commenced nine years outside the primary limitation period and the court should not in all the circumstances exercise its discretion to allow the action to proceed pursuant to s.33 Limitation Act 1980 for the following reasons.

23. It would not be equitable for the court to allow this action to proceed having regard to the degree of prejudice suffered by the defendant in the circumstances of this case. In particular the defendant relies on the following:

(a) The defendant has no access to any relevant documents as a result of the arson attack on its property in 1996, had the claim been brought before 20 July 1993 when the claimant reached 21 years the defendant would not have suffered this prejudice.

(b) Miss Hamilton, an important witness of fact, was killed in 1998 and in the absence of any notification of the claim prior to that date the defendant had no opportunity to take a statement in respect of the allegations made by the claimant that abuse was reported to her.

(c) The evidence likely to be adduced in respect of the regime at The Elms Children's Home and the supervision of staff there is likely to be far less cogent now than it would have been had the claim been brought prior to July 1993, the following members of staff have died: Mr Tree, Mr Bush, Mr Branch and Mr Twig. Further, the documents have been destroyed.

(d) On the claimant's own case he made complaints about the alleged abuse in 1983 and cannot be said to have acted promptly in bringing these proceedings. The police investigation is irrelevant in respect of the claimant's individual case and his ability to commence proceedings within the primary limitation period.

24. The claimant's claim for interest is denied.

I believe the facts stated in this defence are true.

Full Name: ....

Solicitor: ....

Signature: ....

[CASE MANAGEMENT DIRECTIONS]

Claim No. . . .

IN THE HIGH COURT OF JUSTICE

QUEEN'S BENCH DIVISION

IN THE [. . .] DISTRICT REGISTRY

BETWEEN:

JOHN DOE   **Claimant**

– and –

WESSEX COUNTY COUNCIL   **Defendant**

BEFORE   **SITTING AT THE**   **THE DAY OF 2002**

UPON HEARING THE SOLICITORS ON BEHALF OF THE CLAIMANT AND THE DEFENDANT.

AND UPON READING THE DOCUMENTS FILED ON BEHALF OF THE CLAIMANT AND THE DEFENDANT.

IT IS ORDERED as follows:

Allocation

1. The case be allocated to the multi track.

Witness statements

2. There be mutual and simultaneous exchange of the witness statements of the oral evidence which the party serving the statement intends to rely on in relation to any issues of fact to be decided at the trial, those statements and any notice of intention to rely on hearsay evidence are to be exchanged by 23 August 2002.

Expert evidence

3. Permission is given for one expert on behalf of the claimant and one expert on behalf of the defendant to give oral evidence at trial in the field of psychology/psychiatry.

4. (a) The psychological/psychiatric experts' reports shall be exchanged by 23 August 2002.

(b) The experts shall hold a discussion for the purpose of:

(i) identifying the issues, if any, between them; and
(ii) where possible, reaching agreement on those issues.

(c) The experts shall by 25 October 2002 prepare and file a statement for the court showing:

(i) those issues on which they did agree; and
(ii) those issues on which they disagree and a summary of their reasons for disagreeing.

5. Permission is given for one expert on behalf of the claimant and one expert on behalf of the defendant to give oral evidence at trial in the field of social care.

(a) The social care expert reports shall be exchanged by 25 October 2002.

(b) The experts shall hold a discussion for the purpose of:

(iii) identifying the issues, if any, between them; and
(iv) where possible, reaching agreement on those issues.

(c) The experts shall by 20 December 2002 prepare and file a statement for the court showing:

(iii) those issues on which they did agree; and
(iv) those issues on which they disagree and a summary of their reasons for dis-agreeing.

Disclosure of documents

6. Each party to provide by 23 August 2002 standard disclosure to every other party by list.

Inspection of documents

7. Any requests for inspection or copies of disclosed documents shall be made within 14 days after service of the list.

Trial and listing questionnaires

8. (a) The trial of the claim take place within [   ] after [   ] between [   ] and [   ] 'the trial window'.

(b) The claimant make an appointment to attend on the clerk of the lists at room [ ] in order to fix a trial date within the trial window, such appointment to be requested by the 8 November 2002 and give notice of the appointment to all other parties.

(c) The claim to:

(i) be entered in the Trial List, Category [ ] with a time estimate of five days;

(ii) take place in London.

(d) Each party to file his completed listing questionnaire by 8 November 2002.

(e) The parties to inform the court forthwith of any change in the trial time estimate.

Trial bundle

9. The parties agree and file a trial bundle and exchange and file skeleton arguments and chronologies not more than seven and not less than three days before the start of the trial.

Trial timetable

10. The parties agree a timetable for the trial, subject to the approval of the trial judge and file it with the trial bundle.

Settlement

11. If the claim or part of the claim is settled, the parties must immediately inform the court, whether or not it is then possible to file a draft consent order to give effect to the settlement.

Costs

12. Costs in the case.

Date order made:

Date order sealed:

[STATEMENT OF CASE IN SUPPORT OF CICA]

<u>**MR JOHN DOE**</u>

<u>**APPLICATION TO THE CRIMINAL INJURIES**</u>
<u>**COMPENSATION AUTHORITY**</u>

<u>**STATEMENT OF CASE**</u>

We enclose the following:

1. Mr John Doe's CICA application.

2. Statement of John Doe made for the purposes of criminal proceedings against Mr Reginald Smith dated 6 July 2000.

3. Statement of John Doe made for the purposes of his action against Wessex County Council (Civil Statement) dated 14 September 2001.

4. Psychiatric report of Dr Thomas Hardy dated 30 November 2001.

5. Occupational psychology report of Mr Geoffrey Pleasance dated 15 December 2001.

6. Copy sets of Mr Doe's GP and hospital notes.

7. Schedule of loss dated 15 January 2002.

The background to the claim

Mr John Doe is a former resident of the The Elms Children's Home, in Casterbridge, Wessex. He alleges that he was sexually abused from 1983 to 1987 by Reginald Smith, a former officer in charge of the home. In June 2001, Smith was convicted of sexual offences against numerous children in the home including Mr Doe. Mr Doe's allegations and the details of the abuse are set out in paras. 5–9 of his statement made for the purposes of the criminal proceedings.

We refer to paras. 50–55 of Mr Doe's civil statement and paras. 4.1–4.4 of the report of Dr Thomas Hardy, consultant psychiatrist, which deals with the impact of the abuse on Mr Doe and his ability to obtain employment. Dr Hardy states that Mr Doe will need at least five years of treatment before he can begin to find new employment.

It is submitted that Mr Doe has suffered a 'permanent mental illness confirmed by psychiatric prognosis' which is 'seriously disabling' (p. 27 of the 2001 scheme). As a consequence, he has suffered a loss of earnings longer than 28 weeks, which he seeks to recover under para. 30 of the 2001 scheme.

A schedule of loss dated 15 January 2002 is submitted with this application.

Mr Doe's reasons for delay in reporting the abuse and his cooperation with the police

At the time of the abuse, Mr Doe did make two complaints about what was happening (see paras. 24 and 25 of his civil statement), however, nothing was done about the abuse. He was a child in care, without any appropriate adult to whom he could look for support. Paragraphs 3.1–3.2 of the report of Dr Hardy also deals with the issue of non-disclosure when Mr Doe was at The Elms.

Paragraphs 3.5–3.9 of the report of Dr Hardy deal with Mr Doe's reasons for not disclosing what had happened throughout his adult life until he was contacted by the police in June 2000.

Mr Doe describes his reasons for non-disclosure in detail in his civil statement at paras. 54–61. He goes on in the following paragraphs to describe how he gave evidence to the police and how he first approached solicitors in 2001 after the conviction of his abuser.

As soon as Mr Doe was contacted by the police in June 2000, he cooperated with them in full and this led to the conviction of his abuser.

Mr Doe's criminal convictions

Mr Doe has a number of criminal convictions from 1987 to 1993, which consist of drug-related offences together with convictions for theft. We would refer the authority to the following points:

1. The comments of Dr Hardy as at paras. 3.6–3.9 which deal with the link between Mr Doe's history of offending.

2. The fact that since 1993, Mr Doe has not offended at all.

3. The fact that Mr Doe's cooperation with the police and his evidence was instrumental in securing the conviction of his abuser despite the ordeal of giving evidence.

Other applicants and the civil litigation case

Mr Doe's present solicitors are aware of some 10 other claimants who are bringing proceedings in a group action against Wessex County Council. These claimants will also be bringing applications to the CICA.

Civil proceedings are about to be issued in the High Court in Christminster District Registry.

It is understood that the police have already registered a number of potential applicants with the CICA.

20 January 2002

The case of Richard Doe

[CLAIMANT'S STATEMENT OF CASE]

Introduction

Richard Doe is placed in an approved school in the early 1970s where he is physically and sexually abused by four members of staff. He brings proceedings against Wessex County Council.

<u>Claim No. . . .</u>

<u>IN THE HIGH COURT OF JUSTICE</u>

<u>QUEEN'S BENCH DIVISION</u>

<u>IN THE [. . .] DISTRICT REGISTRY</u>

BETWEEN:

<table>
<tr><td></td><td align="center">**RICHARD DOE**</td><td>**<u>Claimant</u>**</td></tr>
<tr><td></td><td align="center">– and –</td><td></td></tr>
<tr><td></td><td align="center">**WESSEX COUNTY COUNCIL**</td><td>**<u>Defendant</u>**</td></tr>
</table>

<u>PARTICULARS OF CLAIM</u>

A. SUMMARY OF CLAIM

1. The claimant was born on 1 January 1959.

   He was at Wessex Approved School ('the school') between approximately January 1971 and September 1973.

He alleges that:

(a) he was sexually abused by Mr Brown;

(b) he was physically abused by:
 (i) Mr Black;
 (ii) Mr Green; and
 (iii) Mr Red.

The claimant also suffered emotional abuse while at the school.

2. The particulars of the claimant's claim are set out as follows:

B. INTRODUCTION

3. The particulars of claim have been drafted without sight of the documents held by the defendants in relation to the claimant. Disclosure of these documents has been requested but not been given by them. If necessary, the claimant will apply to amend this document after disclosure has occurred.

C. SEQUENCE OF EVENTS

4. The events contained in this section are those which the claimant is able to recollect from his childhood as no documentation relating to him has been disclosed by the defendants.

5. The claimant was born on 1 January 1959.

6. The claimant had an unhappy childhood. His father abandoned the family when the claimant was 2 years old. The claimant and his two sisters were raised by their mother. At school, the claimant was bullied.

7. At the age of 11 or 12, the claimant began to commit a number of petty crimes, usually involving stealing sweets and drinks from shops and on one occasion stealing a pedal cycle.

8. As a result of these matters, the claimant was removed from home and placed into the care of the defendant. He was sent to Wessex Approved School in January 1971.

9. The claimant was discharged from care on 1 January 1977 when he reached 18 years of age.

D. THE STATUTORY BACKDROP

10. The claimant's claim is for breach of a common law duty of care. No claim is specifically made for breach of statutory duty. It is alleged, however, that the statutory backdrop is relevant to the common law duty of care owed by the defendants to the claimant. The following provisions are therefore relevant background to this claim.

11. The claimant was committed to the defendant's care prior to being sent to the school under the provisions of the Children and Young Persons Act 1969. The defendant owed him, therefore, the statutory duties set out in s.12 Children Act 1948 (as amended by the Local Authority Social Services Act 1970 and the Children Act 1975) and s.24 Children and Young Persons Act 1969.

12. Further, once the claimant was transferred to the school, the defendant owed him various statutory duties contained in:

    (a) the Approved School Rules 1933;

    (b) the Approved School Rules 1949;

    (c) the Approved School Rules 1963;

    (d) the Children and Young Persons Act 1969; and

    (e) the Community Homes Regulations 1972.

E. THE DIRECT DUTIES OWED BY THE DEFENDANT TO THE CLAIMANT (OR TAKEN OVER BY THE DEFENDANT)

13. Until 1 April 1973 when the Cessation of Approved Schools (Wessex Approved School) Order 1973 was implemented, the Home Office was responsible for the management, control, supervision and inspection of Wessex Approved School. The school was administered by a Committee of Managers, known as the Wessex Approved School Managers.

14. The *Handbook for Managers of Approved Schools*, published by the Home Office in 1961, described the nature and purpose of approved schools as follows:

The schools provide care and training under residential conditions. They give a general education with considerable attention to craft training for the older groups, but their primary objects are the readjustment and social re-education of the boys in preparation for their return to the community. The aim is to base this process of rehabilitation on understanding of the personality, history, abilities and aptitudes of each boy, and on knowledge of the family situation and to promote it by stable environment in the school enabling remedial influences to be brought to bear and progressive training to be given, by contact with the home and by help and supervision after the boy leaves the school. The main ingredients of approved school training are education (in the more formal sense) religious education and guidance, practical or vocational training, attention to health and to the use of recreation and leisure, social training (how to live with others) and personal casework (help with personal problems).

15. The *Handbook for Managers* further described to managers how:

> The school managers are in *loco parentis* to the boys; and the statutory *Approved School Rules 1933 as amended by the Approved School Rules 1949* specify certain requirements regarding the managing body, the treatment and discipline of the boys and other matters designed to safeguard the welfare of those who have been deprived of their full liberty by order of a court.

16. Pursuant to Rule 14 Approved School Rules 1933 the managers of an approved school were responsible for the appointment, suspension and dismissal of all staff at the school.

17. The *Handbook for Managers* described the duties of the managers as follows:

> The managers are required to maintain an efficient standard throughout the school, and for this purpose to take into consideration any report communicated to them by or on behalf of the Secretary of State. It is their duty to ensure that the condition of the school and the training and welfare and education of the boys under their care are satisfactory, and for this purpose to pay frequent visits to the school (Rule 10(1) and (2)). To do their work effectively, managers should know the school and should be known to the staff and to the boys.

18. On and after 1 April 1973, Wessex Approved School became a community home under the management, supervision and control of the defendant. Pursuant to the Cessation of Approved Schools (Wessex Approved School) Order 1973 the defendant assumed responsibility from the Wessex Approved School Managers for liabilities incurred while the claimant attended Wessex Approved School prior to April 1973. References to the defendant's duties set out below include reference to those duties taken over by the defendant from the Managers of Wessex Approved School pursuant to the Cessation Order and include the duties set out above.

19. The defendant therefore owed to the claimant a duty of care (or has taken over responsibility for the duty owed by the managers) during the periods when: (a) he was resident at the school; and (b) during the period when he was receiving after care after he had been discharged from the school.

20. The defendant's duty included a duty to:

(a) Ensure that the claimant was kept reasonably safe from physical or psychiatric injury while he was a pupil at the school.

(b) A duty to ensure that the staff employed by the school were suitable for the tasks for which they were employed which included, teaching boys at the school, supervising boys in leisure and sporting activities, taking boys on activity holidays including camping and mountain climbing.

(c) A duty to ensure that any punishment inflicted on children within the school was reasonable and proportionate to the act for which they were being punished; and within the statutory provisions in force at the time and any local authority direction or policy which had been issued at the time.

(d) A duty to ensure that staff working with children reported any inappropriate physical abuse or sexual abuse that they were aware of whether perpetrated by boys or staff in the school.

(e) A duty to ensure that any complaints made by boys in the school in respect of physical or sexual abuse were properly recorded and thereafter investigated.

(f) A duty to ensure that boys at the school received an adequate level of medical care and attention for physical or psychiatric injury or illness.

(g) A duty to ensure that boys at the school received an adequate and suitable level of education for their needs and abilities and that a suitable curriculum was provided at the school and adhered to by the school.

(h) A duty to employ staff that were adequately trained and sufficiently experienced to provide a suitable level of education for the various and differing needs of the boys at the school.

(i) A duty to employ staff who were sufficiently trained and experienced to deal with the varied behaviour of boys at the school including experience and training in restraining boys appropriately if this became necessary.

21. At all relevant times after the defendant received the claimant into its care or after the claimant was committed to its care, the defendant was responsible for the claimant and owed him a common law duty of care until he reached the age of 18 years.

22. The defendant's duty of care to the claimant included:

(a) A duty to act in the place of the child's parents and to provide the claimant with the standard of care which could be expected of a reasonable parent.

(b) A duty to assess the claimant properly and competently on his admission into care and to plan his placements with regard to his long-term welfare.

(c) A duty to provide assessment of the claimant by competent and experienced staff.

(d) A duty to take reasonable steps to protect the claimant from physical, emotional, psychiatric or psychological injury while he remained in the care of the defendant.

(e) A duty to provide a home and education for the claimant for such period as he remained in the care of the defendant.

(f) A duty to place the claimant at all times in a home where his safety would be secured and/or monitored by the defendant.

(g) A duty to safeguard and promote the claimant's development in a manner appropriate to the claimant's stage of development at any given time.

(h) A duty to provide any medical treatment which the claimant required by arranging referral to a suitable medical specialist or otherwise.

241

(i) A duty to secure the claimant's right to family life.

(j) A duty at all times to provide a competent and suitably qualified and/or experienced social worker or workers whose responsibility it was to monitor regularly by adequate contact with the claimant his physical, psychiatric and psychological welfare.

F. THE VICARIOUS DUTIES OWED BY THE DEFENDANT TO THE CLAIMANT THROUGH THE VICARIOUS DUTIES OF ITS SERVANTS OR AGENTS

23. The defendant exercised control over the appointment or termination of employment of staff employed at Wessex Approved School and over their salaries and duties. In the circumstances, such staff were the servants or agents of the defendant .The servants or agents of the defendant employed at Wessex Approved School who were responsible for the teaching and/or care or supervision of the claimant each owed to him a duty of care. The defendant, as employer, is vicariously liable for any breach of such duty.

24. The duties of such servants or agents employed at Wessex Approved School included:

(a) A duty not to injure the claimant and to take reasonable steps to keep the claimant safe from physical or psychiatric injury.

(b) A duty to provide a reasonable level of supervision for the claimant to ensure that he was kept reasonably safe from injury by other boys at the school or by other staff at the school.

(c) A duty to ensure that in respect of any complaint made by the claimant that he had been injured by any boy or member of staff such complaints were properly recorded and investigated and appropriate action taken following such investigation.

(d) A duty to ensure that the claimant was given adequate medical treatment for any physical or psychiatric injury or illness.

(e) A duty to ensure that for such period as any employee had responsibility for the care, supervision or welfare of the claimant, that employee: assessed the claimant's needs appropriately; dealt with the needs that were identified or ought to have been identified appropriately; and/or referred the claimant to such other member of staff as could and should have dealt with such needs appropriately.

(f) A duty to ensure that the claimant's educational abilities were competently assessed and that he received a level of education that was appropriate to his abilities and potential.

(g) A duty to ensure that, before and immediately after the claimant was released from the school, he was given appropriate aftercare help and training so as to enable him to cope appropriately with independent living.

25. Further, at all relevant times, each of the social workers employed by the defendant who was allocated as the social worker for the claimant owed him a duty of care. The duty of care of each social worker for the period for which they were allocated to the claimant included:

(a) A duty not to injure the claimant and to protect the claimant from physical, emotional, psychiatric and psychological damage.

(b) A duty to monitor regularly the claimant's physical, emotional, psychiatric and psychological welfare.

(c) A duty to make arrangements to provide such medical (including psychiatric and therapeutic) treatment as was reasonably necessary for the claimant's welfare and to arrange for his referral to such medical specialists as he required.

(d) A duty to visit the claimant regularly and sufficiently frequently to ascertain his views, wishes, anxieties and complaints in as far as was appropriate to his age and understanding.

(e) A duty to have regard to long-term planning for the claimant and for his long-term welfare in addition to his immediate needs.

G. COMPLAINTS OF ABUSE

26. Instead of providing the claimant with the care which he required at the school he was subjected to distressing and damaging experiences in that he was:

(a) subjected to a harsh and uncaring regime; and

(b) sexually and physically abused.

27. At Wessex Approved School the claimant was sexually abused by Mr Brown.

28. The claimant came to know Mr Brown shortly after he arrived at the school. At first, he believed that Mr Brown was sympathetic and was befriending him. However, just before Christmas 1971, Mr Brown assaulted him for the first time and, thereafter, regularly and repeatedly assaulted him as follows:

(a) After a game of football at Wessex Approved School, Mr Brown asked the claimant to stay behind for extra practice. After a short period of extra practice, Mr Brown approached the claimant placed his arm round his waist and then placed his hands inside the claimant's trousers and touched his penis.

(b) On a training trip to Scotland in August 1972, Mr Brown took the claimant alone to the river bank where he sat him down, removed his trousers, lay on top of him and buggered him. The claimant was in extreme pain and was bleeding. Mr Brown told him to go and wash in the river.

(c) Thereafter Mr Brown buggered the claimant on two further occasions while he was at Wessex Approved School; once in the grounds of the school; once when he took the claimant from his dormitory to the staff sleep-over room.

29. The claimant attempted after returning from Scotland to report the sexual abuse by Mr Brown to Mr Black. Mr Black's response was to punch the claimant, to throw him to the floor and to accuse him of being a liar.

30. As well as being assaulted sexually by Mr Brown and physically by Mr Black in the manner described above, the claimant was exposed to a regime at the school which he describes as being brutal. The claimant was constantly hungry and often cold; he was

forced to wear shorts and suffered from chilblains and chapped skin. The claimant was struck by a member of staff at least once or twice each week while he was at the school. He recalls the following assaults in particular:

(a) Being grabbed by Mr Green and punched in the stomach very shortly after he arrived at the school which hurt him so badly he had stomach pains for three days thereafter.

(b) Being struck by Mr Green across the shoulders with a plank of wood while being required to help with building works in the grounds of Wessex Approved School.

(c) Being slapped and punched frequently by Mr Red for no apparent reason whenever he walked down the same corridor.

(d) Being caned by Mr Black on his bare buttocks in part because he continued to report that he was being abused by Mr Brown.

31. The harsh regime at the school together with the above acts of abuse caused the claimant to suffer pain, suffering and injury.

32. The said damage was caused by the deliberate acts of Mr Brown, Mr Black, Mr Green and Mr Red, each of whom was allocated by the defendant the task of caring for the claimant while he was at Wessex Approved School. Such assaults, including sexual assaults and buggery as described above, were carried out by Mr Brown, Mr Black, Mr Green and Mr Red while they were acting in the course of their employment. The defendant is vicariously liable for these assaults.

33. Further, the claimant relies in support of the allegations set out above on the fact that on 1 January 2001, Mr Brown was convicted by a jury sitting at Wessex Crown Court of 14 counts of indecent assault, four counts of attempted buggery and three acts of buggery in respect of boys resident at Wessex Approved School in the 1960s and 1970s. Mr Brown was sentenced to a term of 15 years' imprisonment. The claimant relies, pursuant to the provisions of the Civil Evidence Act 1968, upon the conviction of Mr Brown as evidence that he was sexually abused by Mr Brown.

34. Further, the claimant suffered damage as a result of the negligence of the defendants.

H. PARTICULARS OF NEGLIGENCE OF THE DEFENDANT EITHER DIRECTLY OR THROUGH EMPLOYEES FOR WHOM THE DEFENDANT IS VICARIOUSLY LIABLE

35. The defendant was negligent in that it, its servants or agents:

(a) Employed Mr Brown, Mr Black, Mr Red and Mr Green at the school when they were unsuitable employees in a children's home or school or at all.

(b) Allowed the members of staff identified in (a) above to work unsupervised with children before ascertaining whether they were suitable to do so and failing to ascertain that they were not.

(c) Employed other staff at the school who were not sufficiently vigilant to prevent the claimant being sexually and physically abused.

(d) Failed to take reasonable steps to implement a proper system of care and supervision at the school designed to ensure that children at the school were reasonably safe from injury and abuse.

(e) Failed to arrange for regular and adequate medical examinations to ensure that any injury (whether physical or psychiatric) to the claimant at the school was identified, diagnosed and suitably and adequately treated.

(f) Failed to inspect the school regularly or vigilantly enough to ascertain that the claimant and other children were suffering injury, by adequate interviews with the children or otherwise.

(g) Failed to provide for the claimant with a social worker or other suitable responsible adult while he was at the school in whom the claimant could place sufficient trust and respect to report the abuse he suffered.

(h) Failed to monitor the claimant's placement so as to have regard to his long-term welfare.

(i) Failed to deal with the claimant's welfare in a suitable or appropriate manner when it was known or ought to have been known that he was a vulnerable child.

(j) Failed to make adequate or suitable arrangements for the claimant's welfare after he had left the school.

36. As a result of the negligence of the defendant, its servants or agents for whom the defendant is vicariously liable, the claimant has suffered injury, loss and damage.

I. PARTICULARS OF INJURY

37. The claimant sustained pain and suffering at the time of the abuse set out above, and distress and injury, in the form of severe post-traumatic stress disorder, as set out in the report of Dr............., Consultant Psychiatrist, date ....

J. PARTICULARS OF LOSS AND DAMAGE

38. Details of the claimant's losses are contained in the appended statement of expenses and losses.

K. LIMITATION

39. In the circumstances, the claimant did not have the requisite knowledge to commence proceedings pursuant to ss.11 and 14 Limitation Act 1980. The claimant attempted to report the abuse at the time as set out above, but was not believed and was punished for doing so. The first time he appreciated that Wessex Approved School was subject to police investigation was when he read about it in the paper in about May 1999. He then contacted the police and solicitors. This was the first occasion he had been able to discuss the details since he left Wessex Approved School.

40. Alternatively, the claimant asks the court to exercise its discretion pursuant to s.33 Limitation Act 1980 to allow this action to proceed in all the circumstances of the case

and having regard to the fact that:

(a) The reason time has elapsed has been the difficulty that the claimant has in discussing the events set out above. This difficulty was contributed to by the lack of assistance he had from the defendant by way of counselling or social work support which would have helped him to discuss the abuse.

(b) The evidence remains sufficiently cogent for:

(i) the police to investigate the events which occurred at Wessex Approved School and to charge Mr Brown with criminal offences; and

(ii) a jury to convict Mr Brown.

(c) The defendants have failed to respond to requests for the records relating to Wessex Approved School that have been requested.

(d) The claimant remained under a disability by reason of his minority until 1 January 1977 and thereafter he has been suffering psychiatric injury as a result of the events set out above whether or not he has for any of this period been under a disability by reason of mental disorder. The claimant reserves the right to argue in respect of any or all of the period that his psychiatric disorder has been such as to render him under a disability.

(e) The claimant acted promptly and reasonably once he understood that his complaints of abuse were part of a wider police investigation.

(f) The claimant acted promptly in seeking legal and expert advice.

(g) The claimant will further rely on the fact that pursuant to Article 3 of the European Convention for the Protection of Human Rights and Fundamental Freedoms the defendant as a public authority was and remained under an obligation to investigate the abuse Mr Smith perpetrated on the claimant and thereby subjecting him to inhuman and degrading treatment.

41. Further, the claimant contents that, where it is alleged that the defendant is vicariously liable for physical and/or sexual abuse, the existence of a duty of care between the defendant and the claimant prior to the abuse taking place results in a special relationship and/or assumption of responsibility for the claimant so that any injury caused to the claimant in such circumstances whether by a deliberate act or otherwise constitutes a breach of duty, and the claim is properly categorised as one of breach of duty coming within ss.11, 14 and 33 of the Limitation Act 1980.

L. INTEREST

42. The claimant claims interest on the damages as follows:

(a) on general damages at 2 per cent from the date of service of these proceedings; and

(b) on special damages at the full special account rate.

And the claimant claims:

(a) damages exceeding £50,000. More than £1,000 is likely to be awarded to the claimant for his pain, suffering and loss of amenity.

(b) interest.

M. STATEMENT OF TRUTH

43. The claimant believes the facts stated above are true to the best of his knowledge and belief.

Full name: ....

Solicitors: ....

Signed: ....

Table of reported cases from *X (Minors)* v. *Bedfordshire CC* to date

No.	Title of case	Reference	Date of decision	Cases in this list referred to in the judgments	Type of proceedings	Summary
1	*X (minors)* v. *Bedfordshire CC*	[1995] 2 AC 633	29 June 1995		Defendant application to strike out RSC Ord 18 r. 19	HL consideration of novel claims against public authorities in the area of child care and education
						Examination of principles to be applied in respect of statutory duty/common law duty of care, justiciability, strike out
						Claims related to failure to remove children from home struck out, claims in respect of educational services provided by local authority not struck out
2	*H* v. *Norfolk CC*	[1997] 1 FLR 384	10 May 1996	*X* v. *Bedfordshire CC*	Application for permission to appeal by claimant from striking out proceedings	The claimants alleged abuse by foster parents with whom the local authority had placed them; Harrison J. struck out the claim on the basis that applying the policy considerations in *X* v. *Bedfordshire* it was unarguable, CA refused permission to appeal

	Case	Citation	Date	Related cases	Application	Outcome
3	*W* v. *Essex CC*	[1998] 3 WLR 534	2 April 1998	*X* v. *Bedfordshire CC; H* v. *Norfolk; Barrett* v. *Enfield (CA)*	Appeal by defendants from refusal to strike out claims by children and appeal by parents against striking out	Found by majority (Stuart-Smith LJ dissenting) children's claims should not be struck out, policy considerations different from *X* v. *Bedfordshire*, held unanimously parents' claims should be struck out (parents' appeal later allowed by HL)
4	*Culwick* v. *Devon CC*	Unreported	29 June 1998	*H* v. *Norfolk*	Defendant's application for permission to appeal from refusal to strike out, permission refused	Case distinguishable from *H* v. *Norfolk* on the facts where the claimant was resident in a school run by the defendant at the date of the alleged abuse
5	*Osman* v. *UK*	[1999] 1 FLR 193	28 October 1998		Application to ECHR for breach of Articles 2, 8, 6	Court found there was a breach of Article 6 where the CA had ruled out a claim against the police following *Hill* v. *Chief Constable of West Yorkshire*; CA held it was not just, fair and reasonable to impose liability on the police in respect of the investigation of crime
6	*Gallagher* v. *Berrow Wood School and Sec. of State for Education*	Unreported	9 February 1999	*X* v. *Bedfordshire CC; Barrett* v. *LB of Enfield (CA); H* v. *Norfolk*	Application by Sec. of State for Education to set aside order joining him as sixth defendant	Claimant attended an independent school owned by a private individual, placement was made by Kent CC (but the claimant was never in care); Jackson J. set aside order joining Sec. of State on basis claimant could not establish proximity or that it was just, fair and reasonable to impose liability nor could it be said the Sec. of State was acting outside the ambit of his discretion

No.	Title of case	Reference	Date of decision	Cases in this list referred to in the judgments	Type of proceedings	Summary
7	*Barrett v. London Borough of Enfield*	[1999] 3 WLR 79	17 June 1999	*X v. Bedfordshire; H v. Norfolk; Phelps v. Hillingdon (CA); Osman v. UK*	Claimant's appeal against striking out pursuant to RSC Order 18 r.9 allowed	The claimant was in the care of the local authority from 10 months to 17 years and claimed to have suffered psychiatric damage from the negligence of the local authority in respect of his placements. To decide whether what was alleged was justiciable it was necessary to have the facts investigated at trial
8	*Palmer v. Tees HA*	[2000] PIQR p.1	2 July 1999	*Barrett v. Enfield; Osman v. UK; X v. Bedfordshire CC; Phelps v. Hillingdon (CA)*	Claimant appeal from striking out of claim pursuant to Order 18 r. 19 dismissed	Claimant suffered bereavement and psychiatric damage when her daughter was murdered by a patient of the defendant, CA accepted the claim could not be struck out after Barrett on the ground it was not just, fair and reasonable to impose liability but could be struck out for lack of proximity
9	*Z v. UK*	Report of European Commission Application No 29392/95	10 September 1999	*X v. Bedfordshire; W v. Essex*	Claim before European Commission of Human Rights by children in *X v. Bedfordshire CC* for breaches of Articles 3, 6, 8, 13	The children whose claims were struck out in *X v. Bedfordshire CC* alleged violations of article 3 (inhuman and degrading treatment) and article 6 (lack of fair trial/access to court) and breaches were found by the Commission of articles 3 and 6 and no separate issue arose under articles 8 and 13

10	*Gallagher v. Berrow Wood*	Unreported 17 October 1999		*Barrett v. Enfield; Palmer v. Tees HA*	Application for permission to appeal by claimant refused	Claimant above appealed against removal of fifth and sixth defendants from claim, no ground of appeal in respect of lack of proximity or the finding that acts of Sec. of State within ambit of discretion
11	*S v. Gloucestershire CC*	[2000] 3 All ER 346	14 March 2000	*Barrett v. LB of Enfield; H v. Norfolk CC; Osman v. UK; Z v. UK*	Claimant's appeal against striking out of claim allowed; defendant's application for summary judgment under CPR part 24 allowed in one case and refused in the other	Claimant in *S v. Gloucestershire* case alleged abuse by foster parent, claim not suitable for summary judgment unless all facts before the court, facts undisputed or could not be successfully disputed, no real prospect of oral evidence affecting the position. In case of *L v. London Boroughs of Tower Hamlets and Havering* all facts before court and no real prospect of success *H v. Norfolk CC* stated to be wrongly decided
12	*Phelps v. LB of Hillingdon*	[2000] 3 WLR 776	2 July 2000	*Barrett v. Enfield; Osman v. UK; W v. Essex CC; X v. Bedfordshire CC*	Claimant's appeal from CA reversing finding of Garland J. as to liability, other appeals from strike out and summary judgment	Claims in respect of education sustainable both on basis of vicarious liability and arguably in respect of direct liability
13	*Z v. UK*	App No 29392/95	10 May 2001	*W v. Essex CC; Barrett v. LB of Enfield*	Referral by Grand Chamber to the Court of the decision by the Commission	Violation of article 3 confirmed (not contested by the government) – there was a failure of the system to protect the children from long-term neglect and abuse. No separate issue arose under Article 8. No breach of Article 6, HL had carried out a balancing of the policy reasons for and against imposing liability in the particular circumstances of this case and in subsequent cases had found a duty could arise in other factual situations (para. 99). Breach of article 13.

APPENDIX D

List of useful organisations

The Association of Child Abuse Lawyers
PO Box 467
Chorleywood
Rickmansworth
Herts WD3 5YW
Telephone 01923 286888
Website *www.childabuselawyers.com*

The Association of Lawyers for Children
No. 60 Wyndham Street
Barry
Vale of Glamorgan
CF63 4EL
Telephone 01446 746973
Webside *www.alc.org.uk*

The British Association of Behavioural
  and Cognitive Therapists
PO Box 9
Accrington
BB5 2GD
Telephone 01254 875266
Website *www.babcp.com*

The British Association for Counselling
37a Sheep Street
Rugby
Warwick
CV21 3BS
Telephone 01788 550899
Website *www.counselling.co.uk*

The Children's Legal Centre
University of Essex
Wyvenhoe Park
Colchester
CO4 3FQ
Telephone 01206 872466
Website *www.childrenslegalcentre.com*

The Criminal Injuries Compensation
  Authority
Tay House
300 Bath Street
Glasgow
G2 4LN
Telephone 0141 331 2726
Website *www.cica.gov.uk*

Directory and Book Services National
  Resource Directory
79 Copley Road
Doncaster
South Yorkshire
DN1 2QP
Telephone 01302 768689
Website *www.dabsbooks.co.uk*

The National Institute for Social Work
Tavistock Square
London
WC1H 9FN
Telephone 0207 387 9681
Website *www.nisw.org.uk*

The Commission for Local Administration
  in England
21 Queen Anne's Gate
London
SW1H 9BU
Telephone 0207 430 8400
Website *www.lgce.gov.uk*

Updates

Child abuse compensation claims is a fast moving and new area of law. The authors recognise this and have kindly agreed to provide their readers with periodical updates to the book.

It is hoped that these updates will keep readers informed of new case law, changes in procedure and funding, and any developments in legislation.

When ready, each update will be posted to a website which supports the book. The website can be found at the following address:

> *www.ccclaims.pwp.blueyonder.co.uk*

You will be able to download each update to your PC.

If you have any problems accessing the site from your PC, please send an email to: *publishing@lawsociety.org.uk.*

If you do not have access to the Internet and still wish to receive updates to the book, please contact the editor at the address below:

Ben Mullane
Law Society Publishing
The Law Society
113 Chancery Lane
London WC2A 1PL

Suggested reading list

Everett, B. and Gallop, R., *The Link between Childhood Traumas and Mental Illness, Effective Interventions for Mental Health Professionals*, Sage Publications Limited.

Fergusson, D. and Mullen, P.E., *Childhood Sexual Abuse: An Evidence Based Perspective*, Sage Publications Limited.

Furniss, T., *The Multi Professional Handbook of Child Sexual Abuse*, Routledge.

Neeb, J. and Harper, S., *Civil Action for Childhood Sexual Abuse*, Butterworths Law (Canada).

Reder, P., Duncan, S. and Gray, M., *Beyond Blame: Child Abuse Tragedies Revisited*, Routledge.

Wroe, A., *Social Work, Child Abuse and the Law*, Amazon.

Index